T0326503

Islamic Finance as a Complex System

Islamic Finance as a Complex System

New Insights

Edited by
Haider Ali Khan and Karamo N. M. Sonko

Foreword by
M. Kabir Hassan

LEXINGTON BOOKS
Lanham • Boulder • New York • London

Published by Lexington Books
An imprint of The Rowman & Littlefield Publishing Group, Inc.
4501 Forbes Boulevard, Suite 200, Lanham, Maryland 20706
www.rowman.com

6 Tinworth Street, London SE11 5AL, United Kingdom

British Library Cataloguing in Publication Information Available

Library of Congress Cataloging-in-Publication Data

Names: Khan, Haider, editor. | Sonko, Karamo N. M., editor.
Title: Islamic finance as a complex system : new insights / edited by Haider Ali Khan
     and Karamo N. M. Sonko ; foreword by M. Kabir Hassan.
Description: Lanham : Lexington Books, [2020] | Includes bibliographical references
     and index. | Summary: "Islamic Finance as a Complex System is a unique collection
     that provides theoretical, empirical, and policy insights into Islamic finance. The
     contributors are theorists and practitioners from prominent institutions, including
     the world's biggest Islamic and non-Islamic financial institutions, and well-known
     academic/research institutions"— Provided by publisher.
Identifiers: LCCN 2020011662 (print) | LCCN 2020011663 (ebook) |
     ISBN 9781793608659 (cloth ; alk. paper) | ISBN 9781793608666 (epub)
Subjects: LCSH: Finance—Islamic countries. | Finance—Religious aspects—Islam. |
     Financial institutions—Religious aspects—Islam.
Classification: LCC HG187.4 .I828 2020 (print) | LCC HG187.4 (ebook) |
     DDC 332.0917/67—dc23
LC record available at https://lccn.loc.gov/2020011662
LC ebook record available at https://lccn.loc.gov/2020011663

Dedicated to the memory of the late Professor Sulayman S. Nyang of Howard University, Washington, D.C., a proud Muslim, Gambian brother, American citizen, champion of Islamic studies and interfaith dialogue!

Contents

Foreword

There has been a very rapid increase in the interest in Islamic finance in the world in recent years, resulting in an equally rapid increase in such finance. By the end of 2017 global industry assets had reached $2.4 trillion and were forecasted to reach $3.2 trillion by 2020.

This collection of eight chapters (including the introduction) provides some key theoretical, empirical, and policy insights into Islamic finance from an overall complex financial and economic systems perspective. Within the complex financial and economic systems framework, the book addresses theoretical, empirical, and policy questions such as how to conceptualize Islamic financial institutions in a nonlinear general equilibrium system, how to promote Islamic finance in Africa, how "Islamic" is Islamic finance, and how it affects price stability, among other things. The book provides case studies in Africa and Asia, addresses the subject in a structural financial CGE model, demonstrates the development impact of Islamic finance, and presents an Islamic version of the Iceland Plan for Monetary Reform.

The main purpose of the book is to assist the beginner as well as the expert in academia, policy making, business, and the economic media to benefit from a single publication which is easy to read and understand, with some background in economics and finance, while simultaneously offering sophisticated theoretical and empirical/quantitative analysis. Therefore, a unique feature of the book is that it would appeal to a diverse range of readers—from the beginner looking for the definitions of basic Islamic finance concepts to the average reader wanting to understand different aspects of Islamic finance, and the sophisticated scholar of mathematical and statistical methods in economics and finance.

Apart from the novel complex systems perspective, for the first time in the literature on Islamic finance, it addresses the question of knowledge in promoting sustainable Islamic finance in sub-Saharan Africa, the impact of Islamic finance on inflation, and other key issues. The empirical evidence covers a long list of countries in Africa, Europe, the Middle East, and other parts of Asia such as Malaysia. The book also includes the case study from an award-winning research project on Islamic finance in The Gambia, for the first time. The authors of the book include theorists and practitioners, critical and moderate, from prominent academic, research, and international development finance institutions in Europe, the Middle East, and North America. For a small collection of its size this is indeed rich.

As the world's needs for ethical and socially responsible investments increase, I hope that there will be more and more research into Islamic finance and continuous increase in such financing around the world. Islamic finance is for both Muslims and non-Muslims!

M. Kabir Hassan
Professor of Finance
University of New Orleans

Chapter 1

Introduction

Haider Ali Khan and Karamo N. M. Sonko

Islamic finance as an academic field is of relatively recent origin. It started as a subfield of Islamic economics in the 1980s and remained mainly limited to a few specialist papers. With the spread of practical banking, explorations began but until now have mainly been restricted to an analysis of Sha'ria-compliant finance. There has been a very significant increase in the interest in Islamic finance in the world in the twenty-first century, resulting in a dramatic rise in financing since the last decade, as various chapters in this book document. This is happening despite the historic challenges to Islam itself during the same period. The main stimuli for this practical interest in Islamic finance seem to be the need for large-scale infrastructure financing and the concerns about conventional finance arising from recurrent financial crises in the global economy.[1]

Therefore, even pundits of conventional finance are increasingly realizing the potential and hope for Islamic finance in Islamic and non-Islamic economies. At the same time, there are many paradoxes with respect to how "Islamic" the Islamic finance really is and the broader, human well-being enhancing implications—if any—of such finance. Such paradoxes and ambiguities are not accidental but relate to tensions in the moral economy of Islam in the capitalist world of the early twenty-first century. This book is the first one to examine these emerging issues both theoretically and empirically and begin a conversation between the theorists and practitioners. It is also the first attempt to analyze Islamic finance within the broad framework of a complex adaptive financial system approach, as the theoretical chapter by Khan in this book makes clear.

The book is, therefore, intended to begin the much-needed dialogue regarding the contemporary relevance of Islamic finance within the complex system of global finance. The chapters illustrate the various approaches and experiences of Islamic finance in different parts of the world, identify the opportunities and constraints involved in such finance, critically assess how Islamic it is, provide guidance on how to tap the potential, address some of the constraints, and nurture the efforts in promoting the well-being enhancing part of it in the global economy. The contributors include practitioners and scholars of Islamic finance from Africa, Asia (including the Middle East), Europe, and North America. One distinguishing mark of this book is its wide geographical coverage in spite of its relatively small number of chapters. Theorists such as Sonko and Sonko and Ahmad and practitioners such as Diagana (the World Bank group) and Cham (Islamic Development Bank) provide a very broad coverage of African and Asian countries. For a book of its modest length, this is a tremendous achievement.

Without any claims to be exhaustive and definitive, the country and regional chapters, some more critical than others: (1) present an overview of the forms of Islamic finance in the countries or regions; (2) provide detailed data/information; (3) examine the pros and cons of the experience in the country or region; (4) recommend how to make further progress in the promotion of Islamic finance in the country concerned. The theoretically grounded chapters address concepts, theoretical understanding, strategy, and other issues that are crucial in the efforts to understand and promote Islamic finance in the global economy for enhancing human well-being. In order to address the important aspects of human well-being, refinements of the Nobel laureate Amartya Sen's capabilities approach are presented in Khan's chapter as well. We predict that this one-way normative work based on scientific modeling of Islamic finance will proceed in the future.[2]

It needs to be emphasized that the very purpose of this project includes the provision of diverse analyses of the subject in terms of rigor (e.g., Khan's mathematical model of a complex Islamic financial system which is the first time ever for this subject, and Cham's econometric modeling of Islamic banking and inflation, and Ahmad's evaluation of Sukuk in Malaysia). These rigorous analytical approaches are illustrated through the geographic coverage and relevant empirical evidence (Africa, Asia, and other countries). Here, too, the geographical coverage includes countries that have been neglected so far. Sonko and Sonko's chapter, for example, covers a country on which there is not a single publication with regards to Islamic finance. This chapter also has comprehensive coverage of Islamic finance and Islamic financial institutions (IFIs) in sub-Saharan Africa (SSA), illustrating to a great extent the experience throughout the continent. This book can stand on its own as a monograph on Islamic finance in Africa. The extensive geographic coverage is maintained through most of the other chapters (e.g., Ahmad on Malaysia, Cham using data on all the countries of the Gulf Cooperation Council (GCC), Iran, and the Sudan, and Diagana's empirical evidence on GCC countries,

Turkey, and Africa); thus, showing harmony between the chapters with regard to many of the countries cited or geographic coverage in the book.

The theoretical challenges raised by the diverse empirical evidence from a wide swath of the planet are addressed using conventional, nonconventional, and Islamic economic theories that tie together Khan's, Zaman's, Tobin's, and Cham's chapters without the straitjacket of a single mid-range theory. As mentioned earlier, all these approaches are integrated under the rubric of the complex systems approach to global and Islamic finance by Khan which also addresses the important issues emerging from the uneven development of the Islamic financial systems in various parts of the world. According to the theory of complex financial systems developed by Khan, diverse practices are possible and functional within limits. Thus, just as the string theories in physics explain gravity that is ubiquitous, the theory of complex financial systems shows unevenness of financial development to be a "natural" aspect of the process of evolution of financial practices and institutions.

Thus, there is a deeply thematic and theoretical unity in this diversity of Islamic finance that this book brings out. Theoretically, Khan's chapter acts as an anchor for all the chapters structurally in a rigorous way from both economic theory and Islamic financial institutional angles. Cham's econometric approach illustrates the need for and achievements in rigorous empirical analysis based on sound econometric modeling. Other chapters illustrate these points and connections as well. Finally, the policy angles are brought out in each chapter in its own manner. But two angles are particularly worth mentioning.

First, the complex systems approach makes clear that simple state versus market political economy is inappropriate for the policies in the complex field of Islamic finance. We need a blend of well-functioning markets and well-regulated financial institutions. In particular, the corporate governance of Islamic financial institutions should receive much more attention than it has received so far. Khan[3] pioneered a complexities approach to corporate governance in the context of Asia. Future work in Islamic finance will need to follow up on this within the complex financial systems framework. Secondly, Zaman's work breaks new ground in suggesting an entirely appropriate twenty-first-century plan to rationalize Islamic finance.

We now turn to a brief synopsis of individual chapters. As alluded to before, the key conceptual and technical analytical chapter is by Khan at the beginning (chapter 2). The main purpose of this chapter is to incorporate the key characteristics of the Islamic banking and financial system in a larger systemic model of a mixed economy with both Islamic and other characteristics. One aspect is to begin with the complexities of IFIs. This serves a dual purpose. On the one hand, it acquaints the reader not familiar with many IFIs, with enough of them quickly to provide a foundation for further learning.

On the other hand—and more importantly—for all readers, both beginners and experts, this section emphasizes the actual institutional complexities of the IFIs from economic and social points of view.

Next, is the task of formalizing the argument and the framework of analysis. To this end, Khan constructs a structural computable general equilibrium (CGE) model with banking and financial sectors including the IFIs. Here it is demonstrated mathematically that a modern Islamic banking sector can be defined and included in a sophisticated nonlinear structural CGE model with multiple equilibria and path dependence.

Both technically and from a social perspective, efficient and egalitarian Islamic economics are shown to be feasible. This type of banking and financial system with socially oriented Islamic characteristics can also support modern innovation systems. The technical model allows incorporation and scientific testing of important features of Islamic finance in a general equilibrium setting. The section on IFIs presents a succinct and critical summary of the main Islamic financial instruments in addition to the purely formal modeling which is necessary for a rigorous analysis but not sufficient.

Through a case study of The Gambia in chapter 3, Sonko and Sonko employ statistical surveys, economic and financial analysis, with comparative assessments, in order to achieve the objectives of (1) gauging the perceptions and understanding of Gambians with regard to Islamic banking; (2) assessing the performance of an existing Islamic banking sector in relation to the conventional banking sector; and (3) understanding the policies and practice of the government (central bank) in a dual banking system.

The authors explain what Islamic finance refers to, trace its history and evolution in the world economy, and outline causes of its growth worldwide and in SSA. They illustrate the various types of IFIs and their geographic distribution. Their chapter also shows the many challenges which still hinder the advancement of Islamic finance in Africa, even in North Africa, where the national populations are almost entirely Muslims. These challenges include domestic political issues associated with Islam. There are other challenges too. In Africa, the institutions that exist are generally small, with narrow and often exclusive customer bases. Generally, they are expensive and have difficulties in competing with conventional institutions. They face capacity constraints in finding the necessary skills for Islamic products and services, directly and indirectly, required in Islamic finance. The regulatory framework for Islamic finance rarely exists.

The Gambia provides a very good mirror for viewing the understanding of, and the behavior of a populace toward, Islamic banking and for assessing the potential of such banking in a non-Arab, but mostly Muslim, sub-Saharan African country. It offers useful lessons for SSA countries where the populations are largely Muslims and the banking industries are dominated by conventional banks. The results show that the largest number of Gambians have little or no knowledge of Islamic banking.

Overall, their analysis of the Arab Gambia Islamic Bank (AGIB), in comparison with the conventional banks, through financial soundness indicators tells a somewhat mixed story, but indicates good relative performance by AGIB. It shows that the bank is doing better than or equal to the conventional banks, by most of the measures. On the most positive side are its relative performance in terms of liquid assets and regulatory capital.

The authors also conduct an analysis of T-Bills versus Salaam al-Sukuk and find an overwhelming emphasis on T-Bill issuances by the central bank, but higher yields on Sukuk. They draw conclusions and provide practical recommendations for policymakers, investors, and researchers with regard to the promotion and development of Islamic finance in The Gambia and, by implication, SSA as a whole. As in Khan, Cham, and Ahmad, chapter 3 helps the reader in understanding the various concepts in Islamic finance, while providing a portrait of Islamic finance in SSA and, addressing for the first in the literature on the subject, the question of knowledge in promoting sustainable Islamic finance in the continent.

In chapter 4 Tobin helps us to understand the diverse array of criticisms against Islamic finance, an important area of scholarship which students of Islamic finance are unfamiliar with. This chapter focuses on an analysis of the main criticism against Islamic finance; that is, how Islamic it is, a thread that runs three other chapters in the book (Khan, Sonko and Sonko, and Zaman). She observes that Islamic banking and finance institutions (IBFI) are highly criticized for lacking what is perceived to be a "real Islamic authenticity." Such criticisms tend to fall into three categories: (1) institutional emphases that are informed by economic policy and often exclusionary against the poor; (2) the aesthetics of the physical elements of the facilities that the customers witness and experience; and (3) the ethical or scriptural/theological emphasis of the institutions.

The chapter examines exactly what is at hand in claims of authenticity, especially in their Middle Eastern and Islamic understandings. Then it examines each of these criticisms in turn and proposes alternatives that best remedy the concerns and more closely approximate a "real" or authentic Islamic practice in IBFIs. The chapter concludes with a discussion of what the criticisms reveal about authenticity and their calls for a distinctly Islamic alternative. The conclusions to this chapter explore the possibilities for IBFIs to bring in elements of an Islamic authenticity for the Middle Eastern populace in order to grow the industry, attend to religious concerns of the public, and commit to a more equitable and just economic system for all.

Chapter 5 addresses another important question with regard to Islamic finance—inflation. There are a lot of studies that look into the determinants of domestic prices in the GCC, Iran, and the Sudan applying various methods. Many of these studies investigated the linkages in money demand, money supply, exchange rate, and inflation. However, there seems to be none that includes Islamic finance as one of the determinants of inflation, despite the importance of the Islamic mode of finance in the demand for money in the region.

Therefore, Cham in chapter 5 investigates whether Islamic finance through extending credit could affect domestic price inflation. This research aims to address the empirical gap and to provide an insight into the relationship between Islamic banking and inflation. He assesses whether Islamic banking growth has been one of the contributing factors to high inflation in these countries, by studying the relationship between Islamic banking growth and inflation in the GCC, Iran, and the Sudan, using monthly time series and unbalanced monthly panel data covering the period 2001–2015. Several econometric models are applied including single equation model, panel ordinary least squares (OLS), and Vector error correction model (VECM).

The empirical findings reveal that Islamic banking does not increase domestic prices in all the models applied. According to the single equation OLS results, Islamic banking growth dampened domestic prices in Oman, Qatar, and Iran. From VECM analysis, in the short run, Islamic banking decreased inflation in Iran and the Sudan, and in the long run Islamic banking growth dampened inflation in Bahrain and Iran. The panel regression results reveal no indication that Islamic banking growth increases inflation. Five out of a total of seven countries considered in the study revealed that Islamic banking dampened domestic price inflation. Inflation inertia, monetary growth, and exchange rate depreciation are the main factors that increase inflation in these economies. The results offer new views and insight for further empirical work on Islamic banking and macroeconomic stability.

Diagana in chapter 7 addresses Islamic finance from an ethical perspective, which is in line with the World Bank's viewpoint and those of non-Muslims generally. In fact, this is also the main reason behind the growth of Sukuk in non-Muslim countries, where non-Muslim investors seek ethical opportunities. The phenomenal growth of Islamic finance in general and Sukuk, in particular, is captured in Sonko and Sonko (chapter 3) and Ahmad (chapter 6).

The author's approach differs from the common view in recent years which treats ethics as a sort of byproduct of compliance in order to avoid the worst in organizations. Instead, he treats ethics as a way first bringing out the best in people and, therefore, in the organizations where they are active. According to the author, ethics must show the way; it must inspire staff to care deeply for the ultimate objectives of the organization. For international organizations, this means that ethics must promote a culture of active altruism, which he argues is essential for international organizations, such as the

World Bank, that are committed to building a better world and are involved in Islamic finance.

He goes on to stress the importance of Islamic finance in funding infrastructural challenges. He reports that the World Bank has estimated that the undersupply of infrastructure in developing economies is at around US$1 trillion per year, through 2020, with an additional US$200 to US$300 billion required annually to ensure that infrastructure investments are low emitting and climate-resilient. The Africa Progress Report (2015) estimated that 620 million people in Africa have no access to electricity, and the report estimates that $55 billion per year is needed, until 2030, in order to meet the demand and provide universal access to electricity in the region.

He also points out that Islamic finance is equity-based, asset-backed, ethical, sustainable, environmentally and socially responsible finance. It promotes risk sharing, connects the financial sector with the real economy, emphasizes financial inclusion and social welfare, focuses on social justice, and contributes to the diversity of the offer of financial services which increases the financial market's resilience. The chapter also cites earlier studies which compared the performance and associated risks of Islamic banks with conventional banks during global financial crises and argues that the two have different strengths and weaknesses and benefit from coexisting.

As also alluded to earlier, Zaman in chapter 8 breaks new ground in suggesting an entirely appropriate twenty-first-century plan to rationalize Islamic finance. The current fractional reserve banking system allows creation of credit by private banks. As shown by the financial fragility theory of Minsky, this leads to repeated banking crises. After the Great Depression which was caused by excess credit creation, economists created the Chicago Plan for 100 percent reserve banking. After hundreds of minor banking crises, and the major Global Financial Crisis of 2007, the plan was revived and updated by Iceland. This plan also proposes a 100 percent reserve banking system supplemented by the concept of sovereign money. He designs a modification of the plan which eliminates interest to bring the whole system in conformity with Islamic principles. The purpose of Zaman's chapter is to show that, with minor modifications, the Iceland Plan can serve as a model for a genuinely Islamic approach to money and banking, suitable for the modern world.

He shows that current monetary theories make no mention of the banking sector because of fallacious assumptions about the role of banking. The harms of the current system of credit creation by banks are enumerated, and historical evidence provided to document these harms. He provides theoretical evidence along several dimensions where the Islamic version of the Iceland Plan (i.e., an Islamic plan) would be far superior to current banking systems—both Islamic and conventional.

The author argues that the root cause of current massive and increasing inequality is the power of credit creation by banks. This inequality causes tremendous negative social damage by destroying democracy and impoverishing the already poor for the benefit of the rich. The practical implication is that current efforts to create Islamic banking are being made in the wrong direction, because these efforts are also within a fractional reserve setup, which is not Islamic, and has harmful socioeconomic consequences. Therefore, Islamic banking as currently practiced offers no solutions, according to Zaman. He maintains that the alternative Islamic plan outlined in his chapter does offer a solution to these problems. In particular, the 100 percent reserve banking would prevent banking crises, reduce income inequality, direct money toward productive investments, lead to increased prosperity, and avoid speculative bubbles.

Finally, it is important to point out that the aim of this book is not to present a single perspective of Islamic finance. Instead, the aim is to provide the reader with diverse viewpoints, as shown by the contents of the selected chapters, some of which are more critical than others. However, in spite of the differences, all the authors share a common view of the importance of Islamic finance in the global economy and almost all of them agree on the need to make it fully Islamic and more effective in transforming economies and lives. In the long term this serves the interests of both investors and clients or customers. It is our hope that in these difficult times, an authentic, dynamic and cosmopolitan Islamic finance can help build some of the bridges that can prevent future crises and lead to a diverse global civilization for peaceful human flourishing. Our effort can be best seen as a small contribution toward a conversation for building a better future for all at a time of perilous global crises as clearly demonstrated by the COVID-19 pandemic.

NOTES

1. For a discussion of financial crises in the complex systems framework, see the works by H. A. Khan listed as follows: H.A. Khan, "Development Strategies: Lessons from South Korea, Thailand, Malaysia and Vietnam," in Augustin Fosu (ed.), *Lessons from Successful Development Strategies* (Oxford: Oxford University Press, 2013), in particular, develops a complex nonlinear systems approach that is more comprehensive. Earlier, C.S. Lin and Khan, "A New Approach to Modelling Early Warning Systems for Financial Crises," *Journal of International Money and Finance* (2008): 1098–1121, had developed a complex systems approach to global finance via a fuzzy set-theoretic nonlinear neural network modeling. H.A. Khan, *Global Markets and Financial Crisis: Towards a Theory for the 21st Century* (Basingstoke, UK: Macmillan/Palgrave, 2004), developed a multisectoral nonlinear model in the context of the Asian Financial Crises; H.A. Khan, "Complex Financial Governance with an Application to the BRICS," forthcoming in P. Anand, F. Comim and S. Fennel (eds.), *The BRICS Handbook* (Oxford: Oxford University Press, 2019); H.A. Khan, "Critical

Macroeconomic and Multisectoral Perspectives on US Infrastructure: Challenges and Directions for the 21st Century," forthcoming in Aman Khan and Klaus Becker (eds.), *US Infrastructure: Challenges and Directions for the 21st Century* (London: Routledge, April 2019); H.A. Khan, "Development Orders and Disorders: Real Competition in Complex Global Capitalist System," paper presented at the New School University, NYC, January 30, 2018; H.A. Khan, "Challenges of Urbanization: Building Healthy Sustainable Smart and Resilient Cities," presented at the British Academy Workshop on Smart Cities, July 12–15, 2017, Bradford University, UK; H.A. Khan, "A Strategy for Development as Freedom," in Robert Lensink, Stefan Sjogren and Clas Wihlborg (eds.), *Paths for Sustainable Development* (Gothenburg: University of Gothenburg, 2017); H.A. Khan, "Macroeconomic Multisectoral Perspectives on US Infrastructure: Challenges and Directions for the 21st Century," Discussion chapter, JKSIS, University of Denver, Denver, USA (2017); H.A. Khan, "Social Accounting Matrix: A Very Short Introduction for Modeling," in EconPapers (2007); Khan, *Global Markets and Financial Crisis*; H.A. Khan, "Innovation and Growth in a Schumpeterian Model," *Oxford Development Studies* 30, no. 3 (2002): 289–306; H.A. Khan, "Corporate Governance: The Limits of the Principal-Agent Model," Working Paper, GSIS, University of Denver, 2002; H.A. Khan, "Corporate Governance in Asia: Which Road to Take?" Paper presented at 2nd high-level symposium in ADBI, Tokyo, 1999; H.A. Khan, "A Note on Path Dependence," unpublished manuscript (2001).

2. See D. Judzik, "Social Capabilities-Based Flexicurity for a Learning Economy." *Sage Economic and Labour Relations Review* 27, no. 3 (2016): 333–348; H.A. Khan, *Technology, Development and Democracy* (Cheltenham: Edward Elgar, 1998); Khan, "Development Strategies"; H.A. Khan, "Basel III, BIS and Global Financial Governance," *Journal of Advanced Studies in Finance* 2, no. 8 (Winter 2013); Khan, "Challenges of Urbanization"; Khan, "A Strategy for Development as Freedom"; Khan, "Macroeconomic Multisectoral Perspectives on US Infrastructure"; Khan, "Development Orders and Disorders"; Khan, "Complex Financial Governance with an Application to the BRICS"; Khan, "Critical Macroeconomic and Multisectoral Perspectives on US Infrastructure"; and most importantly, Amartya Sen, *Inequality Re-Examined* (Oxford: Oxford University Press, 1992); Amartya Sen, *Development as Freedom* (Oxford: Oxford University Press and New York: Alfred A. Knopf, Inc., 1999); and Amartya Sen, *The Idea of Justice* (Cambridge, MA: The Belknap Press of the Harvard University Press, 2009).

3. Khan, "Corporate Governance in Asia."

BIBLIOGRAPHY

Africa Progress Panel. *Africa Progress Report: Power, People, Planet.* Geneva: APP, 2015.

Judzik, D., H. A. Khan, and L. Spagnolo. "Social Capabilities-Based Flexicurity for a Learning Economy." *Sage Economic and Labour Relations Review* 27, no. 3 (2016): 333–348.

Khan, H. A. "Basel III, BIS and Global Financial Governance." *Journal of Advanced Studies in Finance* 2, no. 8 (Winter 2013): 121–144.

———. "Challenges of Urbanization: Building Healthy Sustainable Smart and Resilient Cities." Presented at the British Academy Workshop on Smart Cities, Bradford University, UK, July 12–15, 2017.

———. "Complex Financial Governance with an Application to the BRICS." Forthcoming in P. Anand, F. Comim and S. Fennel (eds.), *The BRICS Handbook*. Oxford: Oxford University Press, April 2019.

———. "Corporate Governance in Asia: Which Road to Take?" Paper presented at 2nd High-level Symposium in ADBI, Tokyo, 1999.

———. "Corporate Governance: The Limits of the Principal-Agent Model." Working Paper, GSIS, University of Denver, 2002.

———. "Critical Macroeconomic and Multisectoral Perspectives on US Infrastructure: Challenges and Directions for the 21st Century." Forthcoming in Aman Khan and Klaus Becker (eds.), *US Infrastructure: Challenges and Directions for the 21st Century*. London: Routledge, April 2019.

———. "Development Orders and Disorders: Real Competition in Complex Global Capitalist System." Paper presented at the New School University, NYC, January 30, 2018.

———. "Development Strategies: Lessons from South Korea, Thailand, Malaysia and Vietnam." In Augustin Fosu (ed.), *Lessons from Successful Development Strategies*. Oxford: Oxford University Press, 2013.

———. *Global Markets and Financial Crisis: Asia's Mangled Miracle*. Basingstoke: Macmillan/Palgrave, 2004.

———. *Global Markets and Financial Crisis: Towards a Theory for the 21st Century*. Basingstoke: Macmillan/Palgrave, 2004.

———. "Innovation and Growth in a Schumpeterian Model." *Oxford Development Studies* 30, no. 3 (2002): 289–306.

———. "Macroeconomic Multisectoral Perspectives on US Infrastructure: Challenges and Directions for the 21st Century." Discussion chapter, JKSIS, University of Denver, Denver, USA (2017).

———. "A Note on Path Dependence." Unpublished Manuscript, University of Denver, Denver, 2001.

———. "Social Accounting Matrix: A Very Short Introduction for Modeling." In EconPapers (2007). https://econpapers.repec.org/paper/tkyfseres/2007cf477.htm (Last visited on December 24, 2018).

———. "A Strategy for Development as Freedom." In Robert Lensink, Stefan Sjogren and Clas Wihlborg (eds.), *Paths for Sustainable Development*. Gothenburg: University of Gothenburg, 2017.

———. *Technology, Development and Democracy*. Cheltenham: Edward Elgar, 1998.

Lin, C.-S., H. A. Khan, R.-Y. Chang, and Y.-C. Wang. "A New Approach to Modelling Early Warning Systems for Financial Crises: Can a Machine-learning Fuzzy Expert System Predict the Currency Crises Effectively?" *Journal of International Money and Finance* 27, no. 7 (2008): 1098–1121.

Sen, Amartya. *The Idea of Justice*. Cambridge, MA: The Belknap Press of the Harvard University Press, 2009.

———. *Development as Freedom*. Oxford and New York: Oxford University Press and Alfred A. Knopf, Inc., 1999.

———. *Inequality Re-examined*. Oxford: Oxford University Press, 1992.

Chapter 2

Human Capabilities and Islamic Finance in General Equilibrium

A Critical-Structural CGE Model for Policy-Making within a Complex Socioeconomic System

Haider Ali Khan

The main purpose of this chapter is to incorporate the key characteristics of the Islamic banking and financial system in a larger systemic model of a mixed economy with both Islamic and other characteristics. To this end, I construct a structural computable general equilibrium (CGE) model with banking and financial sectors. Thus, I demonstrate mathematically that a modern Islamic banking sector can be defined and included in a sophisticated CGE model. Furthermore, through an application of socially embedded capabilities analysis (SECA)—an extension of the Nobel laureate Amartya Sen's capabilities theory by the present author—incorporating institutional socioeconomic characteristics of various types of households and their capabilities, an assessment of the human capabilities impacts of Islamic finance can also be carried out.

Both technically and from a social perspective, efficient and egalitarian Islamic economics are shown to be feasible. This type of banking and financial system with socially oriented Islamic characteristics can also support modern innovation systems. The technical model allows incorporation and scientific testing of important features of Islamic finance in a general equilibrium setting. The section on Islamic financial institutions presents a succinct and critical summary of the main Islamic financial instruments.

Work on Islamic economic systems is advancing quite rapidly. Recent books have explored many aspects including finance.[1] One relatively unexplored area, however, is how the critically *Islamic* features of the financial and banking systems in many Islamic countries can be theoretically included in a disaggregated multisectoral *economy-wide model* that is implementable in the real world. This is the task I set myself in this chapter. As a further bonus, the proposed model is applicable to gauging the impact of the Islamic financial institutions on human well-being as well. In the model below, SECA or socially embedded capabilities analysis can examine rigorously the human capabilities impacts of Islamic finance.

Accordingly, the main purpose of this chapter is to incorporate the key characteristics of the Islamic banking and financial institutions in a larger systemic model of a mixed economy with both Islamic and other characteristics. To this end, I construct a structural computable general equilibrium (CGE) model with banking and financial sectors. Thus, I demonstrate mathematically that a modern Islamic banking sector can be defined and included in a sophisticated CGE model. Using a social accounting matrix (SAM) incorporating the capabilities as well as achieved freedom will allow an evaluation of the Islamic banking and other financial institutions in terms of their impact on human well-being.

Both technically and from a social perspective, efficient and egalitarian Islamic economics are shown to be feasible. This type of banking with socially oriented Islamic characteristics can also support modern innovation systems. The technical general equilibrium model shows how such an economy can lead the Muslim-majority countries to rapid augmentation of both efficiency and social capabilities of people[2] in an egalitarian manner.

This chapter is organized in the following manner. The next section presents following Sen and others the concept of the freedom-oriented concept of development consistent with the Islamic ideas of unity (*Tawheed*), justice (*Al-adl*), and truth/reality/right/justice (*Haqq*, الحق) within the socioeconomic complex systems framework.[3] Section 3 presents the concepts of Islamic banking and finance focusing on both *mudarabah* and *riba*. Section 4 presents a detailed typology of important Islamic financial instruments and contracts arrived at through critical reflections on the above-mentioned Islamic concepts and principles. The following section presents the CGE model incorporating inter alia an Islamic banking sector in five equations specific to this sector. These equations can be further disaggregated, and extra modules related to insurance, real estate, equity, debt, and other social risk-sharing institutions and organizations can be added. Thus, the model presented is relatively flexible with respect to adding further institutional details.

SECTION 1: DEVELOPMENT AS A COMPLEX SOCIAL-ECONOMIC-STATE SYSTEMIC PROCESS IN BOTH ISLAMIC AND NON-ISLAMIC CONTEXTS:

Writing in 1926, in a biographical essay on Edgeworth, Keynes underlined some of the problems of complex human systems:

> We are faced at every turn with problems of organic unity, of discreteness, of discontinuity—the whole is not equal to the sum of the parts, comparisons of quantity fail us, small changes produce large effects, the assumptions of a uniform and homogeneous continuum are not satisfied.[4]

If anything, the developing part of the world economy today shows to even a greater degree the kind of complexity captured in Keynes's words. Fortunately, systems theory and economic theory have both made some progress since those dark days. Although we are far from a genuinely complete theory of complex economic systems, efforts are underway that have already borne some interesting fruit in several limited areas.[5] A review of even partially successful set of country experiences such as are contained in Fosu (2013)[6] can be seen as case studies that reveal many facets of complex developing economies—each with its own sub-systemic characteristics to be sure, but also sharing some common strategic features.

The purpose of this chapter is to incorporate Islamic finance and banking within a complex systems model and draw some appropriate lessons. The main claim is that such an approach can lead to a theoretical view of an enabling developmental state that includes many features from the East Asian developmental state model. But in our theoretical model in section 4, we go beyond that model. In particular, it turns out that the theoretical basis of the East Asian developmental state model must be crucially augmented by considerations of deepening of democracy according to Islamic precepts and instituting social justice or *Adl* against *Zulm* or oppression in conformity with Islam during the developmental process. These are features of Islam relatively unknown to Western-trained economists. Furthermore, our theoretical model in section 4 shows the possibilities of the systemic financial crises in the twenty-first century that Islamic finance and banking can address more effectively than the old East Asian model.[7]

However, at this point in our discussion, some clarification of the key term "development" is necessary in order to avoid ambiguities and confusions. In the rest of this chapter, I will be referring to three concepts of development that are implicit in much of the discussion in the political economy of development literature. The first is the idea of development as growth with some structural change or at least the idea that this type of growth is the most crucial necessary condition for development. The second concept is derived by adding explicit distributional elements to growth—particularly inequality and poverty. Both these ideas are shared by many development economists—for example, many of the authors of the chapters in Fosu[8]—at least implicitly. Fields was one of the earliest in being explicit in discussing all three—growth, absolute poverty, and inequality—and his thoughtful model in the *Quarterly Journal of Economics* (Fields 1979) article alerts the reader to the performance of a developing economy in all three areas and derives—at least partly—a logic of further necessary reforms following from his cogent analysis of the three aspects of development in this sense. Warr[9] is a more recent example for the case of Thailand. He concludes:

> Not all aspects of the Thai development strategy have been similarly successful. Inequality has increased at the same time as absolute poverty has declined. The underlying causes of this increase in inequality are still not well understood.[10]

The third—and the broadest approach to development discussed here—is in terms of Sen's idea of capabilities and its further extensions. In this view, development is really an extension over time and space of freedom, particularly the positive freedom to lead a certain type of life an individual has reasons to value. Sen and his coauthors have, of course, used this idea, and following Sen, many others have done so as well.[11] Yet, in so far as there is a normative aspect about development being a "(public) good" that is a premise for the whole project such a view is consistent with the analyses of the East (and to some extent Southeast) Asian development. Warr's essay on Thailand again is quite explicit in mentioning both the positive achievements and the shortcomings of Thailand's record and its strategy which can fit into this broad systemic capability approach. For Korea, Keun Lee has gone further. In fact, Keun Lee's perceptive comments on the possible role of democracy in development extend considerably the terrain of discussion in the direction of the "development as freedom" perspective when he writes:

> We see obvious advantages in democracy, amongst which is the convenient feature that citizens are not subject to arbitrary arrest and torture. Truly strong states get it wrong more often than they get it right. Thus, the military dictatorships of Latin America left little in the way of legacy, whereas the military dictatorships in Korea and Taiwan (while not on anything like the same scale of brutality) left a powerful legacy of development. The difference lies clearly in strategic orientation and in institutional capacity in formulating and implementing a program of national industrial development. Our point is that this is an option available to the political leadership of any developing country

today. On top of this, the key to the Korean or Asian success was institutional longevity.[12]

It would seem, therefore, that there is an implicit agreement that development is "growth plus" other things.[13] While the list of "other things" may vary somewhat, none of the thoughtful scholars of development would want to equate growth and development. Yet, as the East Asian experience shows, generating high growth may be a useful means toward development. But one must also pay careful attention to what can be called "the political economy and the well-being consequences of growth." Consideration of these factors leads inevitably to the role of the state. The East Asian experience suggests that the role of states in their developmental process was "enabling" but the transition from an authoritarian to more democratic forms of state was slow. In terms of class character, these states are still bourgeois with accommodations for popular interests that are the results of long and hard struggles by the masses from below.[14] This suggests a change in strategic orientation for the progressives in the twenty-first century. Such an approach necessarily will need to take differences—particularly class, gender, racial-ethnic differences—seriously in a critical theory of equalizing capabilities.[15] It will proceed differently with different institutional mix in different parts of the world. But in all cases, the fundamental dynamics will have to be capabilities-enhancing. It can be argued that an Islamic financial and banking system in a mixed economy can move in this enabling direction.

What precisely can be the character and role of such an "enabling" financial and banking system in an Islamic mixed economy in the twenty-first century? We try to answer this question in the next section.

SECTION 2: ISLAMIC BANKING AS A KEY PART OF AN ISLAMIC ENABLING DEVELOPMENTAL STATE

Islamic banking (مصرفية إسلامية) is generally defined as banking activity that is consistent with the principles of Shari'ah (Islamic social sanctions consistent with *fiqh* or [Islamic] legal system). Economics and finance scholars are attempting to match the *fiqh* prescriptions in practical applications by developing the disciplines of Islamic economics and finance. Many of these scholars claim that a more correct term for Islamic banking and finance is Shari'ah-compliant banking and finance.

The Institute for Islamic Banking and Insurance explains: Islamic banking refers to a system of banking or banking activity that is consistent with the principles of the Shari'ah (Islamic rulings) and its practical application through the development of Islamic economics. The principles which emphasize moral and ethical values in all dealings have wide universal appeal. Shari'ah prohibits the payment or acceptance of interest charges (riba) for the lending and accepting of money, as well as carrying out trade and other activities that provide goods or services considered contrary to its principles. While these principles were used as the basis for a flourishing economy in earlier times, it is only in the late twentieth century that a number of Islamic banks were formed to provide an alternative basis to Muslims although Islamic banking is not restricted to Muslims.

Islamic banking has the same purpose as conventional banking except that it operates in accordance with the rules of Shari'ah, known as *Fiqh al-Muamalat* (Islamic rules on transactions). Islamic banking activities must be practiced consistently with the Shari'ah and its practical application through the development of Islamic economics. Many of these principles upon which Islamic banking is based are commonly accepted all over the world, for centuries rather than decades. These principles are not new but arguably their original state has been altered over the centuries.

There are historical precedents even before the origin of Islam but close to its founding moment in the economic activities of the Prophet himself who acted as an agent for his wife's trading operations in Mecca and beyond, esp. Syria. Under Islam, right from its beginning, but particularly from the Medina period from 622 CE, Islamic partnerships *(mudarabah)* defined the Islamic commercial world for centuries until the domination by the West.

At both the micro and macroeconomic levels such partnerships played significant economic roles. They combined factors of production and allowed for expanded reproduction of the enterprises and the macroeconomy. The organization of production allowed for some to contribute the money and others to manage the business for predetermined shares of the surplus production and sales. Likewise, loss was also shared thereby retaining a productive incentive mechanism.

Thus, it can be argued that it was *Mudarabah* that really is at the heart of a creative production system under Islam. Any model of Islamic economics and finance that takes productivity enhancement and innovation seriously will have to incorporate *Mudarabah*. Fortunately, the model presented in section 4 can accommodate *Mudarabah*.

We now ask the question: for an Islamic society, how do we conceive of a model of Islamic finance and banking as part of an initial strategic plan that starts from a mixed institutional situation that does not contradict *Tawheed* or *Haqq* but incorporates Islamic elements for enhancing both efficiency and social capabilities of people in the twenty-first century?

It may be briefly pointed out that the Muslim-majority countries in the world such as Bangladesh, Tunisia, Morocco, and Indonesia are making the most progress. Turkey if it overcomes the current (2016) crisis stands a good chance also. We approach the challenge of making further progress by seeking the help of an appropriate technical model. Our model incorporates Islamic finance and banking within a complex web of interdependent multisectoral relations. Thus, the task of the policymakers to address the challenges of scientific policy-making consistent with the best teachings of *Al Qur'an* and well-examined and accepted *Ahadith* can be made possible in the complex world of the twenty-first century. Islam and good science are consistent, not contradictory.

SECTION 3: ISLAMIC CONTRACTS AND BANKING:

Before presenting and discussing the formal CGE model for Islamic finance, it is important to understand the complexity of Islamic contracts including financial contracts.

I present here a typology that can serve this purpose without being exhaustive.

Islamic Contracts

Definition: Offering money for the purpose of profit from its owner to another party who manages and acts in return for a permissible return. Permissible return meaning that it is compatible with the Islamic rules.

The objectives of Islamic finance are as follows:

• Meeting the borrower's needs
• Balancing the needs of the individual and society
• Developing the state economy by establishing and operating projects

The following are the characteristics of Islamic finance:

• Staying away from loans that draw interest (usury)
• Investing real money by employing it in support of productive movement
• Diversification of investment in money (cash) and concrete money (i.e., real estate)

The following are the pillars of the Islamic financing contract:

• The lender
• The borrower
• The money: the amount that is given from the lender to the borrower
• The formula of the *Islamic contract*

The following are the trade types in Islam:

Base on the due time concerning the exchange between the payment for the price of the commodity by the buyer and the possession of the commodity itself, there are four types:

The first is the immediate due time for the exchange between the possession of the commodity and the payment of the price of the commodity.
A good example of this is the daily exchange at the supermarket where
you pay the price for one bound of meat for $15 in cash. The possession
of the buyer money goes to the seller and that possession of the meat
goes from the seller to buyer at the same time. This is compatible with
the Islamic rules.

The second is the deferred possession for both the commodity and the payment of its price. This is known as selling debt for a debt which is not
allowed according to Islamic rules. It is not allowed mainly because there
are many issues that could come up from this kind of trade: that is, one
party cannot deliver his obligation or different specifications than what
both the parties have agreed on the first place, like a broken car instead of
a fine one. There are more details about this subject.

The third is the immediate due of the payment (the price) and the deferred
possession for the commodity. This is also known as forward sale or السَّلَم.
It is compatible with the Islamic rules.

The fourth is the immediate due possession for the commodity and the
deferred of the payment (the price). This is the opposite of the third type,
and there are two cases for this type, which are as follows:

- The deferred of the payment (the price) until the due date and then pay
  the full amounts at once.
- The deferred of the payment (the price) and pay it in parts, that is,
  "installment sale"

Trade conditions:

The following are common conditions for trade in Islam:

- There is satisfaction between contractors.
- The contract is permissible to act.
- The commodity or the item should be permissible.
- The commodity or the item must be owned by the seller or is authorized
  to dispose of it
- The commodity or the item shall be known by sight or description.
- The price should be known.
- There is ability to deliver the commodity or the item.

Examples of the Islamic financing contracts are as follows:

- *Installments Sales: (البيع التقسيط)*

Definition: A contract on immediate sale at a deferred price that leads to the separation of the payments based on known amounts and times in the future.

What should be mentioned is that this is similar to the third type, and it is different from the usury because the amount cannot be changed after the agreement is valid, so if the buyer could not pay it at the due time there should be no increase in the amount that the lender or the seller demands.

There are six conditions for the installment sales in addition to the common rule for trade:

- It is not an excuse to usury (i.e., the sale of "Al-Eenah").
- The commodity should be in the seller's possession.
- There is no usury in the exchange, that there is no doubt that it is "riba al-nasee'ah" which basically means they are not sharing the same usury problem as gold in exchange for gold that does not equal in price and weight.
- The immediate delivery for the item.
- The due time/s shall be known for both parties before signing on the contract.
- The possession for every part is considered as exchange for the payment of that part. In other words, they should not demand the full payment before the possession of the commodity, otherwise it will be considered a corrupt contract if the possession is not transferred to the buyer immediately (one part at a time).

The following are the issues in installments selling:

- The increase in deferred price is mentioned alone. That is, the seller says the price of this item is $100 and an increase in case of installments plan equals 20 percent. This has two cases:
  - First case happens during the bargaining and when they (the buyer and seller) write the contract, there will be one price. This is okay according to the Islamic finance rules because the contract is settled on just one deferred price and all debts are transferred to the buyer's liability in exchange for buying the good.
  - The second case is to provide in the contract the amount of the increase either by linking them to the current interest rate in the market or by fixing something like 20 percent of the price. This case is controversial and that the Fiqh Council has agreed that it is haraam to compare it with riba.
- Discount due to accelerating the payment of the installments has four cases:

- ○ First case, they mention this point in the contract: that is, in the contract they add a clause which provides for a discount if the buyer accelerates the payments or pays the full amount earlier. This is not compatible with the Islamic rules because it has two sales in one sale. Second, it has the same interpretation as that of riba because if the buyer chose to pay in two years and then he could not do it and delay the payment for another year for more money the original amount.
- ○ The second case, it is okay if the seller chooses to reduce the price after signing the contract for charity whether the buyer ask for it or not.
- ○ The installment amount is due, but the buyer cannot pay it in full, so both the seller and the buyer agree to give a discount for the immediate payment. This is okay if the seller agrees.
- ○ The last case, the buyer (or the seller) offers to seller (or the buyer) to reduce the deferred amount for an immediate payment, that is, if the buyer has $1,000 as debt due after five months and he offers to pay $850 today to the seller and the latter agrees or vice versa. This is controversial and the author says it is compatible with the Islamic rules.
- The third issue, the discount of commercial papers:

  Commercial papers like checks, bills, and other notes are all considered as a legislative documenting instrument of debts. The main papers here to talk about are bills which can be presented to banks to get a discount. This kind of commercial paper is not compatible with Islamic finance and it is considered as a type of "riba al-nasee'ah." The true picture of this bill according to the Islamic perspective is that the bank lends the one who ask for the bill discount (the beneficiary) for an increase in the drawer when the bill is mature.
- The imposition of a financial fine on delay in payment:

  This is not acceptable from the Islamic perspective because it is similar to the interest rate (riba) which is to ask money for more time.
- The foreclosure for missed payments:

  Foreclosure or refrain from delivering the commodity because of missed payment is prohibited in the Islamic point view for two reasons:
- ○ The seller has dropped his right on the possession of the commodity by agreeing to defer the payment.
- ○ It can be interpreted as being contrary to the contract, which provides for the transfer of ownership of the commodity to the buyer.
- Mortgaging the commodity on its deferred price:

  The buyer has the right to pledge the commodity for its price for many reasons, that is, the possession has transferred to him and he can act as he wants at it.
- *Murabaha Sale for the Purchase Order* (بيع المرابحة للآمر بالشراء)

Definition: Murabaha sale is selling a commodity for its cost in addition to a known profit.

Murabaha sale for the purchase order means that X asks Y to purchase a commodity for him (X) after describing it or showing it to him (Y). Then X would purchase this commodity from Y with additional profit. In other words, he is going to pay more than the original price for Y.

There are four conditions for Murabaha addition to the common conditions for trade in Islam:

• Cost and profit shall be known to both parties
• The first contract should be compatible with the Islamic rules
• The price in the first sale should not be riba-like (exchange for the same type, that is, gold for gold)

A good example of this is when someone (X again) goes to a bank and asks the bank to purchase a house for him. Then X would purchase the house from the bank for a higher price and usually deferred payments.

This means that the bank could be in a position where X has changed his mind, and this is risky for the bank. So, the bank may end up with a commodity (a house for example), which it does not want it but has purchased it for X who now does not want it. The bank cannot contract with X before he purchases the house because that will contradict with the Islamic rule to not sell what you do not have in your possession. Therefore, the bank can enter the first contract (buying the house) with an option to and set a time where he can know if X determines that he wants the house. So, if X choses to buy the house, he can sign a contract with the bank. If otherwise X changes his mind, the bank can return the house because he has a choice in the first contract.

• *Lease to Own Agreement:* (التأجير المنتهى بالتمليك)

Definition: That two parties would agree to lease something for known time and cost, but it will end up with owning that thing.

This contract is subject to dispute and the Fiqh Council has terminated its prohibition. The reason for the prohibition was because it combines two contracts in one at the same time.

Moreover, if, for example, there is a car that has stopped working, who is going to take the responsibility to fix it? There is a conflict between the lease contract and the sale contract: if it is a lease contract that means the seller has to fix it, if it is a sale contract the buyer has to fix it. The solution to this is by leasing the commodity with a promise to sale it at the end of the contract to the renter. The promise is morally binding and not legal. Nevertheless, the commodity would be under the lessor guarantee for the whole time of the lease agreement and under the buyer at the end after signing the sale contract. Another way is to do an installment agreement with a condition that the buyer does not transfer the possession to another one until he pays the full amount, or the contract will be not binding. Moreover, it could be a sale agreement with pledging the commodity for its price.

- *Forward Sale: (السَلَم)*

Definition: A contract on a described object that would deliver in the future for an immediate payment.

Example: A buyer should pay $5,000 in cash (immediately) to a seller in exchange for a hundred pounds of grapes that would be delivered after six months.

Forward sale conditions:

- That future delivering commodity can be described so it will not lead to disagreement.
- To not be specified, for example if the agreement is to deliver grapes with some specification but the delivery does not meet this particular specification.
- To be agreed on the weight and time.
- To take the full payment at the agreed time.
- That it is not something that does not required immediate exchange like gold for silver, dates for wheat, or dollar for yen.
- *Istisna' Contract (عقد الإستصناع)*

Definition: To ask another person for something that has not yet been done to make him apply specific specifications, with materials from the manufacturer, in return for financial compensation.

Differences between the forward sale and Istisna' contract:

- Istisna' contract has something to do with the industry.
- Forward sale requires immediate payment, but it is not necessary in the Istisna' contract where it could be late.

Difference between the forward sale and lease contract:

- Istisna' contract is both on the work and the object but the lease contract is on the object only.

The Parallel Istisna'

When a bank contracts two separate contracts: in one of them the bank is the one who asks the producer to make him an object, and in the other he is the producer in the object at the same specification with a higher price than the one in the first contract and the mature date usually will be after the first contract.

Example:

The first contract: the bank signs an aircraft manufacturing contract from an aircraft manufacturer, and pays $1 billion for six aircraft with specific specifications and asks to deliver it after a year from the date of signature.

The second contract: the bank signs a contract with an airlines company to deliver six aircraft, with the same specifications at the first contract, after a year and a half for $1,000,500,000.

Conditions on the parallel Istisna'

- Separate contract means the aircraft should not be assigned the same aircraft in the first contract, but it should be the same specifications.
- Possession of the objects in the first contract should be before delivery to the airline's company, and the bank should hold full responsibility as an owner of the aircraft.

- *Loans (القروض):*

Definition: To pay money to those who benefit from it and return it.

- *Banker's Draft:(السفتجه)*

Definition: To lend money to someone and get it back from the same person or from the one who represented him at the same or different place or country.

Example: Banks work by taking deposits and lending loans to somebody else.

- Current account in banks are considered as loans because
  - the bank must be returned the amount and not the assigned banknotes.
  - the bank guarantees these loans.
- In the author's opinion since these current accounts are considered as loans it is prohibited to charge interest or benefit from the bank for it otherwise it will consider as riba (loans riba or ابر القروض).
- Issuing bank cards and checkbooks:
    It is compatible with the Islamic rules. It has benefits for both sides.
    Non-bank overdraft commission:
- It is compatible with the Islamic rules because of the cost for the other bank for installing all these ATMs.

- *Credit Cards (البطاقات الائتمانية)*

There are two types of credit cards:
○ Covered credit cards

The covered credit card means the card that requires the customer to have a sufficient amount of money to cover its used. In other words, the bank will not pay for it and get that amount later so the customer has to have enough funds to cover his purchases.
○ Uncovered credit cards

This is like the visa card where a customer purchases and pays at the end of the month. This is like a loan to the customer so the bank should not ask for any money in exchange for this service.

The use of uncovered credit card is compatible with the Islamic rules unless it has used to purchase gold or silver or currencies because the handle is not achieved.

• *Tawarruq* (التورق)

Definition: Buying a commodity in the possession of a seller at a deferred price and then the buyer sells it for cash to another buyer who is not the first seller.

Conditions:

The only condition is that the buyer cannot sell the commodity to the first seller because this would lead to riba (riba Al Eeinah or ربا العينة)

The organized Tawarruq:

A person agrees with the bank that the bank sells him iron for a thousand dollars deferred, and then the bank commits to sell the iron to a third party for a thousand and five hundred dollars immediately and then the bank gives that amount to the customer. In most cases, this is not compatible with the Islamic finance rules because there is no real possession and it is just a trick to riba al Eeinah according to Fiqh Council

• *Diminishing musharakah* (المشاركة المتناقصة)

Definition: Diminishing musharaka is a partnership agreement (musharaka) with provision for gradual buyout of one of the partners. It can be used, for example, when a person wishes to buy a house from a bank.

For example, a real estate company has set up an investment commercial tower costing $70 million having no adequate liquidity. It contracted with a bank to finance the project by diminishing musharaka. By buying a share of the bank every year until the company purchases the whole tower from the other party.

• *Sharecropping and Share-Watering* (المُزَارَعة والمُسَاقاة)

Definition: Sharecropping means to give a piece of land to someone who sows it as an exchange for a common part of the crops of that land.

Share-watering is to give someone land with crops to water it for a common part of its production.

SECTION 4: A CGE MODEL WITH ISLAMIC BANKING

In this section, I present a CGE model implementable by using an appropriate software (Mathematica, GAMS, etc.) through a social accounting matrix (SAM). The key parameters of the model can be calibrated to the SAM for finding the general equilibrium solution. After this step, policy experiments with quantitative results can be carried out.

It is important to note that modules 6, 7, and 8 for the banking sector are where the crucial Islamic banking part occurs. For both state-owned and private commercial banks, we can have both Islamic and other banking subsystems. In modeling these modules in a disaggregated manner, the discussion in the previous section on the complexities of Islamic financial contracts must be kept in mind. What follows is a conceptually clear but empirically compact model that will need further disaggregation to accommodate the concrete realities of actual Islamic finance and banking.

A Financial-Structural Model of General Equilibrium with Islamic Banking

The financial-structural model was developed for applying to the possibility of Islamic banking and finance in the Indonesian economy. However, with some modifications, this can be applied to other Islamic cases as well. The most striking aspect of the model is the *possibility of a financial crisis* that results directly from the forces unleashed by the moves to liberalize finance quickly. With and an enabling developmental state the risk sharing in Islamic banking, such crises can become less frequent or can be avoided altogether. In a non-Islamic setting, a crisis happens because of the weaknesses in the banking sector which cannot cope with the demands arising from sudden liberalization. Significantly, such crises can occur even in a flexible or "managed float" regime. The persistence of the crisis in Asia during 1997–1998 suggests that "structural" factors rather than fixed exchange rates were the underlying causes of the crisis. It is important to recognize that a wisely crafted and implemented Islamic banking and finance strategy can produce stable, less crisis-prone and more egalitarian all-round development.

Equations of the GGE model:

I. Household Agriculture (HAG)

1.
$$NW_{HAG}(t) = KAS_{HAG}(t-1) + DSB_{HAG}(t-1) + DPB_{HAG}(t-1)$$
$$+ P_Z(t)Z_{HAG}(t-1) + P_{HAG}^K(t)K_{HAG}(t-1) + S_{HAG}(t)$$

Household net worth at eop (end of period) is = cash + initial deposit at private, state bank + the value of stock held at eop + the value of capital, which is the amount of capital at the beginning of period multiplied by price at eop to account for capital gain + saving.

Note: Household position is a net position. The assumption is that households do not engage in borrowing activity. Household is a recipient of wages/salary, interest from deposit, and firm's profit. It does not borrow for consumption. A household may borrow for investment in a venture, however, once it takes a loan of this kind, then it no longer is classified as a household. Depending on the type of business the household will be classified under a certain type of firm.

2. $QA_{HAG}(t) = NW_{HAG}(t) - P^K_{HAG}(t)K_{HAG}(t)$

Quantity of financial assets of household agriculture is = household net worth - the value of physical capital at eop.

Note: Physical capital of household at eop $K_{HAG}(t)$ includes investment made during the year. See equations 11, 22, and 33.

3. $q_{HAG} = A^{HAG}_{SB}(i_{sb} / \bar{i}_{sb})^{\sigma_{HAG}-1} + A^{HAG}_{PB}(i_{pb} / \bar{i}_{pb})^{\sigma_{HAG}-1}$

$\qquad + A^{HAG}_{Z}(r / \bar{r})^{\sigma_{HAG}-1} + A^{HAG}_{KAS}$

Agriculture households try to maximize the utility of return q_{HAG}, which is formulated by using CES type harmonic mean return.

A^{HAG}_i = distribution parameter

i_{SB}, i_{pb}, and r = interest rate at private, state bank, and rate of return on capital (profit) respectively

$\bar{i}_{SB}, \bar{i}_{pb}$, and $\bar{r}$ = normal yield on bank (private and state bank) deposits and company's capital.

σ_{HAG} = elasticity of substitution

The agriculture-household asset returns consist of interest from state bank, private bank, the share of the firm's profit, and cash. Government security is not available for households to buy. Therefore, there is no return from government security.

4. $\varnothing^{HAG}_{SB} = A^{HAG}_{SB} \dfrac{(i_{sb} / \bar{i}_{sb})^{\sigma_{HAG}-1}}{q_{hag}}$ $\longrightarrow$ Share of deposit on state bank

5. $\varnothing^{HAG}_{PB} = A^{HAG}_{PB} \dfrac{(i_{pb} / \bar{i}_{pb})^{\sigma_{HAG}-1}}{q_{hag}}$ $\longrightarrow$ Share of deposit on private bank

6. $\varnothing^{HAG}_{Z} = A^{HAG}_{Z} \dfrac{(r / \bar{r})^{\sigma_{HAG}-1}}{q_{hag}}$ $\longrightarrow$ Share of equity

7. $\varnothing_{KAS}^{HAG} = A_Z^{HAG} \dfrac{A_{KAS}^{HAG}}{q_{hag}}$ $\longrightarrow$ Share of currency

The sum of $\varnothing_{sb}^{HAG}, \varnothing_{pb}^{HAG}, \varnothing_Z^{HAG}, \varnothing_{KAS}^{HAG}$ must equal to 1

8. $D_{HAG} = \varnothing_{sb}^{HAG}(QA_{HAG}) + \varnothing_{PB}^{HAG}(QA_{HAG})$
   Total agriculture-household deposit is equal to share of household deposit in state bank multiplied by total financial assets plus the share of household deposit in private bank multiplied by total financial assets.

9. $Z_{HAG} = \varnothing_Z^{HAG}(QA_{HAG})$
   Total agriculture-household stock/equity is share of stock x total financial assets

10. $KAS_{HAG} = \varnothing_{KAS}^{HAG}(QA_{HAG})$
    Total agriculture-household cash is share of cash x total financial assets

11. $K_{HAG}(t) = K_{HAG}(t-1) + I_{HAG}(t)$
    Total capital owned by agriculture household = initial capital + total investment at end of period

II. Household Non-Agriculture (HNAG)

12. $NW_{HNAG}(t) = KAS_{HNAG}(t-1) + DSB_{HNAG}(t-1) + DPB_{HNAG}(t-1)$

$$+ P_Z(t)Z_{HNAG}(t-1) + P_{HNAG}^K(t)K_{HNAG}(t-1) + S_{HNAG}(t)$$

13. $QA_{HNAG}(t) = NW_{HNAG}(t) - P_{HNAG}^K(t)K_{HNAG}(t)$

14. $q_{HNAG} = A_{SB}^{HNAG}(i_{sb}/\bar{i}_{sb})^{\sigma_{HNAG}-1} + A_{PB}^{HNAG}(i_{pb}/\bar{i}_{pb})^{\sigma_{HNAG}-1}$

$$+ A_Z^{HNAG}(r/\bar{r})^{\sigma_{HNAG}-1} + A_{KAS}^{HNAG}$$

15. $\varnothing_{SB}^{HNAG} = A_{SB}^{NHAG} \dfrac{(i_{sb}/\bar{i}_{sb})^{\sigma_{HNAG}-1}}{q_{hnag}}$ $\longrightarrow$ Share of deposit on state bank

16. $\varnothing_{PB}^{HNAG} = A_{PB}^{NHAG} \dfrac{(i_{pb}/\bar{i}_{pb})^{\sigma_{HNAG}-1}}{q_{hnag}}$ $\longrightarrow$ Share of deposit on private bank

17. $\varnothing_Z^{HNAG} = A_Z^{HNAG} \dfrac{(r/\bar{r})^{\sigma_{HNAG}-1}}{q_{hnag}}$ $\longrightarrow$ Share of equity

18. $\varnothing_{KAS}^{HNAG} = A_Z^{HNAG} \dfrac{A_{KAS}^{HNAG}}{q_{hnag}}$ $\longrightarrow$ Share of currency

The sum of $\varnothing_{sb}^{HNAG}, \varnothing_{pb}^{HNAG}, \varnothing_Z^{HNAG}, \varnothing_{KAS}^{HNAG}$ must equal to 1

19. $D_{HNAG} = \varnothing_{sb}^{HNAG}(QA_{HNAG}) + \varnothing_{PB}^{HNAG}(QA_{HNAG})$

20. $Z_{HNAG} = \varnothing_{Z}^{HNAG}(QA_{HNAG})$

    Total nonagricultural-household stock/equity is share of stock x total financial assets

21. $KAS_{HNAG} = \varnothing_{KAS}^{HNAG}(QA_{HNAG})$

    Total non-agriculture-household cash is share of cash x total financial assets

22. $K_{HNAG}(t) = K_{HNAG}(t-1) + I_{HNAG}(t)$

    Total capital owned by non-agriculture-household = initial capital + total investment at end of period.

III. Household Total (h)

23. $NW_h(t) = NW_{HAG}(t) + NW_{HNAG}(t)$

24. $QA_h(t) = QA_{HAG}(t) + QA_{HNAG}(t)$

25. $qh = q_{HAG} + q_{HNAG}$

26. $\varnothing_{SB}^h = Q_{SB}^{HAG} + Q_{SB}^{HNAG}$ $\longrightarrow$ Share of deposit on state bank

27. $\varnothing_{PB}^h = Q_{PB}^{HAG} + Q_{PB}^{HNAG}$ $\longrightarrow$ Share of deposit on private bank

28. $\varnothing_{Z}^h = Q_{Z}^{HAG} + Q_{Z}^{HNAG}$ $\longrightarrow$ Share of equity

29. $\varnothing_{KAS}^h = Q_{KAS}^{HAG} + Q_{KAS}^{HNAG}$ $\longrightarrow$ Share of currency

30. $D_h = D_{HAG} + D_{HNAG}$

31. $Z_h = Z_{HAG} + Z_{HNAG}$

32. $KAS_h = KAS_{HAG} + KAS_{HNAG}$

33. $K_h(t) = K_{HAG}(t) + K_{HNAG}(t)$

IV. Firms

34–37. $DEF = P_i^k I_i - S_i$ i = FAG, FMIN, FTS, FI

38–41. $Z_i(t) = Z_i(t-1) + \alpha_i + \beta_i \left[(DEF_i(t) / P_i^k(t)) \right]$ i = FAG, FMIN, FTS, FI

42–45. $QL_i(t) = DEF_i(t) - P_z(t)\left[Z_i(t) - Z_i(t-1) \right] + LSB_i(t-1)$

$$+ LPB(t-1) + LF_i(t-1) \quad \text{i = FAG, FMIN, FTS, FI}$$

Another part of the deficit must be financed through borrowing. The required amount of total borrowing at time t ($QL_i(t)$ must be equal to the amount of deficit minus the value of outstanding equity increase at the end of period plus last year's outstanding loan from state bank, private bank, and foreign loan.

The firm's total loan comes from different sources. From the state bank, private bank, and from foreign loan, with distribution parameter of A_x^i, and interest rate on bank loan of i_l, interest rate of foreign loan of i_f. Using CES specification, the firms try to minimize the cost function based on capitalized borrowing cost of $\bar{i}_{xi} / i_x$.

46–49. $q_i = A_{sb}^i (\bar{i}_{li} / i_l)^{\sigma_i - 1} + A_{pb}^i (\bar{i}_{li} / i_l)^{\sigma_i - 1} + A_{fl}^i (\bar{i}_{fli} / i_{fl})^{\sigma_i - 1}$

i = FAG, FMIN, FTS, FI

q_i is the average of capitalized interest rates for each type of firm.

Note: It is assumed that interest rate is not the explaining factor for the firm's decision to choose between state bank and private bank. The image of private bank is having better service, faster, and easier to deal with and that of state bank is safer, bigger, and more helpful when a firm is in trouble. Firms borrowing from the state bank are restrained by many requirements, and its reputation for inflexibility must be taken into account when one tries to find out why there are certain preferences toward one or another.

The share of loan from state bank, private bank, and foreign loan of each firm is given in equations 50–61. The sum of the share must equal to 1.

50–53. $\varnothing_{sb}^i = A_{sb}^i \dfrac{(\bar{i}_{Li} / i_l)^{\sigma_i - 1}}{q_i}$ i = FAG, FMIN, FTS, FI

54–57. $\varnothing_{pb}^i = A_{pb}^i \dfrac{(\bar{i}_{li} / i_l)^{\sigma_i - 1}}{q_i}$ i = FAG, FMIN, FTS, FI

58–61. $\varnothing_{lf}^i = A_{lf}^i \dfrac{(\bar{i}_{fli} / i_{fl})^{\sigma_i - 1}}{q_i}$ i = FAG, FMIN, FTS, FI

The demand for loan from each type of bank by each type of firm is given in equations 62–73.

62–65. $LSB_i = \varnothing_{lsb}^i QL_i$ i = FAG, FMIN, FTS, FI

Firm's demand for loan from state bank

66–69. $LPB_i = \varnothing_{lpb}^i QL_i$ i = FAG, FMIN, FTS, FI

Firm's demand for loan from private bank

70–73. $LF_i = \varnothing_{lf}^i Ql_i$ i = FAG, FMIN, FTS, FI

Firm's demand for loan from abroad

74. $L = \sum\limits_{i=FAG}^{FI} LSB_i + \sum\limits_{i=FAG}^{FI} LPB_i$

Total domestic loan = total loan from state bank and from private bank to all firms

75–78. $K_i(t) = K_i(t-1) + I_i(t)$

Total capital stocks held by firms at the end of period = capital stock at the beginning plus investment at the end of period.

V. Government (G)

79. $FL_G(t) = FL_G(t-1) + e(\Delta FL_G^\$)$

Foreign Loan at time t (eop) = outstanding Loan from abroad at the beginning + new loan from abroad in local currency. The additional loan amount is exogenous, valued at foreign currency (dollar) but converted into local currency by multiplication with exchange rate.

80. $QL_G = LPB_G(t-1) + LSB_G(t-1) + LCB_G(t-1)$

$$+ P_G^k(t)I_G(t) - S_G(t) - e(\Delta LF_G^\$)$$

Government demand for domestic credit = government. investment + initial borrowing from the banking system (SB, PB, and CB), less government saving and loan from abroad.

Note: The government demand for domestic credit is a net position with loan payment included (if any). Any amount of loan repayment from the government to the banking system will appear as reduction in saving by the same amount. Government investment is exogenous.

81. $L_G = \left[\alpha_G^{SB} + \beta_G^{SB}(DEP_{SB})\right] + \left[\alpha_G^{PB} + \beta_G^{PB}(DEP_{PB})\right]$

Bank credit to government = initial claims of the government, certain resources in SB and PB + statutory liquidity ratio β multiplied by deposit of SB and PB.

82. $LCB_G = QL_{G\_}L_G$
Central bank loan to government; it is the government balance sheet residual, that is, the portion of total loan to government that is not fulfilled by commercial banking sector.

83. $K_G(t) = K_G(t-1) + I_G(t)$

VI. Commercial State Bank Portfolio (SB)
(Each equation has two components—Islamic and other)

84. $DSB = DSB_{HAG} + DSB_{HNAG}$

Deposits in the state bank come from household, agriculture, and non-agriculture, at a fixed rate of deposit i_d.

85. $RR_{SB} = u_1^{SB} + u_2^{SB}(DEP^{SB})$

Reserve requirement in the central bank = marginal amount u_i + a fraction of deposits.

86. $QL_{SB} = DSB + ADVCB_{SB} - LSB_G - RR_{SB} + LIK_{SB}$

Domestically available resources or the total loan can be given from domestic resources = deposit + advances from central bank + liquidity credit from central bank − loan to government − reserve requirement.

87. $DCB_{SB} = RR_{SB}\left[1 + \theta(i_{lsb} / \bar{i_l})^{-\gamma}\right]$

The state bank reserve at the central bank is always higher than the requisite reserve requirement. The excess reserve is a function of interest rate charged by the state bank for loan. The higher the rate, the lower the excess reserves.

88. $LF_{SB} = \left(L_G^{SB} + DCB_{SB} + \sum_{i=FAG}^{FL} LSB_i\right) - \left(DSB - REDSCNT - NW\right)$

The state bank resources are deposits, rediscounts from the central bank, and net worth. The total resources available will be used to create loans to government; commercial loans to firms; and some will be used as deposits to central bank. If the available resources are less than the loan created, then foreign loan is needed.

VII. Commercial Private Bank Portfolio (PB) (Two Types: (1) Islamic Banks; and (2) Non-Islamic Banks—total of ten equations)

89. $DPB = DB_{HAG} + DPB_{HNAG}$

90. $RR_{PB} = u_1^{PB} + u_2^{PB}(DEP^{PB})$

91. $QL_{PB} = DPB + ADVCB_{PB} - LPB_G - RR_{PB} + LIK_{PB}$

Available resources (domestic) = deposit + advances from central bank − loan to government − reserve requirement + liquidity credit from central bank

92. $DCB_{PB} = RR_{PB}\left[1 + \theta(i_{lpb} / \bar{i_l})^{-\gamma}\right]$

93. $LF_{PB} = \left(L_G^{PB} + DCB_{PB} + \sum_{i=FAG}^{FL} LPB_i\right) - \left(DPB - REDSCNT - NW\right)$

VIII.   *Commercial Bank Total*
          (Each equation has two components—Islamic and other)

94. $DEP = DSB + DPB$

     Total deposit taken by commercial bank

95. $RR = RR_{SB} + RR_{PB}$

     Total reserve deposit at central bank

96. $QL + QL_{SB} + QL_{PB}$

     Total resources available domestically

97. $i_L = \bar{i_L}\left[\dfrac{L(i\,/\,i_F)^{\in}(i_R\,/\,i_R)^{\phi}}{\alpha QL}\right]^{1/\delta}$

     Market clearing interest rate i_L = loan interest rate; i_F = foreign loan inter-
     est rate; i_R = rediscount interest rate.
     $\in$, ϕ, and δ = loan supply interest rate elasticities, α = loan supply
     intercept.

98. $DCB = DCB_{SB} + DCB_{PB}$

     Total deposit of commercial bank at central bank, including required reserve.

99. $LF = LF_{SB} + LF_{PB}$

     Total residual items: The foreign loan needed by the domestic com-
     mercial banking sector to cover excess loan over domestic resources
     available.

IX.   *Central Bank Portfolio*

100. $FL = FL_{SB} + FL_{PB} + FL_{FAG} + FL_{MIN} + FL_{IS} + FL_{I} + FL_{G}$

101. $ADVCB = ADV_{CEL} + \varnothing_4\left[(FL_{SB} + FL_{PB}) - FL_{CEL}\right] - \gamma_4(DEPCB - RR)$

      Total advances available from central bank = ceiling for advances less
      state banks and private bank's advances, less net deposit at central bank.

102. $KAS_{CB} = KAS_{H}$

103. $NWCB(t) = NWCB(T-1) + DISCR$
      DISCR = accounting discrepancy of state-owned firms

104. $CBREV(t) = FL(t) - FL(t-1) - SF(t) + CBRES(t-1)$

      Central bank's reserve = net foreign loan at eop less foreign saving plus
      reserve at the beginning of the period

105. $NWRES = CBLG + ADVCB + CBRES - KASCB + DEPCB - NWCB$

X.   *Other Financial Balance*

106. $P_Z = \dfrac{ZZ_H}{(Z_{FAG} + Z_{MIN} + Z_{FTS} + Z_I)}$

107. $INT = \left(A_{SB}^{H} + A_{PB}^{H} + i_L L_{SB} + i_L L_{PB}\right) + \left(A_{CB}^{SB} + A_{CB}^{PB} + i_L L_{SB} + i_L L_{PB}\right)$

Interest payment.

Other financial institutions—both Islamic and non-Islamic—can be introduced as well. Thus the insurance, real estate and equity, and debt markets can be easily modeled under the general framework given here. Clearly, the flow of funds capturing the flows encapsulating these sectors as these are embedded in the economy will need to be constructed carefully.

XI. Production and Price Formation

108–114. $P_i^k = \xi_4 P_4 + \xi_7 P_7$ $i = 1,2,3,4,5,6,7$

P_i^k = Price indexes for each sector's capital stock; capital goods come from the industrial sector and from import.

115–121
$$P_{i0}^* = [(\Theta_{1i})^{\sigma_i^{int}}(P_1)^{1-\sigma_i^{int}} + (\Theta_{2i})^{\sigma_i^{int}}(P_2)^{1-\sigma_i^{int}} + (\Theta_{3i})^{\sigma_i^{int}}(P_3)^{1-\sigma_i^{int}} +$$
$$(\Theta_{5i})^{\sigma_i^{int}}(P_5)^{1-\sigma_i^{int}} + (\Theta_{6i})^{\sigma_i^{int}}(P_6)^{1-\sigma_i^{int}} + (\Theta_{7i})^{\sigma_i^{int}}(P_7)^{1-\sigma_i^{int}}]^{1/(1-\sigma_i^{int})}$$

$i = 1,2,3,4,5,6,7$; P_{i0}^* = cost indexes for sectoral intermediate uses, input output coefficient = a_{ji}^* and constant elasticities of substitution among

intermediate inputs = σ_i^{int}

122–128. $a_{ji}^* = \left[\dfrac{P_i^* \Theta_{ji}}{P_j} \right]^{\sigma_i^{int}}$ j = sector; i = market participant HAG – FI

a_{ji}^* = input ou tput coefficient.

129–135. $P_i^c = \left[(\Theta_{Li})^{\sigma_i^{FIN}}(W_i)^{1-FIN} + (\Theta_{Ki})^{\sigma_i^{FIN}}(r_i + \delta_i)(P_i^K)^{1-FIN} \right]^{1/(1-\sigma^{1-FIN})}$
$$+ (\Theta_i^*)^{\sigma_i^{FIN}}(P_i^*)^{\sigma_i^{FIN}}$$

CES cost function = labor cost + fixed capital cost + cost of intermediate goods used

i = sector/commodity 1-7

σ_i^{FIN} = elasticities of substitution

136–142. $L_i = (P_i^c \Theta_{Li} / W_i)^{\sigma_i^{FIN}} X_i$ i = Hag – FI

Level of employment

143–149. $r_i(t) = \dfrac{1}{P_i^K(t-1)} \left[P_i^c(t) \Theta_{Ki} \left(\dfrac{X_i(t)}{K_i(t-1)} \right)^{1/\sigma_i^{INT}} \right] - \delta_i$

Sectoral rates of profit are determined by output level X and incoming capital stocks $K_i(t-1)$

i = HAG – FI

150. $\quad r(t) = \dfrac{r_{HAG}(t)P_{HAG}^K(t)K_{HAG}(t-1) + \cdots r_{FI}(t)P_{FI}^K(t)K_{FI}(t-1)}{P_{HAG}^K(t)K_{HAG}(t-1) + \cdots P_{FI}^K(t)K_{FI}(t-1)}$

Average rate of profit (used for household portfolio decisions) depends on sectoral rate of profit

151–157. $\quad X_{ji} = a_{ji}^* \left[\dfrac{P_i^c \Theta_i^c}{P_i^c} \right]^{\sigma_i^{FIN}} X_i \quad$ j = commodity 1–7

I = market participant HAG − FI

Intermediate goods flow using a_{ji}^* coefficient of input output defined with regard to the intermediate aggregate. (Flow of goods j (sector j) to market participant i; that is, demand of good j by market participant i).

158–164. $\quad Mi = \left[\dfrac{P_i \Theta_{0i}}{e(1+t_0)P_0} \right]^{\sigma_i^{FIN}} X_i$

i = sectors 5, 6, and 7 (import mining and import other)

Mi = Derived demand for import

165–171. $\quad P_i = P_i^c(1 - t_i) \quad$ i = 1–7

After-tax prices for each sector/commodity

XII. Income Generation and Saving

172. $\quad W = w_{HAG}L_{HAG} + \cdots w_{FI}L_{FI} + W_{fh} - W_{hf}$

173–179. $\quad \Pi_i(t) = r_i(t)P_i^K(t)K_i(t-1) + \Pi_{fi} - \Pi_{if}$

i = HAG, HNAG, SB, PB, FAG, FMIN, FTS, FI.

Profit income flows

180–185. $\quad OS_i = (1 - \upsilon_i)\Pi_i + SUB \quad$ i = SB, PB, FAG, FMIN, FTS, FI.

Operating surplus of firms i is part of profit after the household share of υ

Government-owned firm (bank) receives subsidy SUB

186–191. $\quad S_i = (1 - d_i - t_i^{dir})OS_i \quad$ i = SB, PB, FAG, FMIN, FTS, FI

Saving of the firm, equal to operating surpluses less dividend d payment less direct taxes t_i^{dir}

192. $Y_{HAG} = W_{HAG} + d_{SB}^{HAG}OS_{SB}^{HAG} + \cdots d_{FI}^{HAG}OS_{FI}^{HAG} + v_{SB}^{HAG}\Pi_{SB}^{HAG} + \cdots v_{FI}^{HAG}\Pi_{FI}^{HAG} +$

$TRAN_{gHAG} + TRAN_{fHAG}$

Household AG income = wages +dividend + share of profit +transfer from G and abroad

193. $Y_{HNAG} = W_{HNAG} + d_{SB}^{HNAG}OS_{SB}^{HNAG} + \cdots d_{FI}^{HNAG}OS_{FI}^{HNAG} + v_{SB}^{HNAG}\Pi_{SB}^{HNAG}$

$+ \cdots v_{FI}^{HNAG}\Pi_{FI}^{HNAG} + TRAN_{gHNAG} + TRAN_{fHNAG}$

194. $Y_h = Y_{HAG} + Y_{HNAG}$

Total HH income is the sum of HAG income and HNAG income

195. $D_{HAG} = D_0^{HAG} + (1 + s_{HAG})Y_{HAG} - TRAN_{HAGf} - t_{HAG}^{dir}Y_{HAG} - (A_5^h + i_L L_5)$

$+ Y_{HAG} NW_{HAG}$

$$\text{Consumption demand} = \frac{\text{initial}}{\text{basic consumption}} + \text{consumption}$$

$$- \text{transfer abroad} - \text{direct taxes}$$

196. $D_{HNAG} = D_0^{HNAG} + (1 + s_{HNAG})Y_{HNAG} - TRAN_{HNAGf} - t_{HNAG}^{dir}Y_{HNAG}$

$- (A_5^h + i_L L_5) + Y_{HNAG} NW_{HNAG}$

197. $D = D_{HAG} + D_{HNAG}$

198. $S_{HAG} = Y_{HAG} - TRAN_{HAGf} - t_{HAG}^{dir}Y_{HAG} - (A_f^{HAG} + i_L L_5) - D_{HAG}$

199. $S_{HNAG} = Y_{HNAG} - TRAN_{HNAGf} - t_{HNAG}^{dir}Y_{HNAG} - (A_f^{HNAG} + i_L L_5) - D_{HNAG}$

200. $S_h = S_{HAG} + S_{HNAG}$

201. $Y_g = \sum_{i=1}^{4} t_i P_i^c X_i + et_0 P_5 M_5 + et_0 P_6 M_6 + et_0 P_7 M_7 + t_h^{dir} Y_h + \sum_{i=SB}^{FI} t_i^{dir} OS_i$

$+ \sum_{i=1}^{4} t_i^{\exp} P_i^c E_i t$

Government income consists of the sum of indirect taxes from all sectors + domestic currency of import indirect taxes + direct taxes from household + the sum of direct taxes of firms + export taxes.

202. $S_g = Y_g - \sum_{i=1}^{7} P_i G_i - TRAN_{gh} - \left(A_5^g + i_l L_g\right)$

203. $S_f = \sum_{i=1}^{7} \Pi_{if} + W_{hf} + \sum_{i=5}^{7} eP_i M_i + TRAN_{hf} + TRAN_{gf}$

$- \sum_{i=1}^{4}(1 + t_i^{\exp})P_i^c E_i - W_{fh} - \sum_{i=1}^{4} \Pi_{fi} - TRAN_{fg} - TRAN_{fh}$

Current account deficit in foreign currency terms is converted to domestic currency, with export tax rate of t_i^{exp}

XIII. *Final Demand Determination*

204. $\tilde{D} = \sum_{i=1}^{7} \Theta_i^{dem} P_i \quad i = 1-7$

205–211. $C_i = \Theta_i^{dem} + (\alpha_i^{dem} / P_i)(D - \tilde{D}) \quad i = 1-7$

212–215. $I_i(t) = \left[I_{0i} + \omega_i \left\{ r_i(t) - i_l(t) \right\} \right] K_i(t-1)$

i = firms; FAG − FI.

Investment demands of firms depend positively on rate of profit r_i and negatively on loan interest rate i_l. The firm investment parameter is ω_i.

216–217. $I_i(t) = \left[I_{0i} + \omega_i \left\{ r_i(t) \right\} \right] K_i(t-1) \quad i = $ SB and PB

State bank and private bank's demand for investment depend positively on the rate of profit. The loan rate is negative and the deposit rate is positive. However, a simultaneous increase in the loan and deposit rate will net a zero effect. The decisive factor in this case is the spread between loan and deposit rate. But the spread will correlate with rate of profit thus the spread effect on investment demand has been reflected through the inclusion of r_i.

218. $I_{HAG} = I_{0HAG} + \omega_{HAG}^i i_l + \omega_{HAG}^y (Y_{HAG} / P_{HAG}^k)$

219. $I_{HNAG} = I_{0HNAG} + \omega_{HNAG}^i i_l + \omega_{HNAG}^y (Y_{HNAG} / P_{NHAG}^k)$

220. $I_h = I_{HAG} + I_{HNAG}$

Household demand for investment is a function of interest rate (with investment parameter ω^i) and real income (investment parameter W^y).

221. $I_g = I_{0g}$

222–225. $E_i = E_{0i} \left[\dfrac{e P_f^E}{(1 + t_i^{Exp}) P_i^c} \right]^{\eta}$

Export depends on the ratio of price of foreign goods and domestic border price, the elasticity is η. i = 1−4

XIV. *Commodity Balances*

226–232. $Xi = \sum_{j=HAG}^{FI} X_{ij} + C_i + G_i + \xi_i \left(\sum_{j=HAG}^{FI} I_j \right) + p_i \left[\sum_{i=1}^{7} \delta_i K_i(t-1) \right]$

i = commodity 1–7; j = HAG – FI

p_i = sectoral composition of depreciation

XV. Saving—Investment Balances

233. $$SI = \sum_{i=HAG}^{FI} S_i + S_f - \sum_{i=HAG}^{FI} P_i^k I_i$$

Saving of all sectors (excluding the G) plus foreign saving less investment of all sectors (foreign saving not included) will be zero if overall macroeconomic balance is to be maintained.

It should be noted that other features of Islamic finance such as Islamic investment, contracts, distribution including Zakat and both short and long Sukuk,[16] insurance, especially *Takaful* and prohibitions against short sales can be included by expanding the model further within relevant financial modules. Running the model analytically shows that without Islamic banking, the system is more fragile, and expanding Islamic banking and risk-sharing reduces the risk of financial crises in a neuro-fuzzy model created by Khan and coauthors.[17]

SUMMARY AND CONCLUSION

The main purpose of this chapter has been to incorporate critically the key characteristics of the Islamic banking system in a larger systemic model of a mixed economy with both Islamic and other characteristics. To this end, I have constructed a structural computable general equilibrium (CGE) model with banking and financial sectors. Thus, I demonstrate mathematically that a modern Islamic banking sector can be defined and included in a sophisticated CGE model.

Furthermore, as discussed in the modeling section, other financial sectors and their interactions can be modeled in this type of CGE model. Other financial institutions—both Islamic and non-Islamic—can be introduced via appropriately specified equations. Thus, the insurance, real estate and equity, and debt markets can be easily modeled under the general framework given here. As I have also emphasized, the flow of funds capturing the flows encapsulating these sectors as these are embedded in the economy will need to be constructed carefully.

In sections 3 and 4 I considered the desiderata and injunctions of Shari'ah-compliant Islamic finance and banking. Islamic banking (مصرفية إسلامية) is generally defined as banking activity that is consistent with the principles of Shari'ah (Islamic social sanctions consistent with *fiqh* or [Islamic] legal system). Economics and finance scholars are attempting to match the *fiqh* prescriptions in practical applications by developing the disciplines of Islamic economics and finance. Many of these scholars claim that a more correct term for Islamic banking and finance is Shari'ah-compliant banking and finance.

However, consistent with the ethical imperatives of both an extension of Sen's capabilities perspective—particularly in the social-spiritual sense by Khan and a few others—we need a flexible model that will have the Shari'ah-compliant banking and finance as a special case. The major mathematical modeling demonstration in section 4 has been to explore the feasibility of such a mathematical model.

From both technical and social perspectives, efficient and egalitarian Islamic economics are shown to be feasible. This type of banking with socially oriented Islamic characteristics can also support modern innovation systems. The technical general equilibrium model shows how such an economy can lead the Muslim-majority countries to rapid augmentation of both efficiency and social capabilities of people[18] in an egalitarian manner.

It has therefore been shown that a complex systems model incorporating Islamic finance and banking can be formulated for the twenty-first century. The model can accommodate Islamic banking and many other Islamic financial features. It can be shown that Islamic banking and risk-bearing reduces the chance of financial and economic crises in such a model augmented by a neuro-fuzzy learning component.

Two further conclusions follow logically for using appropriate technical models in formulating and implementing the Islamic development strategy in the financial and banking sectors in particular. The first is the need for taking a historically grounded pragmatic and diagnostic approach to the technical problems of development on the one hand. The second is that at the same time the Islamic development strategy must make democratic deepening and egalitarianism in accordance with the Islamic concepts of *Haqq, Adl, and the firm Islamic opposition to zulm,* the strategic centerpieces of any progressive Islamic social movement. It is important to make these last two factors the most salient identifying criteria for an innovative institutional mix for the twenty-first century in the Islamic world.

It is necessary to identify distortions from the perspective of deepening democracy in conformity with *Haqq* and Islamic egalitarianism and correct these quickly. It is also equally necessary to identify market failures and other institutional failures. Instead of taking a grand, presumptive approach to development, the role of a mix of heterodox policies with the willingness to revise policies before the cost gets too high seems to be the best recipe for avoiding failures.

Clearly, in order to promote equitable growth and broad development Islamic countries must build institutions that can supply social insurance and safety nets, and create a democratic space for voice and accountability in keeping with the deeper precepts of Islam. But there is no one-size-that-fits-all for any of these functions.[19] Here the role of history of popular movements and institution building will be crucial. While movements in different parts of the world can certainly learn from each other and have ties of solidarity, each part will need to have specific strategic orientation and tactical and organizational specificities in every sphere according to its particular historical trajectory. No predetermined futures are foreordained in this complex twenty-first-century world. This applies with special force to the Islamic world. Islam in its progressive forms can become a force for both local and global peace and prosperity. The technical modeling offered here is one among many instruments for rational policy-making for peace and prosperity.

NOTES

1. See M. Kabir Hasan, "Loan Loss Provisioning in OIC Countries: Evidence from Conventional vs. Islamic Banks," EconPapers (2015); Hossein Askari and Abbas Mirakhor, The Next Financial Crisis and How to Save Capitalism (Houndsmills and New York: Palgrave Macmillan, 2015).

2. Amartya Sen, *Inequality Re-examined* (Oxford: Oxford University Press, 1992); Amartya Sen, *Development as Freedom* (Oxford: Oxford University Press and New York: Alfred A. Knopf, Inc., 1999); H.A. Khan, *Technology, Development and Democracy: Limits to National Innovation Systems in the Age of Postmodernism* (Cheltenham, United Kingdom: Edward Elgar, 1998); H.A. Khan, "Innovation and Growth in a Schumpeterian Model," *Oxford Development Studies* 30, no. 3 (2002): 289–306; H.A. Khan, *Global Markets and Financial Crisis in Asia: Towards a Theory for the Twenty-First Century* (Houndsmills and New York: Macmillan/Palgrave, 2004); H.A. Khan, *Innovation and Growth in East Asia: The Future of Miracles* (Houndsmills and New York: Macmillan/Palgrave, 2004).

3. Sen, *Inequality Re-examined*; Sen, *Development as Freedom*; Khan, *Technology, Development and Democracy*; Khan, "Innovation and Growth in a Schumpeterian Model," 289–306; Khan, *Global Markets and Financial Crisis in Asia*; H.A. Khan and Yi-bei Liu, "Ecological Economics of Water Management in China," in I. Usha (ed.), *Global Law and Economics of Sustainable Development* (Hyderabad: IFCAI Press, 2008).

4. J.M. Keynes, *The Collected Writings of John Maynard Keynes*, 29 vols., ed., D.E. Moggridge for the Royal Economic Society (London: Macmillan), p. 261.

5. See, for example, Khan, *Innovation and Growth in East Asia*; Khan, *Global Markets and Financial Crisis in Asia*; H.A. Khan, "Technology and Modernity: Creating Social Capabilities in a POLIS," in T. Misa (ed.), *Technology and Modernity* (Cambridge: The MIT Press, 2003); H.A. Khan, "What Can the African Countries Learn from the Macroeconomics of Foreign Aid in Southeast Asia?" in E. Aryeetey, J. Court, M. Nissanke and B. Weder (eds.), *Asia and Africa in the Global Economy* (Tokyo: UNU Press, 2003); Khan, *Technology, Development and Democracy*;

H.A. Khan, *Technology, Energy and Development: The South Korean Transition* (Cheltenham, United Kingdom: Edward Elgar, 1997); H.A. Khan, "Ecology, Inequality and Poverty: The Case of Bangladesh," *Asian Development Review* 15, no. 2 (1997); H.A. Khan, "Technology, Energy, Distribution and Balance of Payments: A Macroeconomic Framework," Unpublished dissertation, Cornell University, Ithaca, New York, 1983; H.A. Khan, "Technology Choice in the Energy and Textile Sectors in the Republic of Korea," in A.S. Bhalla (ed.), *Technology and Employment in Industry*, 3rd ed. (1985); H.A. Khan and Erik Thorbecke, "Macroeconomic Effects of Technology Choice: Multiplier and Structural Path Analysis," *Journal of Policy Modelling* 1, no. 1 (1989); H.A. Khan and Erik Thorbecke, *Macroeconomic Effects and Diffusion of Alternative Technologies within a Social Accounting Matrix Framework: The Case of Indonesia* (Aldershot, UK: Gower Publication, 1988); H.A. Khan and Victor Lippit, "The Surplus Approach to Environment," *Review of Political Economy* (1993); H.A. Khan and Victor Lippit, *Sustainability and Surplus* (Storrs, CT: EconPapers, 2007) and the references therein.

6. Augustin K. Fosu, *Achieving Development Success* (Oxford: Oxford University Press, 2013).

7. Giovanni Arrighi, *Adam Smith in Beijing* (London: Verso, 2007); Giovanni Arrighi, *The Long Twentieth Century* (London: Verso, 1994); H.A. Khan, "What Should the AIIB's Priorities Be?" Davos: World Economic Forum, April 2015; Khan, *Innovation and Growth in East Asia*; Khan, *Global Markets and Financial Crisis in Asia*; John Weiss and H.A. Khan, eds., *Poverty Strategies in Asia: A Growth Plus Approach* (Cheltenham: Edward Elgar and ADBI, 2006); H.A. Khan, "China's Development Strategy and Energy Security," in Amelia Santos-Paulino and Guanghua Wan (eds.), *The Rise of China and India: Development Strategies and Lessons* (Palgrave/Macmillan, 2010); H.A. Khan, "Development Strategies: Lessons from the Experiences of South Korea, Malaysia, Thailand and Vietnam," in Augustin K. Fosu (ed.), *Achieving Development Success* (Oxford: Oxford University Press, 2013); H.A. Khan, "Global Financial Governance: Towards a New Global Financial Architecture for Averting Deep Financial Crises," EconPapers (2013); H.A. Khan, "Deep Financial Crises, Reforming the IMF and Building Regional Autonomy: Towards a New Hybrid Global Financial Architecture," EconPapers (2013); Khan and Liu, "Ecological Economics of Water Management in China"; Minqi Li, *The Rise of China and the Demise of the Capitalist World Economy* (New York: The Monthly Review Press, 2008); M. Woo-Cumings, *The Developmental State in Historical Perspective* (Ithaca, NY: Cornell University Press, 1999).

8. Fosu, *Achieving Development Success.*

9. Peter Warr, "Thailand's Development Strategy and Growth Performance," paper prepared for WIDER conference on Country Role Models for Development Success (June 13–14, 2008), Helsinki.

10. Ibid. See also Peter Warr, "The Thai Economy," in Peter Warr (ed.), *The Thai Economy in Transition* (Cambridge: Cambridge University Press, 1993), pp. 1–80; Peter Warr, "What Happened to Thailand?" *The World Economy* 22 (July 1999): 631–650; Peter Warr, "Boom, Bust and Beyond," in Peter Warr (ed.), *Thailand Beyond the Crisis* (London: Routledge, 2005), pp. 3–65, for nuanced analyses of the

various aspects of Thailand's development experience and K.S. Jomo, *Privatizing Malaysia: Rents, Rhetoric, Realities* (Boulder: Westview Press, 1995); and K.S. Jomo, *Malaysian Industrial Policy* (Singapore: Singapore University Press, and Honolulu: University of Hawaii Press, 2007), for Malaysia.

11. Amartya Sen, *The Idea of Justice* (Cambridge: The Belknap Press of the Harvard University Press, 2009); Sen, *Inequality Re-examined*; Sen, *Development as Freedom*; Martha Nussbaum, "Human Capabilities, Female Human Beings," in M.C. Nussbaum and J. Glover (eds.), *Women, Culture and Development* (Oxford: Clarendon Press, 1995), pp. 61–104; Martha Nussbaum, *Women and Human Development: The Capabilities Approach* (Cambridge: Cambridge University Press, 2000); Khan, *Technology, Development and Democracy*; H.A. Khan, "A Theory of Deep Democracy in the Age of Postmodernism," *Readings in Law and Society Journal* 1, no. 1 (2009); H.A. Khan, "Development and Women's Rights as Human Rights: A Political and Social Economy Approach within a Deep Democratic Framework," *Denver Journal of International Law and Policy* 42, no. 3 (August 2014).

12. Keun Lee, "Can Korea Be a Role Model for Development? A 'Capability-based View' on Korea," paper prepared for WIDER conference on Country Role Models for Development Success (June 13–14, 2008), p. 13.

13. John Weiss and H.A. Khan, "Poverty Strategies in Asia: Growth Plus," in John Weiss and H.A. Khan (eds.), *Poverty Strategies in Asia: A Growth Plus Approach* (Cheltenham: Edward Elgar and ADBI, 2006).

14. Vijay Prashad, *The Poorer Nations: A Possible History of the Global South* (London: Verso, 2014), presents a history of the global South. More importantly, the last chapter discusses critically the details of the emerging movements in the global South and their transformational potential.

15. Khan, "A Theory of Deep Democracy in the Age of Postmodernism"; H.A. Khan, "Deepening Democracy During Crisis," *Cosmopolis* (Summer 2012); H.A. Khan, "Enhancing Economic Integration in the Asia-Pacific through the Strengthening of National Innovation Systems – Challenges and Strategies," *Asia-Pacific Technology Monitor* (March–April, 2012); Khan, "Development and Women's Rights as Human Rights."

16. There are controversies among Islamic scholars regarding Sukuk al-Salam. In particular, trading *salam* debt for money is highly controversial. See Zamir Iqbal and Abbas Mirakhor, *An Introduction to Islamic Finance: Theory and Practice* (Singapore: John Wiley and Sons, 2007); Arshad Ismail, "Emergence and Growth of the Sukuk Market," in Kamar Jaffer and Sohail Jaffer (eds.), *Investing in GCC Markets: Regional Opportunities and Challenges* (Dubai: CPI Financial Books, 2007).

17. See C.-S. Lin, H.A. Khan, R.-Y. Chang and Y.-C. Wang, "A New Approach to Modeling Early Warning Systems for Currency Crises: Can a Machine-learning Fuzzy Expert System Predict the Currency Crises Effectively?" *Journal of International Money and Finance* 27 (2008): 1098–1121.

18. Sen, *The Idea of Justice*; Sen, *Inequality Re-examined*; Khan, *Innovation and Growth in East Asia*; Khan, *Global Markets and Financial Crisis in Asia*.

19. See H.J. Chang, *Institutional Change and Economic Development* (Tokyo: UNU Press, 2007), pp. 53–74, for a number of thoughtful contributions on this topic

among other things, in particular, Erick S. Reinert, "Institutionalism Ancient, Old and New: A Historical Perspective on Institutions and Uneven Development," in H.J. Chang (ed.), *Institutional Change and Economic Development* (Tokyo: UNU Press, 2007), pp. 53–74. See also A. Escobar, *Encountering Development* (Princeton: Princeton University Press, 1995); Alberto Gabriele and H.A. Khan, *Enhancing Technological Progress in a Market Socialist Context: China's National Innovation System at the Crossroads* (Berlin: LAP LAMBERT Academic Publishing, 2010); Khan, *Innovation and Growth in East Asia*; Khan, *Global Markets and Financial Crisis in Asia*; Khan, "Enhancing Economic Integration in the Asia-Pacific"; Khan, "Deepening Democracy During Crisis"; Khan, "Development Strategies"; Khan, "Global Financial Governance"; Khan, "Deep Financial Crises, Reforming the IMF and Building Regional Autonomy"; Jayati Ghosh, "Global Crisis and Beyond: Sustainable Growth Trajectories for the Developing World," *International Labour Review* (July 2010); Jayati Ghosh, *After Crisis: Adjustment, Recovery, and Fragility in East Asia* (Delhi: Tulika Books, 2009).

BIBLIOGRAPHY

Arrighi, Giovanni. *The Long Twentieth Century*. London: Verso, 1994.
———. *Adam Smith in Beijing*. London: Verso, 2007.
Askari, Hossein and Abbas Mirakhor. *The Next Financial Crisis and How to Save Capitalism*. Basingstoke: Palgrave Macmillan, 2015.
Chang, H.J., ed. *Institutional Change and Economic Development*. Tokyo: UNU Press, 2007.
Escobar, A. *Encountering Development*. Princeton: Princeton University Press, 1995.
Fosu, Augustin K., ed. *Achieving Development Success*. Oxford: Oxford University Press, 2013.
Gabriele, Alberto and H.A. Khan. *Enhancing Technological Progress in a Market Socialist Context: China's National Innovation System at the Crossroads*. Berlin: LAP LAMBERT Academic Publishing, 2010.
Ghosh, Jayati. *After Crisis: Adjustment, Recovery, and Fragility in East Asia*. Delhi: Tulika Books, 2009.
———. "Global Crisis and Beyond: Sustainable Growth Trajectories for the Developing World." *International Labour Review* 149, no. 2 (July 2010): 209–225.
Hasan, M. Kabir. "Loan Loss Provisioning in OIC Countries: Evidence from Conventional vs. Islamic Banks." EconPapers (2015). http://econpapers.repec.org/paper/pramprapa/61687.htm (last accessed 2016).
Iqbal, Zamir and Abbas Mirakhor. *An Introduction to Islamic Finance: Theory and Practice*. Singapore: John Wiley and Sons, 2007.
Ismail, Arshad. "Emergence and Growth of the Sukuk Market." In Kamar Jaffer and Sohail Jaffer (eds.), *Investing in GCC Markets: Regional Opportunities and Challenges*. Dubai: CPI Financial Books, 2007.
Jomo, K.S., ed. *Malaysian Industrial Policy*. Singapore: Singapore University Press, and Honolulu: University of Hawaii Press, 2007.

Jomo, K.S., ed. *Privatizing Malaysia: Rents, Rhetoric, Realities.* Boulder: Westview Press, 1995.

Keynes, J.M. *The Collected Writings of John Maynard Keynes,* 29 vols., ed., D.E. Moggridge for the Royal Economic Society. London: Macmillan, 1971–79.

Khan, H.A. "A Theory of Deep Democracy in the Age of Postmodernism." *Readings in Law and Society Journal* 1, no. 1 (2009): 47–72.

———. "China's Development Strategy and Energy Security." In Amelia Santos-Paulino and Guanghua Wan (ed.), *The Rise of China and India: Development Strategies and Lessons.* Basingstoke: Palgrave/Macmillan, 2010.

———. "Deep Financial Crises, Reforming the IMF and Building Regional Autonomy: Towards a New Hybrid Global Financial Architecture." EconPapers (2013). http://econpapers.repec.org/paper/pramprapa/49514.htm.

———. "Deepening Democracy During Crisis." *Cosmopolis* (Summer 2012).

———. "Development and Women's Rights as Human Rights: A Political and Social Economy Approach within a Deep Democratic Framework." *Denver Journal of International Law and Policy* 42, no. 3 (August 2014): 451–478.

———. "Development Strategies: Lessons from the Experiences of South Korea, Malaysia, Thailand and Vietnam." In Augustin K. Fosu (ed.), *Achieving Development Success.* Oxford: Oxford University Press, 2013.

———. "Ecology, Inequality and Poverty: The Case of Bangladesh." *Asian Development Review* 15, no. 2 (1997): 164–179.

———. "Enhancing Economic Integration in the Asia-Pacific through the Strengthening of National Innovation Systems – Challenges and Strategies." *Asia-Pacific Technology Monitor* (March–April, 2012).

———. "Global Financial Governance: Towards a New Global Financial Architecture for Averting Deep Financial Crises." EconPapers (2013). http://econpapers.repec.org/paper/pramprapa/49275.htm.

———. *Global Markets and Financial Crisis in Asia: Towards a Theory for the Twenty-First Century.* Houndsmills and New York: Macmillan/Palgrave, 2004.

———. "Innovation and Growth in a Schumpeterian Model." *Oxford Development Studies* 30, no. 3 (2002): 289–306.

———. *Innovation and Growth in East Asia: The Future of Miracles.* Houndsmills and New York: Macmillan/Palgrave, 2004.

———. *Technology, and Democracy: Limits to National Innovation Systems in the Age of Postmodernism.* Cheltenham, United Kingdom: Edward Elgar, 1998.

———. "Technology and Modernity: Creating Social Capabilities in a POLIS." In T. Misa (ed.), *Technology and Modernity.* Cambridge: The MIT Press, 2003.

———. "Technology Choice in the Energy and Textile Sectors in the Republic of Korea." In A.S. Bhalla (ed.), *Technology and Employment in Industry,* 3rd edition. New York, NY: UN, 1985.

———. *Technology, Energy and Development: The South Korean Transition.* Cheltenham, United Kingdom: Edward Elgar, 1997.

———. "Technology, Energy, Distribution and Balance of Payments: A Macroeconomic Framework." Unpublished dissertation, Cornell University, Ithaca, New York, 1983.

————. "What Can the African Countries Learn from the Macroeconomics of Foreign Aid in Southeast Asia?" In E. Aryeetey, J. Court, M. Nissanke and B. Weder (eds.), *Asia and Africa in the Global Economy*. Tokyo: UNU Press, 2003.

Khan, H.A. and Victor Lippit. "The Surplus Approach to Environment." *Review of Political Economy* 25, no. 3 (1993): 122–128.

————. *Sustainability and Surplus*. Storrs, CT: EconPapers, 2007. http://econpape rs.repec.org/paper/tkyfseres/2007cf464.htm (Last accessed on September 15, 2016), No CIRJE-F-464, CIRJE F-Series from CIRJE, Faculty of Economics, University of Tokyo, pp. 1–29.

Khan, H.A. and Yi-bei Liu. "Ecological Economics of Water Management in China." In I. Usha (ed.), *Global Law and Economics of Sustainable Development*. IFCAI Press, 2008.

Khan, H.A. and Erik Thorbecke. "Macroeconomic Effects of Technology Choice: Multiplier and Structural Path Analysis." *Journal of Policy Modeling* 11, no. 1 (1989): 131–156.

————. *Macroeconomic Effects and Diffusion of Alternative Technologies Within a Social Accounting Matrix Framework: The Case of Indonesia*. Aldershot: Gower Publication, 1988.

Khan, H.A. and John Weiss. "Poverty Strategies in Asia: Growth Plus." In John Weiss and H.A. Khan (eds.), *Poverty Strategies in Asia: A Growth Plus Approach*. Cheltenham: Edward Elgar and ADBI, 2006.

Lee, Keun. "Can Korea be a Role Model for Development? A 'Capability-based View' on Korea." Paper prepared for WIDER conference on Country Role Models for Development Success, Helsinki, June 13–14, 2008.

Li, Minqi. *The Rise of China and the Demise of the Capitalist World Economy*. New York, NY: The Monthly Review Press, 2008.

Lin, C.-S., H.A. Khan, R.-Y. Chang, and Y.-C. Wang. "A New Approach to Modeling Early Warning Systems for Currency Crises: Can a Machine-learning Fuzzy Expert System Predict the Currency Crises Effectively?" *Journal of International Money and Finance* 27 (2008): 1098–1121.

Nussbaum, Martha. "Human Capabilities, Female Human Beings." In M.C. Nussbaum and J. Glover (eds.), *Women, Culture and Development*. Oxford: Clarendon Press, 1995: 61–104.

————. *Women and Human Development: The Capabilities Approach*. Cambridge: Cambridge University Press, 2000.

Prashad, Vijay. *The Poorer Nations: A Possible History of the Global South*. London: Verso, 2014.

Reinert, Erik S. "Institutionalism Ancient, Old and New: A Historical Perspective on Institutions and Uneven Development." In H.J. Chang (ed.), *Institutional Change and Economic Development*. Tokyo: UNU Press, 2007: 53–74.

Sen, Amartya. *Development as Freedom*. Oxford: Oxford University Press and New York: Alfred A. Knopf, Inc., 1999.

————. *Inequality Reexamined*. Oxford: Oxford University Press, 1992.

————. *The Idea of Justice*. Cambridge: The Belknap Press of the Harvard University Press, 2009.

Warr, Peter. "Boom, Bust and Beyond." In Peter Warr (ed.), *Thailand Beyond the Crisis*. London: Routledge, 2005: 3–65.

————. "Thailand's Development Strategy and Growth Performance." Paper prepared for WIDER conference on Country Role Models for Development Success, Helsinki, June 13–14, 2008.

————. "The Thai Economy." In Peter Warr (ed.), *The Thai Economy in Transition*. Cambridge: Cambridge University Press, 1993: 1–80.

————. "What Happened to Thailand?" *The World Economy* 22 (July 1999): 631–650.

Weiss, John and H.A. Khan, eds. *Poverty Strategies in Asia: A Growth Plus Approach*. Cheltenham: Edward Elgar and ADBI, 2006.

Woo-Cumings, M., ed. *The Developmental State in Historical Perspective*. Ithaca, NY: Cornell University Press, 1999.

Chapter 3

Promoting Islamic Finance in Africa

"Top-Bottom" or "Bottom-Up"? A Case Study of Islamic Banking in The Gambia

Karamo N. M. Sonko and Mariama Sonko[1]

INTRODUCTION

On October 18, 2016, during a two-day "Africa Islamic Finance Forum" in Abidjan, organized by the government of Cote d'Ivoire (Ivory Coast), the Islamic Development Bank (IDB), the Islamic Corporation for the Development of the Private Sector (ICD), and a number of other international financial institutions, a participant stood up and asked what impact Islamic finance has on the lives of the African people. He complained bitterly that such a conference and even the finance provided through Sukuk were never heard of by most Africans, especially ordinary people. "What is Islamic finance?" he asked.

His comments drew our attention to related questions: "How is Islamic finance perceived in Africa?", "How much is known about Islamic finance in Africa?" and "How is Islamic finance promoted in Africa?" This chapter attempts to answer all of these questions by looking at a particular country in sub-Saharan African (SSA) and the activities of the key players and arguing that Islamic finance, dominated by banking, is promoted through a "top-bottom" approach, focused on a minority of the population, rather than a "bottom-up" strategy which is focused on the vast majority of the population who do not know much about this mode of finance. As a result, the full potential of Islamic finance in Africa's nascent markets is yet to be properly identified and targeted. Without the participation of the majority, sustainable development of Islamic finance in Africa may be impossible.

Through a case study of The Gambia, the study employs basic statistical surveys, economic and financial analysis, with comparative assessments, in order to achieve its objectives of: (1) gauging the perceptions and understanding of Gambians with regard to Islamic banking; (2) assessing the performance of an existing Islamic banking sector/bank in relation to the conventional banking sector; and (3) understanding the policies and practice of the government (central bank) in such a dual banking system.

The chapter is divided into two main parts: after the literature survey, the first part (sections 2–4) provides a presentation of Islamic finance, in general or globally, and SSA in particular. This presentation is concise, although the topic is vast. The second part (sections 5–8) focuses on The Gambia.

Specifically, in section 1 we review the literature. In section 2 we present an introduction to Islamic finance, its global growth, and the key drivers for this. Section 3 provides a brief presentation of the Islamic finance sector in sub-Saharan Africa, in particular, and outlines the potential of Islamic finance in the region as well as the reasons for such potential. Section 4 focuses only on Islamic banking, looking at the types of banks that exist and their geographic distribution.

Section 5 focuses on a case study of The Gambia. We carry out probability cluster sampling of the metropolitan or urban population, to delineate the attitudes of the most educated and affluent population toward, and their understanding of, Islamic banking. Section 6 carries out another survey, specifically of The Gambian business community. Section 7 narrows down the case study further by pinpointing the Islamic banking sector, through a focus on the only Islamic bank in the country, the Arab Gambian Islamic Bank (AGIB). Economic and financial analysis is carried out on the bank in relation to the conventional banking sector. This section also includes a comparative analysis of T-Bills versus Sukuk al-Salaam (Sukuk or SAS for short) in order to highlight the relative importance and performance of Islamic financial instruments available in The Gambia and The Gambia government's policies toward the two.

Section 8 gauges the implications of the findings and draws the conclusions from the study. The section makes practical recommendations for current and future efforts to promote and develop Islamic banking in The Gambia and sub-Saharan Africa as a whole. This study is intended to be beneficial to policymakers, investors, and researchers and students of Islamic finance. Furthermore, the Gambian project is intended to be a first phase or pilot project which may (depending on the availability of funding) be followed by subsequent phases in which the research would look at the experience of Islamic banking in other regions or countries of Africa. A list of Islamic financial institutions, the questionnaires, and selected references are presented in the Appendices.[2]

SECTION 1: LITERATURE REVIEW

Although the literature on Islamic finance, as a whole, is growing, thanks to the IDB (the Islamic Research and Training Institute [IRTI] in particular) and academic/research institutions and a few scholars, there is still very insufficient work on Islamic finance in sub-Saharan Africa and we could not find any on The Gambia. Most of the existing literature is on Islamic finance in general and on parts of the world outside sub-Saharan Africa, particularly Asia, including the Middle East. Many of the exceptions are included in the references below.

In a somewhat related study to ours, Dusuki (2007) examines the ideal of Islamic banking through a survey of stakeholders' perceptions in Malaysia. However, his interest is only in whether stakeholders believe Islamic banking is different from conventional banking or not. Enrique et al. (2014) provide a survey of Islamic finance in SSA. They argue that while not yet significant in most sub-Saharan countries, Islamic finance instruments have several features that make them relevant to the region, citing, in particular, their ability to foster SMEs and enhance microcredit activities. They recommend that, as a first step, policymakers can introduce Islamic financing windows within the conventional system and facilitate Sukuk issuances to tap foreign investment. The entrance of full-fledged Islamic banks requires addressing systemic issues, and the adaptation of crisis management and resolution frameworks to Islamic banking. The Gulf African Bank (2010) also examines the growth, potential, and challenges of Islamic finance in Africa.

Faye et al. (2013) employ a generalized least squares regression model to empirically analyze the differences in performance between conventional banks and Islamic banks operating in Africa. The study uses a sample of 290 banks of which 279 are conventional and 11 Islamic, operating in 45 African countries over the period 2005–2010. Unlike most of the previous empirical studies on the differences in performance between conventional banks and Islamic banks operating in Africa, the sample in their work comprises only African countries.

To measure performance, the authors use bank-level data on business orientation, efficiency, asset quality, and stability. The findings reveal that Islamic banks perform better than conventional banks in terms of efficiency measured by their cost to income ratios and overhead costs. Additionally, Islamic banks are found to have superior performance in stability using the z-score, return on average assets, and equity to assets ratio as measures. They also perform better in asset quality as measured by the level of non-performing loans compared to conventional banks. The results also indicate that there are no statistically significant differences in business orientation between Islamic and conventional banks. This study represents the most comprehensive mapping of the Islamic finance landscape in Africa, although like the rest of the existing literature it focuses on institutions rather than the population.

A study by Kuwait Finance House Research Limited (KFHR) and Malaysia International Islamic Financial Centre (MIFC) (2014) paints a very bright picture of the future of Islamic finance in Africa. The authors look at all the main segments of Islamic finance—Islamic banking, Sukuk, and Takaful. They observe that

> Africa offers exciting growth prospects. In the next few years, 7 out of the 10 fastest growing economies in the world will be in Africa. Growth drivers are becoming increasingly diverse, with the resource-based, construction and services sectors taking the lead. This augurs well for Africa's economic resilience in the face of an increasingly volatile global economy. Of importance, expected favorable demographics and closer regional ties will drive growth. The continent is currently home to more than 1 billion people, and the population of young, middle-class Africans is rising. . . . The measures undertaken, coupled with the natural advantages offered by Africa, are likely to lead to stronger growth of the Islamic finance industry in the region.[3]

The study analyzes the Islamic finance industry and the reasons for the exciting prospects in the continent. However, it only assumes, like all previous studies, that awareness is increasing, without proving it. Although this assumption can be taken to be correct due to the growth of Islamic finance in Africa, there is still very much need to address the question of how much is known about the industry among the majority of Africa's large and growing populations.

With regard to The Gambia, Cham (2015) carried out a study of the banking sector, posing the question whether it is stable or not. He reveals the major credit risks faced by the sector and assesses the soundness indicators. However, his study is not about Islamic banking and does not address the questions raised in our study.

The existing literature embodies criticisms of current Islamic banking practices for a number of reasons, most of which are centered on the similarities between the Islamic and conventional banking. The Islamic banks are believed to replicate conventional financial products and services, disguising interest and other forms of usury. According to Zaman:

> Sukuk provide a perfect example of second-generation thinking in financial matters. . . . Since the bond is an essential element of capitalist finance, it was taken for granted that this was a good thing. It, therefore, became necessary to replicate this instrument within Islamic law. Direct replication was impossible, since it is clearly interest. Therefore, complex indirect methods were found to create something which functions exactly like a bond, but fulfils the formal requirements of Islamic law. Questions about whether or not bonds are needed were not asked, since the optimality and efficiency of capitalist financial systems were taken for granted from the outset.[4]

Islamic windows in conventional banks have also contributed to sometimes very harsh criticisms of Islamic banking: they are seen as far from being authentic and only as means of attracting Muslim clients. In addition to the non-Islamic identities of the banks involved, the commingling of funds has made such a practice vulnerable to criticism.[5]

Private Islamic banks are criticized for not giving enough or any attention to issues of equity, social justice, balanced development, and the ethics embodied in Islam.[6] Concerning some of these issues, Khan (chapter 2) incorporates the key characteristics of the Islamic banking system in a larger systemic model of a mixed economy with both Islamic and other characteristics. To this end, he constructs a structural computable general equilibrium (CGE) model with banking and financial sectors. He demonstrates mathematically that a modern Islamic banking sector can be defined and included in a sophisticated CGE model. Both technically and from a social perspective, efficient and egalitarian Islamic economies are shown to be feasible. He argues that Islamic banking, with socially oriented Islamic characteristics, can also support modern innovation systems. The technical model allows incorporation and scientific testing of important features of Islamic finance in a general equilibrium setting. His chapter makes a very strong case for Islamic finance, particularly innovative and socially inclusive banking.

We found no study in the existing literature on Africa, so far, which combines the approach, *topic*, and scope of analysis equal to our study. We hope this first attempt will lead to more rigorous efforts to addressing similar questions in the continent in the future.

SECTION 2: ISLAMIC FINANCE AND
ITS GLOBAL GROWTH

This section briefly explains what Islamic finance is and traces the evolution of Islamic finance in the world economy. It looks at the history, growth, various forms, and geographical distribution of the finance in different parts of the world.

Although doing business the Islamic way can be traced back formally to the time of the Prophet Mohamed (peace be upon him), modern Islamic finance started only recently. Islamic banking, in particular, is often dated to 1975, with the establishment in Dubai of the Dubai Islamic Bank, although there are reports of some activity in Egypt in the 1960s.[7] Since then it has spread to other countries of the Middle East and the Islamic world, such as Malaysia and the Sudan. More recently Islamic banking has also been started in non-Islamic/Muslim-minority countries, such as France, the United Kingdom, the United States, Australia, Japan, Singapore, South Korea, and South Africa, and by even non-Islamic banks, such as HSBC, Barclays, and

Standard Chartered Banks. However, despite significant progress, the concept and practice of Islamic finance, including banking, are still largely unknown to most of the populations, even in self-declared Islamic states, such as Mauritania and at one time The Gambia.

With the experience of the global economic crises of the early twenty-first century, many people, even non-Muslims, have started to express concern about the negative effects of interest rates on business and household incomes.[8] Therefore, the scope for and potential of Islamic finance have been expanded significantly due to these negative realities.

Islamic finance has now evolved into an array of very sophisticated financial instruments, too long to list. However, all of these instruments revolve around the principles embodied in the following contracts or products, some of which are specific to banking (see figure 3.1):

Murabaha

- Contract in which a customer requests the Islamic financial institution to purchase a commodity and sell it to him/her at cost plus a mark-up.
- Repayment of the cost plus mark-up will be on a deferred payment basis.
- The cost of the commodity is paid to the supplier and goods delivered directly to the institution or to the customer.
- It can be in the form of a sale contract with many applications in banking and financial markets as well as a *Murabaha* financing which is a banking product.

Mudaraba

- Partnership and profit-sharing contract in which one party offers the funds (the investor) and the other (*Mudarib*—the financial institution, individual or other party) invests and manages the fund. The institution may itself sometimes provide the funds.
- The investor is the main partner and the *Mudarib* is the expert and manager of the funds. Profits are shared at a fixed ratio and the investor accepts the risk of a loss provided that the manager is not negligent.
- The *Mudarib* can also be an investor in the same investment.

Musharaka

- Joint venture agreement where the parties contribute toward the fund required for the venture in an agreed proportion.
- In short, it is based on equity participation between the Islamic financial institution and the client(s).

Istisna'a

- The financier/Islamic financial institution agrees to finance and order the manufacture, production, or construction of a product/asset from a manufacturer/contractor in accordance with agreed specifications and delivery schedule.
- Payment is made in advance, upon completion and delivery of the item to the client(s) or in stages, in accordance with the production schedule.
- *Istisna'a* is commonly advanced to staff.
- It can be in the form of a sale contract with many applications in banking and financial markets as well as *Istina'a* financing which is a banking product.

Ijara

- This arrangement is seen by some as not different from conventional finance and operating leases where the income generated is in the form of rented income accruing to the financial institution.

Takaful
Islamic insurance (Takaful) is also a part of Islamic finance because unlike conventional insurance schemes it is based on risk-sharing and the lack of interest.

Shari'ah Compliance
A distinct feature of Islamic finance is Shari'ah compliance, which determines the extent to which the specific Islamic finance product meets the obligatory requirements of Islamic law, based on the Qur'an and traditions of the Prophet (peace be upon him). At the core of this is the ban on *riba* (usury, the most common of which is interest),[9] which is one of the *major* sins in Islam as shown in various verses of the Holy Qur'an, such as:

1) Those who eat riba (usury) will not stand (on the Day of Resurrection) except like the standing of a person beaten by Shaitan (Satan) leading him to insanity. That is because they say: "Trading is only like riba (usury)," whereas Allah has permitted trading and forbidden riba (usury). So whosoever receives an admonition from his Lord and stops eating riba (usury) shall not be punished for the past; his case is for Allah (to judge); but whoever returns [to riba (usury)], such are the dwellers of the Fire—they will abide therein.[10]
2) O you who believe! Eat not riba (usury) doubled and multiplied, but fear Allah that you may be successful.[11]

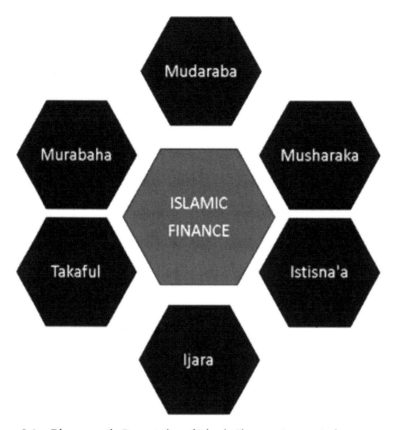

Figure 3.1   Diagrammatic Presentation of Islamic Finance. *Source*: Authors.

The assurance of Shari'ah compliance comes through two channels: (1) internal committees of scholars of the concerned institutions; and (2) regulatory bodies, the most prominent of which are the Accounting and Auditing Organization for Islamic Financial Institutions (AAOIF), Islamic Financial Services Board (IFSB), International Islamic Financial Market (IIFM), and General Council for Islamic Banks and Financial Institutions (CIBAFI).

Growth, Size, and Reasons

Over the decade of the 2000s, the Islamic finance industry grew by more than 10 percent annually to reach an estimated $1.3 trillion by 2011.[12] Generally speaking, the industry can be grouped into (1) banking, $1.5 trillion in 2016; (2) Sukuk (asset-backed/asset-based investment certificates) valued at $318.5 billion in 2016; (3) funds, total assets under management amounting to $56.1 billion in 2016; and (4) Takaful with contributions, equaling $25.1 billion in 2016. Total assets were about $1.9 trillion in 2016 and $2.4 trillion in 2017.[13]

Several factors contributed to this include (1) increasing need of Muslims for Shari'ah-compliant products and non-Muslims for ethical business services; (2) petrodollar surpluses in the Middle East; (3) development of regulatory frameworks in Muslim and non-Muslim countries; and (4) increasing demand for large-scale infrastructure financing.

Therefore, it is not surprising that even non-Muslim countries have risen to become significant centers of Islamic finance and to compete among each other and against Muslim states for such statuses. KFH-Research cites France in one of its reports as one of the new markets that is seeking to join the main players. France is reported to be "working relentlessly" in order to join the major players by making numerous legal and organizational reforms to facilitate the offering of Islamic financial products and services. It notes that 1.5 million clients are interested in Islamic banking, which has a potential market size of $18.2 billion.[14]

SECTION 3: ISLAMIC FINANCE IN SUB-SAHARAN AFRICA

In this section we briefly look at the specific factors contributing to the interest in Islamic finance in SSA, the types of financial institutions and their geographic distribution. Africa has not been left out in the increasing pace of global interest in Islamic finance, although SSA is a latecomer to the scene. The continent has witnessed a significant increase in Islamic finance and financial institutions. According to Gelbard et al. (2014), about thirty-eight Islamic finance institutions—comprising commercial banks, investment banks, and Takaful institutions—operated in Africa, as at the end of 2014. Out of this, twenty-one are in North Africa, Mauritania, and Sudan, and seventeen in sub-Saharan Africa.

The Islamic finance sector is dominated by banking, with insurance and, in particular, Sukuk, recently gathering pace. On the other hand, Islamic funds, such as Qalaa Holdings (Egypt), Oasis Crescent Equity Fund (South Africa), Symmetry Islamic Fund (South Africa), Element Islamic Equity Fund (South Africa), and Stanlib Shari'ah Equity Fund (South Africa), are yet to make their mark as they are very few. Overall and in spite of the progress achieved, however, Africa is far behind other regions, as shown by its share in total global Islamic finance of only 1.6 percent in 2016.[15]

Recent research carried out by the authors of this chapter presents the picture of the numbers and distribution of the different Islamic financial institutions in Africa and is shown in table 3.1 and charts in this section and the list in Appendix C of this book (see figures 3.2, 3.3, 3.4, and 3.5).

Table 3.1　Islamic Financial Institutions in Africa*

Region	Number of Banks	Number of Takaful	Number of Private Equity Funds	Number of Others**
Central Africa	0	0	0	2
East Africa	43	16	0	1
North Africa	9	15	3	0
Southern Africa	2	1	4	2
West Africa	6	2	1	0
Total	60	34	8	5

* Covers parent institutions and their subsidiaries in Africa, classified according to the official regions of the African Union. **Islamic windows. A few of the institutions may not be captured, especially the latest.
Source: Authors' calculations and Islamic Finance Wiki, December 2017.

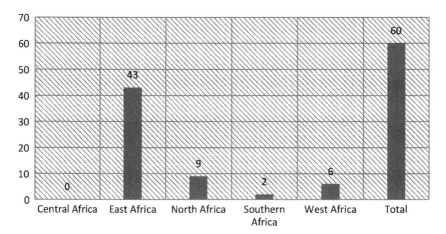

Figure 3.2　Number of Banks. *Source*: Authors' calculations and Islamic Finance Wiki, December 2017.

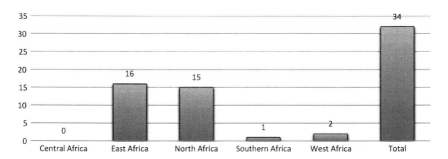

Figure 3.3　Number of Takaful. *Source*: Authors' calculations and Islamic Finance Wiki, December 2017.

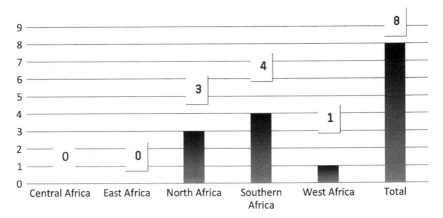

Figure 3.4   Number of Private Equity Funds. *Source*: Authors' calculations and Islamic Finance Wiki, December 2017.

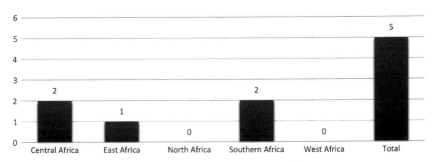

Figure 3.5   Number of Others. *Source*: Authors' calculations and Islamic Finance Wiki, December 2017.

Favorable Factors and Challenges

A number of factors have spurred the progress achieved so far in Islamic finance in Africa. First, regulatory efforts creating the enabling environment have been witnessed in a number of countries. Secondly, market developments globally have had local impact in these countries. Thirdly, a number of conventional African banks have emulated foreign multinational banks, such as HSBC and Standard Chartered Bank, by opening Islamic "windows." Fourthly, the possibility of tapping the international Sukuk market has attracted the attention of many African governments, majority-Muslim and minority-Muslim alike. Finally, large and growing Muslim populations throughout Africa (a total of 250 million, according to the World Bank)[16] have promoted the potential and reality of Islamic finance in the continent. According to the World Bank, Africa's 250 million Muslims are less likely to open bank accounts and save than their non-Muslim counterparts.

Many challenges still face the advancement of Islamic finance in Africa. Even in North Africa, where the national populations are almost entirely Muslim this mode of finance is regarded with suspicion, because of domestic political issues associated with Islam: "Islamic finance has long been held back by a fear that it means introducing Shari'ah law through the back door. . . . (On the other hand) *Evidence suggests that some African Muslims shy away from conventional finance for religious reasons* (emphasis mine)."[17] Even in SSA, the religious implications of Islamic finance can be felt, although seemingly and ironically, to a lesser extent than in North Africa.

There are other challenges. The institutions that exist are normally small, with a narrow and often exclusive customer base. Generally, they are expensive and have difficulties in competing with conventional institutions. They also face capacity constraints in finding the necessary skills for designing and implementing Islamic products and services, directly and indirectly, required in Islamic finance.[18] A well-defined regulatory framework for Islamic finance rarely exists in Africa, even in the case of The Gambia with an Islamic finance sector.

SECTION 4: ISLAMIC BANKING IN SUB-SAHARAN AFRICA

This section presents a snapshot of Islamic banks (specifically) in SSA, which are the predominant institutions of the Islamic finance landscape. Such banking institutions can be put into the following four categories, just as we do with conventional banks. The differences lie in practice and not in form. In fact, as it has been already noted, several conventional banks now provide Islamic products and some of these banks are pioneers or very prominent in the practice. The four categories of Islamic banks are as follows:

1. *Retail Banks.* These banks provide consumer banking, focusing on individuals, and provide their services through local branches. The services include savings and checking accounts, debit/credit cards and certificates of deposit, and mortgages and personal loans. In retail banking, the focus is on mass banking, which makes it attractive for Islamic banking in Africa.
2. *Commercial Banks.* These banks provide various financial services, including deposits and business loans, car loans, and mortgages. They provide a range of investment products such as savings accounts and certificates of deposit. Conventional commercial banks give interest on the

deposits of their customers, which they use for loans with interest rates that are higher than those to their depositors. The spread between the rates offers the bank its net interest income. However, Islamic commercial banks are forbidden to pay or receive interest and, therefore, share instead the net return on investment by the bank. They can also acquire Islamic investment certificates of undivided pro rata ownership in underlying assets (Sukuk). Outside Africa, some examples are Al Rajhi Bank (Saudi Arabia), Mellat Bank (Iran), Dubai Islamic Bank (UAE), Pasargad Bank (Iran), Bank Rakyat (Malaysia), Al Rayan Bank (Qatar), Abu Dhabi Islamic Bank (UAE), and Qatar Islamic Bank (Qatar).

3. *Investment Banks.* These banks create capital for their clients. They underwrite new debt and equity securities and advise in the sale of securities and stock issuances and placements. They also participate in mergers and acquisitions, reorganizations and broker trades for institutional and private investors. As these banks carry out large transactions their clients include governments, and they pay particular attention to Sukuk issuances. Some foreign examples are Samba (Saudi Arabia) and CIMB Islamic (Malaysia), which provide full Islamic banking, and BNP Paribas (France) and Deutsche Bank (Germany), which provide Islamic windows.

4. *Others.* This category include banks that cover a variety of formal financial and quasi-financial and informal institutions or associations which function without *riba* and provide banking-like services.

It needs to be pointed out that a strict division between the different types of banks is not possible as their activities do overlap. It needs to be also pointed out that banking is normally included in Islamic finance and the separation here is only for a better organization of the chapter.

The Islamic banking sector can also be grouped into three categories, based on ownership:

1. Majority government-owned local banks;
2. Majority locally owned private banks, incorporated locally; and
3. Majority foreign-owned banks incorporated locally.

Our interest in this study of The Gambia is in the second type of banks in the second classification/categorization; that is, majority locally owned private *Islamic* banks, incorporated locally. As shown in table 3.1, overall there are about sixty Islamic banks (excluding Islamic windows) presently existing in Africa.[19] The detailed list is presented in Appendix C. In the case of The Gambia, however, only one bank falls into the category of our interest in this study; that is, the AGIB.

SECTION 5: A CASE STUDY OF ISLAMIC BANKING IN THE GAMBIA: SURVEY OF THE POPULATION

This section surveys The Gambia's urban population in order to assess the knowledge of, and attitudes toward, Islamic banking in the country (see figure 3.6).

Why The Gambia?

The Gambia provides a very good example in SSA for a case study of Islamic banking for several reasons. Officially, more than 90 percent of Gambians are Muslims. Islamic schools (formal and informal) can be found throughout the country, especially in the urban areas, and Gambian students in Islamic education are found all over the Islamic world. The Gambia is the first and only country in sub-Saharan Africa which was officially declared by its head of state as an Islamic Republic (December 11, 2015). However, the government was open to Islamic finance even before this declaration, as evidenced by the existence of the AGIB, Sukuk al-Salaam, and Takaful Gambia Ltd. Although there has been a change of policy with regard to the official name, following the December 2016 democratic elections, resulting in the annulment of the "Islamic Republic" by the new government, there has been no policy setback for the promotion of Islamic finance in The Gambia. In fact, the new government is very keen (if not keener) to welcome such finance. Finally, in spite of the small size of the economy, there exist twelve conventional (mostly Nigerian-owned) banks in the country, and, according to Cham (ibid.), the banking industry is nevertheless sound. That there are these many banks in the country is proof of the pudding that the sector potentially holds for Islamic banking in The Gambia.

For all these reasons, The Gambia provides a very good mirror for viewing the understanding and the behavior of a populace toward Islamic banking and for assessing the potential of such banking in a non-Arab, but mostly Muslim, sub-Saharan African country. It offers useful lessons for SSA countries where the populations are largely Muslims and the banking industries are dominated by conventional banks.

Probability Cluster Sampling[20]

In order to gauge the attitudes toward, and understanding of, Islamic banking within The Gambia's metropolitan or urban population, a team of assistants carried out basic sample surveys in the urban conglomerations (Banjul [the capital], Brikama Area Council [BAC], and Kanifing Municipal Council [KMC]) from May to August 2017. These cover the areas where the most educated and affluent Gambian population live. They are mainly the coastal areas shown in the map of The Gambia in figure 3.6, starting from Banjul and ending in Brikama. The survey method was based on probability sampling, using the cluster method. Probability methods rely on random sampling. In random sampling from a population, the selection of a sample unit is based on chance and each unit has a known, non-zero, probability of selection. It enables the researcher to obtain representative samples by eliminating voluntary response bias and protecting against undercoverage bias.

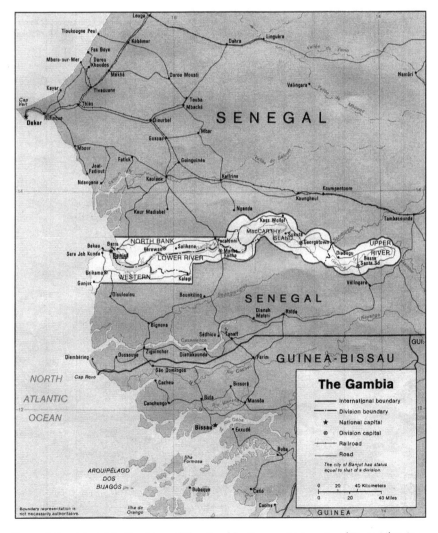

Figure 3.6 **Administrative Map of The Gambia.** *Source*: University of Texas Libraries.

Table 3.2   Major Urban Clusters (Cities) of The Gambia

Cluster	Name	Local Gov./Administrative Area	Population Census (C) April 15, 2013
1	Brikama	BRIKAMA	81,007
2	Bundunka Kunda	KANIFING	55,360
3	Sukuta	BRIKAMA	47,048
4	Talinding	KANIFING	40,562
5	Faji Kunda	KANIFING	38,121
6	Banjul	BANJUL	31,054
7	Nema Kunku	BRIKAMA	28,651
8	Bakau New Town	KANIFING	25,265
Total			347,068

Note: Clusters numbered by authors.
Source: Central Statistics Department (CSD)/Gambia Bureau of Statistics (web).

Through cluster samples, a number of observations can be selected from each cluster by using simple random sampling. Thus, we decided to use the 2013 population census as our sampling frame and base the surveys on the population centers (cities or clusters) identified in the census carried out in the metropolitan or urban areas. The census covered the entire population in eight urban conglomerations in the Banjul-Kombo urban areas mentioned above and shown in table 3.2.

Applications of Cluster Sampling

An example of cluster sampling is area sampling or geographical cluster sampling, in which each cluster is a geographically defined area, such as in this study. As dispersed population can be expensive to survey, so greater economy of scale than simple random sampling can be achieved by putting many respondents within an area into a cluster. Increasing the total sample size, increases precision in the estimators.

Advantages

There are many advantages of cluster sampling over the other sampling methods, such as stratified sampling. These include greater representativeness and hence providing more detailed information through subgroups in the sampling frame. Other advantages are as follows:

• It can be cheaper than other sampling methods—due, for example, to fewer travel expenses and administrative costs in cases of large populations. For instance, compiling information about every household in a town would be very costly, whereas getting such information on blocks of the town would be easier and less costly.

- When the sampling frame of all elements is not available we can resort only to cluster sampling.

Disadvantages

- Sampling error from the "design effect," the ratio between the number of subjects in the cluster in the survey and the number of subjects in an equally reliable, unclustered, and randomly sampled survey.
- If the sampled population has a biased opinion, then the whole population can be inferred to have the same opinion, which may be incorrect.

Our surveys used two different questionnaires, each targeting a different group of respondents: (1) the general or ordinary population; and (2) business community. The questionnaires were personally and directly circulated by the assistants/distributors (students from The Gambia University and other institutions of higher education) to the respondents. They were politely requested to complete them on the spot or collected from the respondents later. The questionnaires are attached in Appendix B of this book.

Statistical Survey of the General/Ordinary Population

A total sample size of 2,500 was decided upon and the shares of 7 of the clusters were based on their proportionate shares in the total metropolitan or urban population. The eighth (Banjul) was given a disproportionate share of 24 percent as opposed to the actual 9 percent as the capital of the country and the heart of the nation's business, education, and politics. Because of the relative ease of access to all areas, we decided to collect data in all instead of some of the urban clusters. The research methodology is further summarized in table 3.3.

The Results

The results show that, as expected, the largest number of Gambians have little or no knowledge of Islamic banking (figure 3.7). However, somewhat surprisingly, Bundungka Kunda and Talinding have bigger numbers of those who say they know very much about it. Banjul comes fourth. However, even these people ignored the follow-up question about the different types of Islamic finance (*Murabaha*, etc.).

Table 3.3 Summary of the Research Methodology, Objectives, and Participants

Participants	Methodology	Sample size	Objectives	Role	Expected Output
The Gambia's Metropolitan/Urban Population	Cluster sampling	2,500	To assess the opinions, understanding of, and attitudes toward Islamic banking (IB)	Observations/ Respondents	Report on what the population knows and thinks about Islamic banking
AGIB	Financial soundness analysis through FSIs	Ten-year analysis (2007–end Q3 2016)	To assess the performance of an existing Islamic bank	Analysis of its data	Report on the performance of AGIB
Business community, incl GCCI	Simple random sampling	353, incl 50 GCCI members	To assess the business community's opinions, understanding of and attitudes toward IB	Observations/ Respondents	Report on what the Gambian business community knows and thinks about IB
CBG	FSI data Comparative analysis of T-Bills and *Sukuk Al-Salaam*	Ten-year FSI data (2007–end Q3 2016), T-Bills vs *Sukuk* (2010–end Q3 2016)	To assess fin soundness of AGIB relative to conventional banks, and Islamic in relation to conventional fin Instruments	Provider of data and bank licenses, and potential post-research co-host of seminar or workshop on IB in The Gambia	Report on performance of AGIB relative to conventional banks, and *Sukuk* in relation to T-Bills
Total/Overall Outputs					Publications Potential Islamic Bank Seminar or workshop on Islamic Finance

Data: Authors.

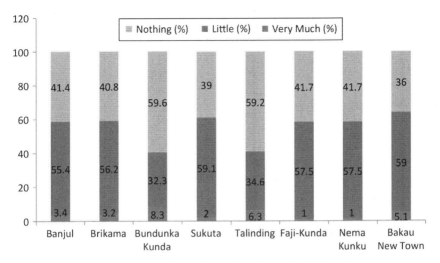

Figure 3.7   How Much Do You Know About Islamic Banking? *Data*: Authors' survey.

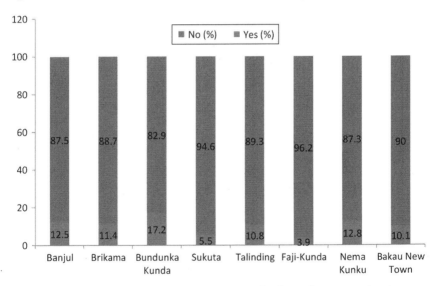

Figure 3.8   Have You Ever Had an Account in an Islamic Bank? *Data*: Authors' survey.

Not surprisingly, Bundungka Kunda also has the largest number of account holders (figure 3.8), Nema Kunku and Banjul follow, respectively. Brikama comes fourth. Figure 3.9 shows that only a small number of account holders were definitely satisfied with their bank, ranging from 3.0 percent (Sukuta and Faji-Kunda) to 12 percent (Bundungka Kunda). Most of the respondents in all the towns said they would open an account in an Islamic bank if they have access to a new one (figure 3.11).

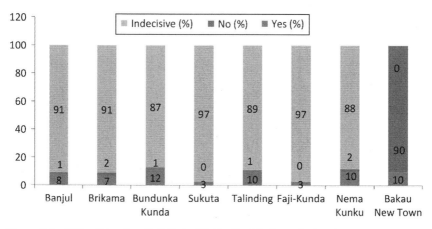

Figure 3.9   If Yes, Were You Satisfied with the Bank? *Data*: Authors' survey.

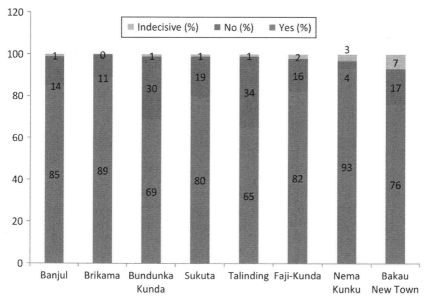

Figure 3.10   Do You Believe That Islamic Banking Is Different from Conventional Banking? *Data*: Authors' survey.

There is a controversy among scholars and laymen worldwide that current Islamic banking practices are not different from conventional banking. We put this to the test in the population and the outcome shows that 65 percent (Talinding) to 93 percent (Nema Kunku) believe that they are different (figure 3.10).

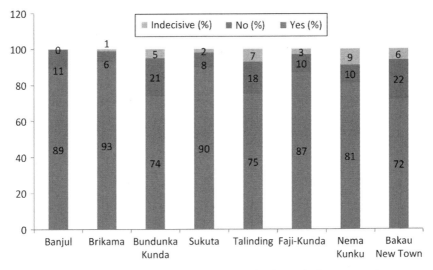

Figure 3.11   Would You Open an Account in an Islamic Bank If You Have Access to a New One? *Data*: Authors' survey.

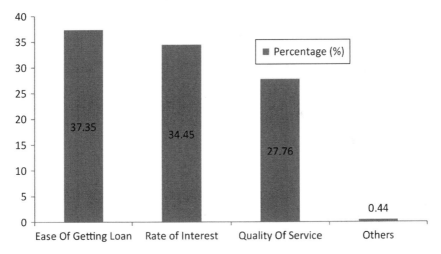

Figure 3.12   Please Rank the Following According to Their Importance to You in Choosing a Bank? *Data*: Authors' survey.

For the population as a whole the ease of getting a loan is more important to most people than the rate of interest (figure 3.12). The quality of services comes as the third most important factor.

Nevertheless, for the overwhelming majority, it matters whether or not their bank is Islamic. This is understandable because they are Muslims and

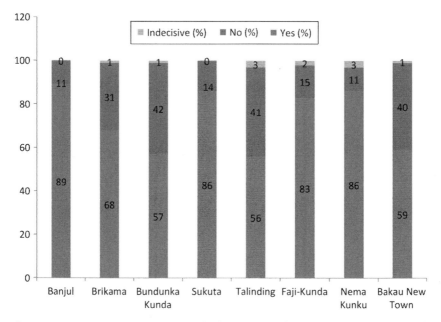

Figure 3.13   Does It Matter to You Whether Your Bank Is Islamic or Conventional?
Data: Authors' survey.

anything "Islamic" may automatically and positively affect the attitudes of most, even with regards to matters they do not practice. It matters the most to people from Banjul and Nema Kunku and Sukuta and the least to those from Talinding (figure 3.13).

SECTION 6: CASE STUDY OF ISLAMIC BANKING IN THE GAMBIA: SURVEY OF THE GAMBIAN BUSINESS COMMUNITY

Statistical Survey of the Gambian Business Community

In order to investigate if the business community's attitudes and understanding are different from those of the general or ordinary population, a snapshot of the business community was taken as an essential part of the study. This was done to distinctly portray the business sector, specifically in terms of what they think, know, or do not know about Islamic banking. For this sector-specific study, some changes were made in the questionnaire for the wider population was adjusted for this sector-specific study and randomly distributed to businessmen and women who are either entrepreneurs or senior employees in private companies. A total of 353 individuals were sampled, including 50 members of The Gambia Chamber of Commerce (GCC), equivalent to 28 percent of their reported active membership in 2017.

The Results

In contrast to the general or ordinary population, a large percentage of The Gambia Chamber of Commerce and Industry (GCCI) members say they know very much about Islamic banking. Most of them also have had Islamic banking experience as account holders. However, given the very small size of the sample as well as the overall membership of GCCI itself, this cannot change our finding that there is very little knowledge, or very few people who know, about Islamic banking. In fact, the percentage of those who say they know little or nothing about Islamic banking in the non-GCCI business community is the same as that of the average for the general population (96%).

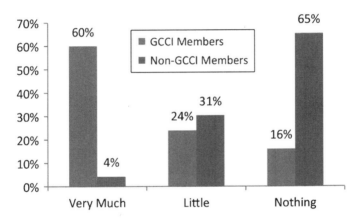

Figure 3.14   **How Much Do You Know About Islamic Banking?** *Source*: Authors' survey.

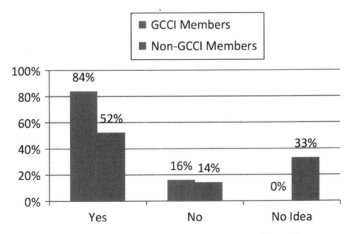

Figure 3.15   **Do You Believe That Islamic Banking Is Different from Conventional Banking?** *Source*: Authors' survey.

The statistical data in figure 3.14 shows the high percentage of GCCI members who say that they know very much about Islamic banking (60%). However, the figure for non-GCCI is only 4 percent. The figure for those who say that they know nothing is much higher for the non-GCCI business community (65%) than each, and the average, of the urban conglomerates.

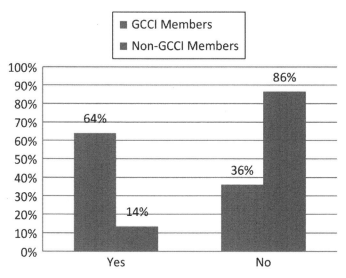

Figure 3.16.1 Have You Ever Had an Account in an Islamic Bank? *Source*: Authors' survey.

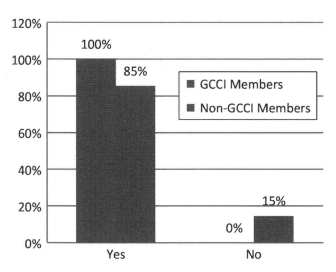

Figure 3.16.2 If Yes, Were You Satisfied with the Bank? *Source*: Authors' survey.

Most of the businessmen and women interviewed believe that Islamic banking is different from conventional banking (84% for GCCI and 52% for non-GCCI) (figure 3.15).

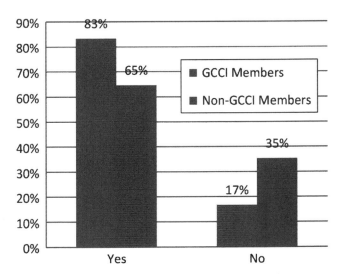

Figure 3.17   Would You Open an Account in an Islamic Bank If You Have Access to a New One? *Source*: Authors' survey.

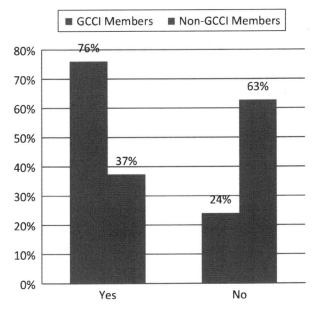

Figure 3.18   Does It Matter to You Whether Your Bank Is Islamic or Conventional? *Source*: Authors' survey.

Most of the GCCI members have had accounts in Islamic banks (64%), but only 14 percent of the non-GCCI members have had accounts (figure 3.16.1). The level of satisfaction among those who have experienced Islamic banking within the business community is very high—100 percent for GCCI and 85 percent for non-GCCI members (figure 3.16.2). Attitudes are also very positive within the business community (83% and 65%, respectively), with regard to the willingness to open an account in an Islamic bank if they have access to a new one (figure 3.17). Although for most non-GCCI members it does not matter whether their banks are Islamic or not, for GCCI members it definitely does (figure 3.18).

SECTION 7: CASE STUDY OF ISLAMIC BANKING IN THE GAMBIA: THE AGIB

The AGIB was incorporated in 1994 and granted a license in 1996. According to the bank's website, AGIB provides its customers with *Murabaha*; *Mudarabah*; *Musharakah*; *Istisna'a*; *Ijarah*; and *Salam*. Its total assets were valued at D2,311,249,000 (2.3 billion dalasis or US$48.15 million) as at the end of June 2018. This represented 5.8 percent of the industry's total asset value, ranking the bank sixth out of twelve banks in The Gambia. For the same period, its total deposits equaled D1,183,851,000 (1.18 billion dalasis or $24.66 million) or 4.8 percent of the industry's total deposits, ranking it sixth out of twelve banks. It has 6 branches and employs a staff of more than 100.

Although the only Islamic bank in the country, its performance and experience are very illustrative in providing useful insights into how an Islamic bank performs in a liberal economy, without very strong institutional, legislative, and/or cultural supports which make it obligatory (as in the cases of Iran and the Sudan[21]) for the population to bank according to Islamic principles. Together with our earlier analysis, this study shows how both the bank and its actual and potential clients behave in such a non-compulsory environment. They also show how free will and understanding, or lack of understanding, with regard to Islamic banking affect the behaviors toward each other (bank and clientele). This study says much about Islamic banking in The Gambia and elsewhere in SSA, where dual banking systems exist and where there is no compulsion.

The key stakeholders (direct and indirect) in Islamic finance as a whole in The Gambia are presented in table 3.4 and figure 3.19.

Table 3.4 Key Stakeholder Analysis

Stakeholders	Segment	Main Institutions	Role and interest
The Ministry of Finance	Government	The central bank	Supervision, regulation, and stability
The Ministry of Trade and Industry	Government	GIEPA	Investment promotion
Business Associations	Private sector	GCC	Membership opportunities of Islamic finance (IF) clientele
Islamic Banks	Private sector	AGIB	Banking and profits
Non-Bank Islamic Business	Private sector	*Takaful*	Insurance and profits
Civil Society	Private non-business sector	Religious educational institutions	Traditional religious education
Civil Society	Private business sector	Secular institutions of education	General business education
Civil Society	Private non-business sector	The media	Information on IF activities

Source: Authors.

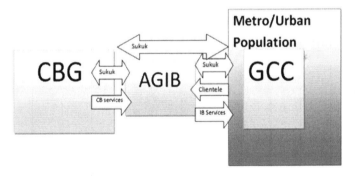

Figure 3.19   Islamic Banking Interactions in The Gambia. *Note*: The sizes of the boxes have no relationship with those of the institutions concerned. *Source*: Authors.

Economic and Financial Analysis of AGIB

For an in-depth analysis, we use standard financial soundness indicators (FSIs) over a ten-year period (2007–2016) to assess AGIB's performance— (1) return on equity (ROE); (2) return on assets (ROA); (3) non-performing loans to total loans; (4) regulatory capital to risk-weighted assets; and (5) liquid assets to short-term liabilities. Since 2010, the CBG has put in place a framework of diagnosing the financial health of banks (the Prompt Corrective Action [PCA]), using these indicators. Using central bank data, our study carries out a comparative analysis of AGIB, in relation to the conventional banks (the average ratios for the industry without AGIB) looking at the historical trend.[22] It should be pointed out that although FSIs provide standard and useful tools of diagnosis for bank health, they can portray the reality only if the data used are credible. The credibility of the data depends on both the quality of reporting by the banks and the effectiveness of central bank supervision.

The Results

All figures for the conventional sector refer to period averages (in percent) for these banks as a whole. In the five out of the ten years under consideration AGIB's returns on equity are higher than that of the industry as a whole (figure 3.20). However, they experience much sharper downturns than the rest of the industry's averages (negative in 2011 and 2013). For the same number of years its returns on assets are higher than that of the conventional sector as a whole (figure 3.21). Again, they experience sharper drops than the conventional sector (negative in 2009, 2011, and 2013).

The ratios of non-performing loans to total loans tell a less positive story (figure 3.22). AGIB's ratios are higher than that of the conventional sector throughout, except in 2016. In terms of the ratios of regulatory capital to risk-weighted assets AGIB exhibits a higher figure for all but three years (figure 3.23). As for the ratios of liquid assets to short-term liabilities, AGIB's are higher for all ten years (figure 3.24).

Overall, our analysis through these financial soundness indicators tells a somewhat mixed story. It shows that the bank is doing better than or equal to the conventional banks, by most of the measures. On the most positive side, are its relative performance in terms of liquid assets and regulatory capital. Definitely mixed are the returns on equity and assets, two of the most important measures for evaluating how effectively a bank's management team is doing with the capital entrusted to them.

On the negative side are its performance in terms of non-performing loans as well as the sharp downturns even in the indicators that it has done better in, during half of the period covered. The results show that there is still room for improvement.

Taking into account the fact that AGIB is still a very small bank in a *potentially* big market, it is clear that the bank has a very long way to go before exploiting the full potential of the Islamic market. This is also shown by our results from the non-GCCI and ordinary population, most of whom exhibit

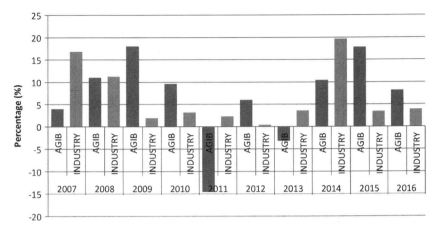

Figure 3.20   Return on Equity AGIB versus Industry. *Source*: Authors, based on CBG data.

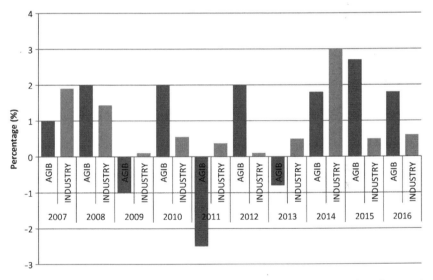

Figure 3.21   Return on Assets AGIB versus Industry. *Source*: Authors, based on CBG data.

(very clearly) little or no knowledge of Islamic banking and never had an Islamic bank account although they would like to.

Recent activities of AGIB provide encouraging signals that the bank is aware that it needs to be more proactive in the market. A $5-million line of finance facility was granted to the bank by the Islamic Corporation for the Development of the Private Sector (ICD) of the IDB in order to finance joint

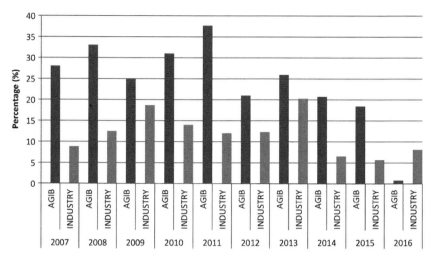

Figure 3.22   Non-Performing Loans to Total Loans AGIB versus Industry. *Source:* Authors, based on CBG data.

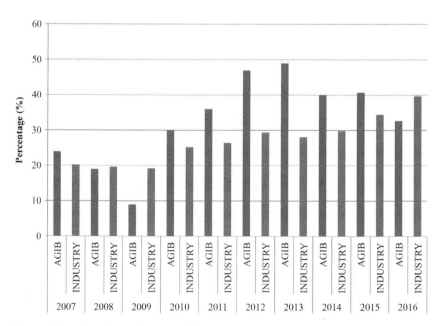

Figure 3.23   Regulatory Capital to Risk-Weighted Assets AGIB versus Industry. *Source:* Authors, based on CBG data.

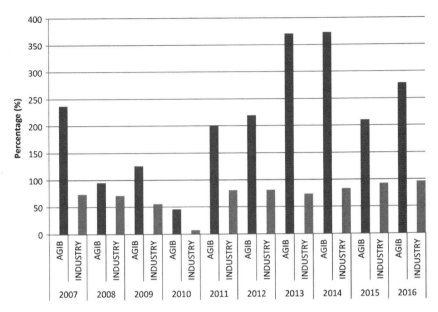

Figure 3.24   Liquid Assets to Short-Term Liabilities AGIB versus Industry. *Source:* Authors, based on CBG data.

strategic cooperation for strengthening AGIB's balance sheet, creating jobs, providing tax revenue, and promoting Islamic banking in The Gambia.[23] The bank has an interest in Islamic microfinance too. The majority shareholder of the bank has also established The Gambia's first privately owned television station, which can be vital in educating the population about *truly* Shari'ah-compliant Islamic finance, a subject which, hopefully, they will pay more attention to in the future.

T-Bills versus Sukuk al-Salaam

Next, we provide an even more comprehensive picture of The Gambia's banking industry by presenting the relative performances of conventional and Islamic financial instruments. We provide a comparative analysis of two types of government securities: Treasury bills (T-Bills) and Sukuk al-Salaam bills issued by the CBG. We cover the period from 2010 to 2016. Sukuk al-Salaam was introduced in 2009 and until 2014 only three-month bonds were issued. The analysis reveals the opportunities available to Islamic and non-Islamic banks and investors as well as the central bank's policies toward the two.

The Results

The data shows that the annual and total issuances of T-Bills *far* surpass those of Sukuk bills (SAS) from 2010 to 2016 (figures 3.25 and 3.26). However, the annual average yields of Sukuk are slightly higher than those of T-Bills when three-month T-Bills and SAS are compared for the same period (figure 3.27).

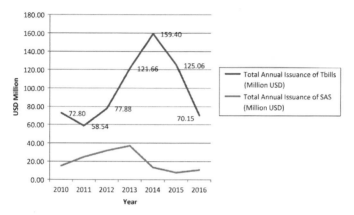

Figure 3.25   Annual Issuances of T-Bills and SAS 2010–2016. *Source*: Authors, based on CBG data.

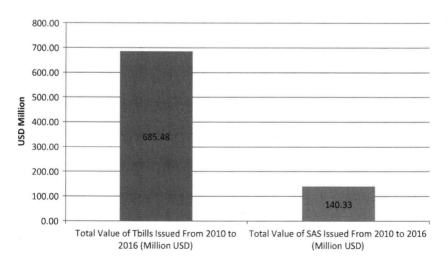

Figure 3.26   Total Issuances of T-Bills and SAS 2010–2016. Source: Authors, based on CBG data.

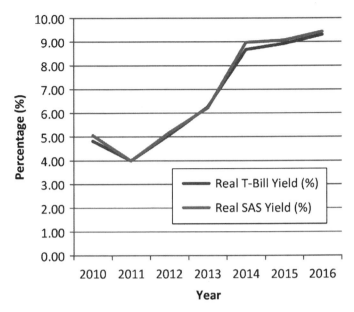

Figure 3.27   Average Yields of Three-Month T-Bills and SAS. *Source*: Authors, based on CBG data.

SECTION 8: IMPLICATIONS, CONCLUSIONS, AND RECOMMENDATIONS

This section enumerates the implications of the results from the surveys and the economic and financial analyses. We draw conclusions and provide practical recommendations for policymakers, investors, and researchers with regard to the promotion and development of Islamic finance in The Gambia and, by implication, sub-Saharan Africa as a whole.

Implications for Promoting Islamic Banking

The pertinent question to ask in this study, based on the evidence from the surveys, is: How do you promote Islamic banking even in a Muslim-majority country if the overwhelming majority knows little or nothing about Islamic banking? In such a situation, the population, in spite of being Muslim, feels no urge to bank according to Islamic principles. They do not see Islamic banking as an alternative and therefore their choices become limited to the banks that they know—the conventional. This is very consistent with the outcome of our study, which proves that in such a situation factors such as the ease of getting loans and the interest rate, rather than Islamic/non-Islamic, affect the choice of a bank.

The key assumption in this study is that there is very little knowledge about Islamic banking in SSA as a result of which the potential for developing the sector is hugely dented. The results from The Gambia have proven this, and, therefore, they have shown that increasing the knowledge about Islamic banking and Islamic finance as a whole could be the best way of promoting it. The GCCI sample (although very small) has shown the largest percentage of those knowledgeable about Islamic banking and also the largest proportion of those with Islamic bank accounts.

Khan observes in chapter 2 that "development is 'growth plus' other things" and "the list of 'other things' may vary somewhat." In Islam both growth and all of the "other things" (whatever they may be) come second to or must be based on spiritual fulfillment; namely, submission to God's will/ commands. Education and work, both of which are critical or essential in development, are obligatory in Islam, but they must meet the requirements of what is judged "*halaal*," according to the Holy Qur'an and the Prophet's (peace be upon him) traditions. The importance of Islamic finance can be better understood in this context. Therefore, knowledge is critical in promoting Islamic banking among Muslims anywhere in the world, because for Muslims it is a matter of faith, which is far more important than business as usual. In other words, it is not a matter of choice but an obligation for Muslims, because *riba* is not "*halaal*," and, in fact, it is among the *major* sins in Islam as pointed out earlier in this chapter. Although the majority of Muslims around the world use conventional banks, it is fair to assume that not all or most of them do so out of choice or in spite of the knowledge that it is forbidden in their religion. We doubt if any serious Muslim, aware of or convinced about the gravity of the sin of *riba,* would willingly and happily choose to bank conventionally (borrow/lend with interest) given the choice, or with the availability, of Islamic banking.

In our surveys, it is shown that there is great potential interest in Islamic banking in The Gambia, because in spite of the small proportion of those who know about Islamic banking, most of the respondents said they would open an account in an Islamic bank if they have access to one. This points to the need for more Islamic banks and wider/more effective marketing by the only existing Islamic bank (AGIB).

The constraints to knowledge about Islamic finance are very serious, because they are structural and historic. In almost all (if not all) Muslim-majority countries, even outside Africa and inside the Arab world, Islamic education focuses on the Five Pillars of the religion, with little attention, if any, paid to business education. In fact, the overwhelming number of the Sheikhs (*Shuyoukh*) themselves know little or nothing about economics or finance. Therefore, there is a need to shape the curricula in institutions of higher education to train Muslims and non-Muslims in Islamic business. As the global surge of Sukuk shows, Islamic finance offers faith, ethics, and profitability, all of which are attractive to Muslims and the latter two of which appeal to non-Muslims too. Therefore, at a time when Islam, in general, is associated with so many negative impressions, Islamic banking and finance can be used to build bridges across the Muslim and non-Muslim worlds. It can also be used to empower the unbanked who keep away from conventional banks because of habit or religious choice. Thus, Islamic finance can be shaped into a multipronged tool to achieve multiple objectives.

Government Policy

It is clear from the huge differences between the central bank's annual issuances of T-Bills and Sukuk al-Salaam where the government's priorities lie when it comes to conventional and Islamic financial instruments. This is historical and convenient, but also, to some extent, a reflection of the attitudes of the population toward Islamic banking, as revealed in this study. Again knowledge is critical: during our study, we found out that even within the central bank itself the knowledge about what Sukuk al-Salaam is based on is not widespread.

There is currently one banking law enacted in 2009 and one set of licensing requirements for banks, which were designed for conventional banks and applied to Islamic banking. While this simplifies things, it does not provide the attention necessary to deliberately regulate, encourage, and promote Islamic banking. However, there is, undoubtedly, much interest in the central bank and the Ministry of Finance as a whole to see more Islamic financial institutions in the country, especially banks and microfinance institutions. In fact, in this regard, The Gambia government tends to be far more accommodating than most governments in the world, including Arab countries.

The central bank and other relevant departments of the Ministry of Finance should be more active in promoting education about Sukuk and Islamic finance as a whole through conferences, seminars, and other fora or channels. The government through the Ministry of Higher Education, Research, Science and Technology should go beyond this by integrating Islamic business education into the curricula of its educational institutions. This can only encourage private institutions to follow suit.

The Gambian Sukuk al-Salaam is open to serious criticisms because there is no evidence that it is based on any underlying asset as required by Shari'ah. It looks very much like a T-Bill with a different name. In order to attract more sophisticated Islamic investors in the long run, the central bank has to address this concern. The bank's staff are very receptive to Islamic finance and with more attention and trained specialists, they can introduce and promote *fully* Shari'ah-compliant Islamic finance in The Gambia.

Strategic Approaches for Investors and Bankers

The assessment of The Gambia's banking industry carried out by Cham (ibid.) concluded: "The analysis revealed the banking system is relatively stable. . . . The analysis further highlighted that the banking system as a whole is well capitalized and has ample liquidity" (pp. 6–7). Although this is not our objective here, the data used for our analysis prove that in spite of the room for improvement for both AGIB and the conventional banks, this conclusion tends to be generally correct, assuming that the official data used in our study and Cham's are reliable. The finding may be seen as somewhat surprising for many, because of the large number of banks in such a small economy. However, it may not be surprising for others who may attribute this soundness to the concentration of investments on, and the high yields of, T-Bills, as well as conservative banking practices of the industry. As Cham (ibid.) recommended: "Banks need to look into new investment opportunities and increase their lending to the private sector rather than investing heavily in government securities such as treasury bills. This will enhance private sector-led growth, which will enhance economic growth going forward" (p.7).

The more relevant point we are trying to make here with regard to Islamic banking is that if so many conventional banks can be doing so well in a population that is more than 90 percent Muslim, with only one Islamic bank, there must be potential for Islamic banking that remains untapped. Islamic bankers and investors can exploit this potential through educational banking policies, which can help the population to perceive the need and benefits of Islamic banking better. Although AGIB is not doing badly, it still has a long way to go in that direction. Because of the low per capita GDP and the low monetary savings rate of the population, Islamic microfinance should be of particular appeal in The Gambia, if properly designed.

A strategic approach to Islamic banking, based on innovation and education, would be the best way of boosting Islamic banking in The Gambia and other sub-Saharan African countries. Innovation here refers to the ability to introduce creative and competitive products and services that can attract the existing clientele of conventional banks. It also, perhaps equally or more important, refers to the ability to tap into the wealth of the largely unbanked Muslim population by encouraging them to save and bank according to Islamic principles.[24]

The Gambia as a Regional Hub for Islamic Banking and Finance

The Gambia has many advantages that can transform it into the gateway to West Africa and a regional hub for Islamic finance, in spite of its small size. These advantages include the following:

1. A warm and welcoming people;
2. Strategic location and airport in West Africa;
3. Proximity to the developed world and North Africa;
4. Untapped agricultural potential;
5. A small area, which naturally facilitates infrastructural development;
6. A well-established tradition of port management, telecommunications, trade, and tourism;
7. A young and energetic population;
8. A tradition of peace;
9. Beautiful beaches, nice climate, and diverse flora and fauna;
10. An uncomplicated bureaucracy;
11. Relatively low costs in several sectors compared to many other countries in West Africa;
12. Significant investment incentives; and
13. A well-trained diaspora scattered all over the world in spite of the country's tiny size. Remittances amount to about $200 million and account for more than 20 percent of GDP, per annum. Many of these men and women have started coming home (or want to do so) since the change of government in 2016 and some of them represent a pool of potential Islamic finance talent.[25]

Some of the above-mentioned and other advantages and disadvantages are shown in the SWOT analysis in figure 3.28.

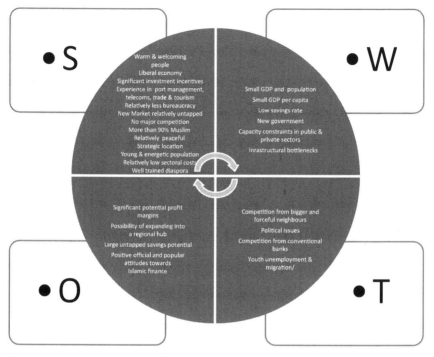

Figure 3.28   SWOT Analysis of The Gambia. *Source*: Authors.

NOTES

1. Pa M. Baldeh, senior economist, Ministry of Finance (Banjul) and Awudu Sumaila, Heeno International (Banjul), assisted by Mariama Daffeh, senior assistant secretary, Ministry of Finance (Banjul) and financial controller, Heeno International, comprise the research team. Survey assistance was provided by students from The Gambia University and other institutions of higher learning in The Gambia. Logistical advice was received from Molifa Sanneh, secretary general, Insurance Association of The Gambia (IAG) and Lamin Sanyang, managing director, Fresh Start Foundation. Dr. Asya Sharief, professor of Statistics and dean, Faculty of Economics and Management Sciences, the University of Garden City, Khartoum, Sudan, provided very helpful advice on cluster sampling. The authors would like to acknowledge and express their gratitude to the central bank of The Gambia (in particular its former governor, Amadou Coley, and his team) for the invaluable data used in this study and a related feasibility study. We are also grateful to various commentators on the draft of this chapter, especially two anonymous referees to whom the *Islamic Economic Studies Journal* has sent it to for review on behalf of the Islamic Research and Training Institute of the Islamic Development Bank, which partially funded this

study. We are equally grateful to Dr. Omar Touray and Abou Jallow of the IDB for their comments.

2. The answers to all the key questions (to which we got 100% rates of responses for the population and business samples) are charted in this study. There were a very few follow-up questions the respondents were not forthcoming on. These were about the meanings of different types of Islamic finance concepts for those who claimed to know very much about the subject and personal questions such as the sex, age, education and employment of respondents. The answers to these questions were so few that they were excluded from the main text and most of them placed in Appendix A instead.

3. See Kuwait Finance House Research Limited (KFHR) and Malaysia International Islamic Financial Centre (MIFC) (2014).

4. A. Zaman, "Logical Positivism and Islamic Economics," *International Journal of Economics, Management and Accounting* 21, no. 2 (December 2013): 1–18. Also, see chapter 8 of this book.

5. For a discussion of the criticisms against Islamic finance also, see A. Tobin, "Making Islamic Finance "Islamic": Authenticity in Islamic Banking and Finance Institutions," Chr. Michelsen Institute, Bergen, Norway, 2018, published as chapter 4 in this book.

6. For the critical literature, see, for example, Zaman (ibid); A.W. Dusuki and N.I. Abdullah, "*Maqasid al-Shari`ah, Maslahah,* and Corporate Social Responsibility," *The American Journal of Islamic Social Sciences* 24, no. 1 (2007): 25–48; B.S. Chong and M.H. Liu, "Islamic Banking: Interest-Free or Interest-Based?" *Pacific-Basin Finance Journal* 17 (2009): 125–144; and Hafiz Muhammad Zubair and Nadeem Ghafoor Chaudhry, "Islamic Banking in Pakistan: A Critical Review," *International Journal of Humanities and Social Science* 4, no. 2 (Special Issue, January 2014).

7. The IDB was established in the same year.

8. See, for example, Brian Kettle, *Sukuk: A New Sharia'a Compliant Asset Class* (London, 2013).

9. Riba can be translated as usury or unjust gains made in business.

10. Al-Baqara, chapter #2, Verse #275 (Mohsin Khan translation).

11. Aal-i-Imraan, chapter #3, Verse #130 (Mohsin Khan translation).

12. *Islamic Finance Europe*, Wednesday, April 18, 2012.

13. Islamic Finance Services Board (IFSB), *IFSI Stability Report 2017*. Also see MIFC, *Islamic Finance in Africa: Impetus for Growth*, June 13, 2017; and for a more recent publication, DIFC, see Thomson Reuters and DinarStandard, *State of the Global Islamic Economy Report 2018/19*.

14. Reported in *Islamic Finance Europe*, Wednesday, April 18, 2012.

15. IFSI Stability Report 2017.

16. Cited by *The Economist*, "Africa is Islamic Banking's New Frontier; Islamic Banking in Africa," July 15, 2017.

17. *The Economist*, ibid.

18. Ibid.

19. Based on update on August 13, 2019, from IDB.

20. For more information on cluster sampling refer to http://research-methodolo gy.net/sampling-in-primary-data-collection/cluster-sampling/, among numerous sources.

21. Iran and the Sudan are two of the pioneers of Islamic finance. In 1983, four years after the end of the revolution in 1979, the Iranian government passed the Riba-Free Banking Act, forcing local banks into Shari'ah-compliant products. In the following year, the Sudan passed the Civil Transactions Act making it mandatory for all financial institutions in the country to comply with Islamic laws.

22. Data for 2016 cover first to third quarters only. Source: Central Bank of The Gambia.

23. ICD, June 8, 2017/APO/.

24. On Africa's unbanked Muslim majority, see Enrique Gelbard, Mumtaz Hussain, Rodolfo Maino, Yibin Mu, and Etienne B. Yehoue, "Islamic Finance in Sub-Saharan Africa: Status and Prospects," IMF Working Paper 14/149, 2014; and for how Gambians save, see Parker Shipton, "How Gambians Save and What Their Strategies Imply for International Aid," Policy, Research, and External Affairs working papers, no. WPS 395, 1990.

25. See Karamo N.M. Sonko, "The 'New Gambia': Reflections on the Road Ahead," Conference & Networking Event—Third Edition: "Opportunities and Challenges in The Gambia- an Entrepreneurship Perspective," Coral Beach Hotel— The Gambia, December 27 and 28, 2017.

BIBLIOGRAPHY

Alam, Nafis. "The Impact of Regulatory and Supervisory Structures on Bank Risk and Efficiency: Evidence from Dual Banking System." *Asian Journal of Finance and Accounting* 4, no. 1 (2012): 215–244.

Chapra, Umer. "The Global Financial Crisis: Some Suggestions for Reform of the Global Financial Architecture in the Light of Islamic Finance." *Thunderbird International Business Review* 53, no. 4 (September 2011): 565–579.

Chong, Beng Soon and Ming-Hua Liu. "Islamic Banking: Interest-free or Interest-based?" *Pacific-Basin Finance Journal* 17, no. 24 (2009): 125–144.

Cihák, Martin and Heiko Hesse. "Islamic Banks and Financial Stability: An Empirical Analysis." *Journal of Financial Services Research* 38, nos. 2–3 (December 2010): 95–113.

Datul Rifaat, Ahmed A. K. "Islamic Finance: An Alternative Funding Source for the African Development Bank?" *Africa Capacity Development Brief* 3, no. 3 (December 2012).

Deming, William Edward. *Some Theory of Sampling.* Hoboken, NJ: John Wiley, 1950.

DIFC, Thomson Reuters, and DinarStandard. *State of the Global Islamic Economy Report 2018/19.* Dubai: Thomson Reuters and DinarStandard, 2019.

Dow Jones Islamic Market Indexes. "The Challenges and Opportunities of Islamic Banking in Africa." *Quarterly Newsletter* (July, 2012).

Dridi, Jemma and Maher Hasan. "The Effects of the Global Crisis on Islamic and Conventional Banks: A Comparative Study." *Journal of International Commerce, Economic, and Policy* 2 (December 2011): 163–200.

Dusuki, Asyraf Wajdi. "The Ideal of Islamic Banking: A Survey of Stakeholders' Perceptions." *Review of Islamic Economics, Special Issue* 11 (December 2007): 29–52.

El Galfy, Ahmed and Khiyar Abdalla Khiyar. "Islamic Banking and Economic Growth: A Review." *The Journal of Applied Business Research* 28, no. 5 (September, 2012): 943–956.

Enrique Gelbard, Mumtaz Hussain, Rodolfo Maino, Yibin Mu, and Etienne B. Yehoue. "Islamic Finance in Sub-Saharan Africa: Status and Prospects." *IMF Working Paper,* 14/149 (2014).

Faye, Issa, Thouraya Triki, and Thierry Kangoye. "The Islamic Finance Promises: Evidence from Africa." *Review of Development Finance* 3 (2013): 136–151.

Fowler, Floyd J. *Survey Research Methods (Applied Social Research Methods)* (5th Edition). Washington, DC: Sage, 2014.

Gulf African Bank. "Islamic Finance: The African Experience (Growth, Potential, and Challenges)." 2nd East and Central African Islamic Finance Conference, Kenya, May, 3rd and 4th, 2010.

Hesse, Heiko, Andreas A. Jobst, and Juan Solé. "Trends and Challenges in Islamic Finance." *World Economics* 9, no. 2 (2008): 175–193.

Imam, Patrick and Kangni Kpodar. "Islamic Banking: How Has it Diffused?" *IMF Working* Paper 10/195 (2010).

Iqbal, Zubair and Abbas Mirakhor. "Islamic Banking." *IMF Occasional Paper* 49 (1987).

Islamic Development Bank (IDB) and The World Bank Group (WBG). *Global Report on Islamic Finance 2016; Islamic Finance: A Catalyst for Shared Prosperity?* Jeddah and Washington, DC: IDB and WBG, 2016.

Islamic Finance Services Board (IFSB). *Islamic Finance Industry Stability Report.* Kuala Lumpur: IFSB, 2017.

Khaf, Monzer, Ausaf Ahmad, and Sami Homud. *Islamic Banking and Development: An Alternative Banking Concept?* Jeddah: Islamic Research and Training Institute (Islamic Development Bank), 1998.

Khan, Feisal. 2010. "How 'Islamic' is Islamic Banking?" *Journal of Economic Behavior and Organization* 76 (2010): 805–820.

Khan, H.A. 2018. "Islamic Banking in General Equilibrium: A Structural CGE Model for Policy-Making within a Complex Socio-economic System." JKSIS, University of Denver, CO, unpublished (May 2018) (chapter 2 of this book).

Kuwait Finance House Research Limited (KFHR) and Malaysia International Islamic Financial Centre (MIFC). *Islamic Finance in Africa: Unlocking Opportunities for Growth.* Safat: KFHR, 2014.

Lewis, Mervyn K. "In What Ways Does Islamic Banking Differ from Conventional Finance?" *Journal of Islamic Economics, Banking and Finance* 4, no. 3 (2008): 9–24.

MIFC. *Islamic Finance in Africa: Impetus for Growth*. Kuala Lumpur: MIFC, June 13, 2017.

Mohieldin, Mahmoud. *Realizing the Potential of Islamic Finance*. Washington, DC: The World Bank, 2012.

Pew Research Center. *Mapping the Global Muslim Population*. Washington, DC: Pew, October 2009.

Pew Research Center. *The Future of the Global Muslim Population*. Washington, DC: Pew, January, 2011.

Shipton, Parker. "How Gambians Save and What Their Strategies Imply for International Aid (English)." *World Bank Policy, Research, and External Affairs Working Papers, WPS 395*. Washington, DC: The World Bank, 1990.

Yaacob, Hakimahand others. "International Convention for Islamic Finance: Towards Standardisation." ISRA Research Paper 29/2011 (2011).

Zulkhibri, Muhamed. "Islamic Financing and Bank Behaviour in a Dual Banking System: Evidence from Malaysia." *IRTI Working Paper* 2016–08 (May 1, 2016).

Chapter 4

Making Islamic Finance "Islamic"

Authenticity in Islamic Banking and Finance Institutions

Sarah A. Tobin

INTRODUCTION: ISLAMIC AUTHENTICITY

Rooted in the philosophical traditions, authenticity is defined by the quest for "self-fulfillment." Individuals take on this inward endeavor while taking into account the importance and influence of common values and moral commitments to one's social environs.[1] The self is in harmony with its environs and historical traditions. The literature on the process is rife with the language of a "quest for" or "searching for" authenticity, fears and an aversion to an authenticity that is "staged" or "artificial," and—by contrast—a pursuit for one that is "sincere" and "real." Authenticity is understood as a singular, objective experience based in a hermetic knowledge for only the persons who come from said tradition. An individual can really only find an authentic self and apprehend the authenticity of something if one encounters it in a pristine, untouched, and unpolluted form.

Such understandings of authenticity largely derive from Western traditions and overlook the many ways that traditions have come into existence historically, as well as the ways that individuals wield them for particular social, political, or economic gain. This is certainly true in studies of cultural authenticity in the Middle East. The Arabic word for authenticity, *asala*, derives from the root *asl*, which references social, familial, or geographic origins: one's "roots." Such linkages have scaled up to other levels such as in references to an "Arab spirit" (*ruhi 'araby*) or in nationalist fashion such as referring to Cairo as the "mother of the world" (*Um Al-Dunya*). Authenticity in Middle Eastern writings references both high cultural knowledge and elite understandings of "truth" (often as a counterpoint to Western forms), as well as in forms of nativist nostalgia, often in folkloric ways.[2] Cultural authenticity in the Middle East is locally rooted and political in what it both includes and excludes and has often been used in geopolitical conflicts between the region and the West.[3]

When applied to the question of religion, it is believed by scholars that an Islamic authenticity can be attained "by cutting away all accretions, which have clouded and disinformed the original message of Islam."[4] This is a "stripping down" of Islamic understandings to some core messages and beliefs (or, perhaps one might argue, an "orthodoxy"). Islamic authenticity, which is about reestablishing a direct linkage that is deemed pure and untainted by politics, is the main objective. It is about connecting to an imagined—Islamic—community[5] of the past, complete with its recorded rituals, social groupings, and moral exhortations.

When it comes to the question of authenticity and Islamic economy in the Middle East, as I have discussed at length elsewhere,[6] many middle-class Muslims assert that there is a "real" and authentic Islam that is both normative and timeless. In their beliefs, values, and practices, they develop and invoke Shari'ah-based evidence that they are following, as one informant said, "The same Islam of the Prophet Mohammed (Peace be upon him [PBUH]), his Companions, and the true Muslims of our past." As a result, authenticity and truth claims are grounded in one's ability to establish credible and reliable discursive links and references to the past through Shari'ah.[7]

Islamic economics and Islamic banking and finance institutions (IBFIs) are subject to these in debates about Islamic and Middle Eastern cultural authenticity, particularly as they relate to the invocation and usage of Shari'ah.[8] The literature in the field has taken great pains to examine not only the distinctly Islamic points of the movement but also the political-economic and cultural aspects.[9] As this work has shown, protestors have sought Islamic economic justice from corrupt political regimes, using Shari'ah: Islamic clerics have sought political authority by imposing it. Corrupt national and public leaders have claimed legitimacy in adopting it. Social critics and nationalists have used it as a marker of their own cultural authenticity and Islamic identity.[10]

These efforts often focus on the *production* of certain types of knowledge, services, or products as distinctly Islamic, rather than their public receipt as such. In other words, Islamizing economic offerings at IBFIs, and the ensuing contests for its control, does not necessarily guarantee an authentically Islamized public. These concerns with "supply-side" Islamic authenticity in the economy preclude many attempts to establish and grow Islamic banking and finance. In these instances, the public does not deem IBFIs to be sufficiently or convincingly "Islamic," and thus are not necessarily worthy of their patronage.

Khan (chapter 2), Sonko and Sonko (chapter 3), and Zaman (chapter 8) provide the critical arguments against Islamic finance as currently practiced. In this chapter, I am going to focus on three criticisms that are waged against IBFIs as a result of the supply-side versus demand-side disjuncture in authenticity. First, there are criticisms against the institutional emphases that are informed by economic policy. That is, many see the institutional composition of IBFIs to be insufficiently Islamic and not reflecting Islam in the economy. Secondly, many find the experience of the IBFIs do not convey their understandings of what an IBFI should feel like in an Islamic form, as the experience of the physical elements of the facilities that the customers witness and experience does not have an Islamic aesthetic. Finally, in the ethical or scriptural emphasis of the institutions, for those who have a working knowledge of the Shari'ah norms and proscriptions invoked in IBFIs, they often find them to overemphasize some nonessential aspects and underemphasize those that they perceive to be more critical to the enterprise. After I explore each criticism, I offer a recommendation to remedy it and establish something that more closely approximates a demand-side authenticity in the Islamic economic institutions. Sonko and Sonko carries out a case study of Africa in chapter 2. The conclusions to my chapter explore the possibilities for IBFIs to bring in elements of an Islamic authenticity for the Middle Eastern populace in order to grow the industry, attend to religious concerns of the public, and commit to a more equitable and just economic system for all.

INSTITUTIONAL

From For-Profit, Elite Institutions to Postal Savings Systems Alternatives

IBFIs are often criticized for their institutional status as for-profit banks and financial institutions. A survey of the literature demonstrates that while many articles have been and continue to be published about the possibilities and promise for Islamic finance to promote socioeconomic equity and financial inclusion,[11] very few demonstrate that Islamic finance is actually doing this.[12] IBFIs are neither charities nor are they necessarily inherently oriented toward inclusion of the poor.[13] This runs contrary to what many see as the main attraction of a distinctly Islamic form of banking and finance.

Many authors who write on Islamic economics are quick to point out that Islamic economics and actions by Muslims in any modern economy result in remarkably similar types of actions and outcomes.[14] This is because, despite rhetoric to the contrary, Muslim economies and secular economic equivalents are not greatly different.[15] Profit shares in Islamic banks parallel interest rates on commercial markets. Islamic banking and financial institutions face and respond to competition among customers. Residents face burgeoning bureaucracies in countries where *zakat* is controlled by government agencies, and they too engage in tax evasive measures—only couched in terms of an Islamic justification—that resonate with those seen in non-Muslim-majority countries. In other words, there is no evidence that implementing Islamic economic policies have "brought about the behavioral changes envisioned in Islamic texts."[16]

Solutions to these concerns are diverse. In my previous work,[17] I suggested that public-private partnerships (PPPs) ameliorate the risks inherent in the Islamic banking and financial endeavors specifically in Jordan, including risks associated with mistrust of the government, financial inclusion for the so-called high-risk poor,[18] and risks associated with capital loss through interest, or *riba.*[19] In this particular case, the PPP is in the form of postal savings. Postal savings systems continue to be one of the most unexplored and underrepresented possible alternatives for making Islamic financial institutions more just and equitable for larger populations. The basic premise is to make use of the brick and mortar presence and public service orientation of post offices in order to provide infrastructure for deposits and savings throughout both urban and rural areas. This system is coherent with the types of financial infrastructure called for in an Islamic institution.

Postal savings programs are particularly important in countries where bank service fees are high or there are weak or unreliable banking institutions, as is the case in much of the Middle East and North Africa (MENA) region. These services are particularly important, as other savings facilities are often difficult to find and access in rural areas throughout many parts of Asia and Africa. They are also important in instances where market liberalization has weakened confidence in banks, as was the case in Vietnam in the 1990s, or in instances where the privatization of national banks resulted in the closure of rural branches, as was the case in Kazakhstan.[20] As a result, it is surprising that postal savings often receives little attention, despite the fact that Adam Smith himself—the icon for neoliberal policy drivers—praised the post office as "both a necessary and successfully managed government-run mercantile project."[21] Of obvious and immediate concern are the implications and outcomes of privatization efforts and neoliberal reforms that threaten to contract and withdraw postal service offerings from the costliest populations, and also undermine savings infrastructure.

While financial inclusion has not been a priority in financial sector development or in economic development generally, microfinance and Islamic microfinance efforts have attempted to extend such services, albeit to a limited degree. In the Arab world there are three types of organizations that provide financial products to low-income consumers. They include financial institutions, such as banks; nongovernmental microfinance institutions; and state-owned postal savings systems.[22] Microfinance efforts have brought in approximately 2.5 million active borrowers in MENA, with 1.2 million of them in Morocco, which is quite low when compared to the 39 million in South Asia or the nearly 12 million in Latin America and East Asia.[23] However, there is a desire for more in the MENA. In Yemen 52.6 percent and in Lebanon 35.8 percent of enterprises surveyed would like to obtain a loan.[24] Some of these microfinance programs have been Islamized.[25] For example, the *sanadiq* system in Syria's Jabal Al-Hoss region is one of the few, if not the only, microfinance membership-based model in the region that pays dividends to shareholders in a profit-sharing scheme of *musharaka*.[26]

In 2009, I interviewed the director general of the Postal Savings System, Sheikh Ahmed,[27] as well as the Jordanian economist who spearheaded the movement to Islamize the investment methodologies, Sheikh Barakat. Sheikh Barakat had a bit of a following while I was conducting research in Jordan. He gave regular lectures, which were quite popular with the staff at a local Islamic bank. I had befriended a number of employees, who added to my information on Islamic economics, banking, and finance, as well as the Postal Savings Fund with copies of Sheikh Barakat's lectures that they had attended and the documentation they had collected. A number of my friends who were also employees at a local Islamic bank in Amman expressed jealousy at my meeting with these notable gentlemen from the Postal Savings Fund. In fact, the bank employees talked about Sheikh Barakat and his teachings in ways that echoed strongly the way young people respond to other regional preachers who are quite popular with young adults and have collected a bit of a cult following.

During the course of the interview with Sheikh Ahmed and Sheikh Barakat, they gave me a large number of electronic books, reports, and powerpoints, as well as brochures and flyers. In addition, I received a short lecture from Sheikh Barakat that modeled how moving away from a credit-based economic system will prevent inflation, and therefore, stabilize the economy and create opportunities for a more equitable society.[28] After the short lecture, Sheikh Ahmed jumped in, extolling the values of using Islamic banking methodologies in the Postal Savings Fund. He said:

> Islamizing our Postal Savings Fund makes a difference, you know? It makes a difference for our society, that's true. But it also makes a difference in the lives of the people who invest. They are making money *the Islamic way*. They don't have to have much money at all—2 JDs, 3 JDs. They can deposit it. We take any amount. You know who this helps? Women in the rural areas. It's true. Women in the rural areas don't have much money and there's no Islamic bank in their village. But there's a post office, and they can invest it there. You know what

else? The women who deposit their money are the only people who can take it out again. Their husbands can't take their money from them. We're giving women independence and freedom and doing it *the Islamic way.*

As the quote demonstrates, not only are there structural aims in place at the transformation of society away from credit-based interactions, but also the intent is to extend such opportunities to financially vulnerable populations, including poor, rural, and Muslim women. In fact, the angle that Sheikh Ahmed is promoting is one that supports using Islamic financial methods to bolster economic development and microfinance through postal savings. Furthermore, Sheikh Ahmed is promoting "modern" ideas, as mediated by an Islamic ethic: women should be financially independent from their potentially domineering husbands, and they can do it because Islam allows for it.[29]

EXPERIENTIAL: AN ISLAMIC AESTHETICS?

My own research found that skepticism of the banks often emerged from customers' affective experiences within the banks.[30] Complaints ranged from spaces that prioritized families, to consideration for gendered sensitivities and preferences for segregation, and to spaces for prayer for both men and women. While the bank might technically adhere to some agreed-upon principles of Islamic banking and finance as displayed in the arrangements of *murabaha, mudaraba, musharaka, ijara,* and others, the aesthetic experience as a customer of an Islamic bank leaves many uncertain about the authenticity of the self-proclaimed Islamic status.[31]

The most commonly cited critique that I encountered was *"Al-kharaji Islami, wa al-dakhali ribawi"* which roughly translates to "the exterior is Islamic, but the interior is of interest." The idea that the IBFIs are doing the minimum required to technically fulfill the mandates of an Islamic banking system was pervasive, and it permeated all the other critiques that I encountered. However, there was also a sentiment that several "obvious" adjustments could be made that would enable a more authentically Islamic aesthetic experience within the banks. There are two common areas in which the experiential aspects of IBFIs could be improved to convey Islamic authenticity and counter the idea that IBFIs are only doing the minimum demanded in the religion.[32]

The first idea relates to the physical layouts and spatial experiences of the IBFIs. As most IBFIs resemble conventional (non-Islamic) institutions, the experiences in Islamic banks and other financial institutions are strikingly similar to those in conventional institutions or, in some instances, even worse. I frequently heard complaints that women with children suffered long waits without children's play spaces or privacy for women to remove their face coverings or sufficiently adjust their head coverings. Some women I spoke with complained about being subjected to male employees, when they would prefer to work with female employees. And, finally, a third common complaint that I heard was that women disliked having to wait in lines in close proximity to male customers.

Such complaints may strike the reader as obvious in the context of creating an Islamic space: of course, there should be a consideration for women and families. It is unsurprising that women prefer to conduct business with and around other women. However, the exclusion of women from the planning and implementation of spatial characteristics in Islamic banks can result in these often-gendered complaints. Ways to counter this would include creating and prioritizing spaces for families and women. This might include play areas for children or small waiting rooms for the families to have measures of privacy while awaiting their services. Women that I spoke with indicated that they far preferred to use ATM machines so that they would not need to wait in lines next to male customers or to deal with male employees.

Another seemingly obvious observation is that physical spaces in the banks must also account for ritualized religious life, namely wash and prayer rooms for both employees and customers. Deep trust between corporation or business and both employees and customers comes from the enactment of good business norms of predictability and transparency. The inability to find sufficient prayer spaces at Islamic banks, when one can often find such places in malls in major Muslim-majority cities, often decreases one's trust in IBFIs as authentically Islamic.

The second area in which physical improvements may be made to enhance the experience of IBFIs is in the institution's interior and aesthetic style. Customer satisfaction of the Jordan Islamic Bank (JIB) has been reported as relatively low.[33] This is at least in part because the buildings were described by one of my interviewees as "dark and drab, with nothing but a rusty ceiling fan for ventilation." A former Jordan Islamic Bank employee informed me, "We used to take the contracts, print them out on paper with green trim and put a '*Bismillah*' at the top and—boom—it became 'Islamic!'" Corruption is considered common and management poor due to these aesthetic styles and experiences.[34] The presentation of the professional qualities of the IBFIs in the form of proper ventilation and updated fixtures or even in the quality of the contracts and letterhead, in fact, reflects on the proposed Islamic nature of the facility.

These aesthetic experiences strike many customers as "inauthentic" and insufficiently Islamic. While the Qur'an might not have much to say about the necessity of making business exchanges particularly aesthetically pleasing, the fact remains that customers turn to those experiences in order to assess the value of the underlying principles. Customers demand a correspondence between the internal states of purity and Islamic ethics and morals with the aesthetic and physical expressions. A bank, it seems, cannot be Islamic if the Muslims themselves are turned off from practicing and engaging their ritual and ethical religious life within the building. IBFIs need to be attentive to their customers' needs and adhere to Islamic standards not only in institutional or structural ways but also in the immediate and relevant—even aesthetic—ways that the banks realize their Islamic aspirations of the abstract idea in the textures of an Islamic institution.

ETHICS, SCRIPTURES, AND THEOLOGICAL EMPHASES

IBFI take great pride in pursuing what many have referred to as the "moral economy."[35] The moral Islamic economy takes the ideals of a moral economy—that the economy is based on the cultural norms and values that it considers good, fair, and just—one step further. The Islamic moral economy states that the underpinning virtues enacted in the economy are Islamic in nature; that they are dictated in the mandates of the Almighty Allah, His Messenger (PBUH), and transmitted over time in Shari'ah.

The case of water in the Muslim world is an important one for exploring the contours of the Islamic moral economy.[36] It reveals some important ways Islamic goods and services are both administered and capitalized on while simultaneously underpinning the Islamic importance. In Islamic theology, history, and political economy, water is of profound importance.[37] Given that the revelation of Islam occurred in one of the driest and hottest parts of the world, references to and stories about the miraculous nature of water and its symbol as a miracle of God come as no surprise. From the stories of the spring of Zamzam,[38] to the stories of drowning in sweat on the Day of Judgment,[39] water has the power to both give and take life.

Historically, Islamic governance has provided for legal protections of private water rights, even protecting prices determined by the market, which can be quite high.[40] At the same time, the Islamic injunctions to protect the poor often make full privatization of water markets undesirable. As I have proposed elsewhere, private-public partnerships are one avenue by which Islamic governments may maintain "ownership" of the water for the communities while simultaneously allowing the private sector to determine delivery methods, transparency, and accountability.[41]

In Islamic banking and finance, the underpinning of Islamic ethics, values, and morality most often emerge in the set of screens or categories for the industry's activities. The nine most commonly cited contradictions of current practices are as follows:[42]

1. Committing business with conventional banks in such a way that violates Islamic fundamentals such as through interest payments or debts; derivatives, futures, or securities, and foreign exchange for fixed-terms;
2. Engaging in conventional insurance or accompanying activities;
3. Profiting from alcohol production, consumption, selling, and marketing;
4. Dealing in illicit drugs;
5. Profiting from gambling, even if it falls under names like "lotto," sports betting, or financing the structures for that purpose;
6. Profiting from pork production, processing, or sales;
7. Promoting any sexually explicit entertainment, prostitution, nightclubs, and other related activities that usually include pornography, but not beaches or lingerie sales;
8. Engaging in any transactions that lack appropriate levels of knowledge and awareness, or take on excessive risk, or involve interest; and
9. Engaging in any transaction involving weaponry.

This last item, "Any transaction involving weaponry," is highly debatable. Some sources do not reference this at all.

These nine screens all hold some measure of grounding in Islamic theology.[43] The critiques of these screens, however, are that they overlook other important—and theologically grounded—Islamic mandates as well. A focus on alcohol, pork, and sexual purity comes at a deemphasis or purposeful ignoring of concerns for the environment, employment law, and professionalism and anti-corruption. These too are grounded in Shari'ah.[44]

CONCLUSION

Such paradoxes and problematized understandings of the relationship between the actions of Muslim actors and the structural intents of Islamic economics raise the question of where the movement can go from here in order to fulfill its aims for an economic reformation. Oft-overlooked sites of negotiation for Islamic economics—and the potential sites for the widespread structural reformation Islamic economists hope for—are not only in the banking, finance, taxation, or "production side" of the economy. The Islamization of the economy also must involve reshaping consumption practices in which each actor uses goods and services to create and sustain his/her own identity as a certain type of "Muslim" and to communicate that identity with others.[45] There are three primary areas of consumption that are subject to Islamization by Muslim actors but are currently not being included in the overall structural agenda of Islamic economics: knowledge, services, and products.[46] Knowledge-based modes of communication include print media, multimedia advertisements, internet-based resources and their content such as notions of appropriate correct religious practices, and prophetic traditions. Services may include conferences, social services, ministries, poverty relief, pedagogical tools for children's education, and education more generally, among others. Products include religious commodities and signs of the body, such as dress, hairstyles, cosmetics, or tattoos, and other visual symbols of identity.

The consumptive actions that result from these competing Islamic understandings and debates by Muslims as they attempt to engage in ethically informed manners, however, are not always simple or straightforward. Tracing the development of the points of hybridity and negotiation of Islamic identity formation, by way of consumption, helps to demonstrate that neither are identities simply cultivated by the powerful forces that produce Islamic knowledge,[47] nor are they the result of *homo economicus* in a free-market society.[48] Instead, the theoretical aims of an Islamic economics and an anthropology of Islamic consumption can illuminate the complex processes by which Islamic markers of identity are produced in various contexts of capitalism and can be held together despite contradictions and inimicalities, as well as hybridized and negotiated in very specific ways that, in turn, shape the culture, communities, and everyday practices of consumers.

NOTES

1. Charles Taylor, *The Ethics of Authenticity* (Cambridge, MA: Harvard University Press, 1992).

2. Christa Salamandra, *A New Old Damascus: Authenticity and Distinction in Urban Syria* (Bloomington, IN: Indiana University Press, 2004).

3. Roel Meijer, *Cosmopolitanism, Identity and Authenticity in the Middle East* (Abingdon-on-Thames, UK: Routledge, 2014).

4. Ibid., 8.

5. Benedict Anderson, *Imagined Communities* (London and New York, NY: Verso, 1991).

6. Sarah A. Tobin, *Everyday Piety: Islam and Economy in Jordan* (Ithaca, NY: Cornell University Press, 2016).

7. Salamandra, *A New Old Damascus*.

8. Timur Kuran, "Islamic Economics and the Islamic Subeconomy," *Journal of Economic Perspectives* 9, no. 4 (1995): 155–173; Timur Kuran, *Islam and Mammon: The Economic Predicaments of Islamism* (Princeton, NJ: Princeton University Press, 2004).

9. See, for example, Jonathan Benthall and Jérôme Bellion-Jourdan, *Charitable Crescent: Politics of Aid in the Muslim World* (I.B. Tauris, 2003); Bill Maurer, "Re-formatting the Economy: Islamic Banking and Finance in World Politics," *Islam in World Politics* 1 (2005): 62.

10. Sami Zubaida, *Law and Power in the Muslim World* (London, UK: I.B. Tauris, 2003), 5.

11. See, for example, Sami Ben Naceur, Adolfo Barajas, and Alexander Massara, "Can Islamic Banking Increase Financial Inclusion?" *IMF Working Paper* No. 15/31. Posted: March 24, 2015; Mahmoud Mohieldin, Zamir Iqbal, Ahmed Rostom, and Xiaochen Fu, *The Role of Islamic Finance in Enhancing Financial Inclusion in Organization of Islamic Cooperation (OIC) Countries* (Washington, DC: The World Bank, 2011).

12. Munawar Iqbal and Philip Molyneux, *Thirty Years of Islamic Banking: History, Performance and Prospects* (New York, NY: Springer, 2016).

13. Tobin, *Everyday Piety*.

14. Feisal Khan, "How 'Islamic' is Islamic Banking?" *Journal of Economic Behavior & Organization* 76, no. 3 (2010): 805–820.

15. Kuran, *Islam and Mammon*, 43–49.

16. Ibid., 47.

17. Sarah A. Tobin, "Islamized Postal Savings: A Model for Risk-Sharing," in Luna Khirfan (ed.), *Order and Disorder: Urban Governance and the Making of Middle Eastern Cities* (Montréal: McGill-Queen's Press-MQUP, 2017).

18. Mayada El-Zoghbi, "Advancing Financial Access in the Arab World: Opportunities and Challenges," CGAP Advancing Financial Access for the World's Poor, Savings and Credit Forum, SDC, October 17, 2012, available at: HYPERLINK "https://www.shareweb.ch/site/EI/Documents/Events/SC-Forum/SC-Forum%20 2012-10%20Financial%20Inclusion/SC-Forum%202012-10%20Financial%20Inclu sion%20-%20fsd%20s%20c%20forum%20october%202012%20-%20scforum%20f i%20in%20arab%20world%2017%2010%202012.pdf" https://www.shareweb.ch/s ite/EI/Documents/Events/SC-Forum/SC-Forum%202012-10%20Financial%20Incl usion/SC-Forum%202012-10%20Financial%20Inclusion%20-%20fsd%20s%20 c%20forum%20october%202012%20-%20scforum%20fi%20in%20arab%20 world%2017%2010%202012.pdf (accessed May 3, 2019); Mayada El-Zoghbi and Meritxell Martinez, "Can Postal Networks Advance Financial Inclusion in the Arab World?" 2012, available at https://www.cgap.org/research/publicatio n/can-postal-networks-advance-financial-inclusion-arab-world (accessed May 3, 2019).

19. Ziauddin Ahmad, "The Theory of Riba," *Islamic Studies* 17, no. 4 (1978): 171–185.

20. Mark J. Scher and Naoyuki Yoshino, eds., *Small Savings Mobilization and Asian Economic Development: The Role of Postal Financial Services* (Routledge, 2015).

21. Ibid., xvi.

22. El-Zoghbi, "Advancing Financial Access in the Arab World"; El-Zoghbi and Martinez, "Can Postal Networks Advance Financial Inclusion in the Arab World?"

23. Shamshad Akhtar and Douglas Pearce, "Microfinance in the Arab World: The Challenge of Financial Inclusion," MENA Knowledge and Learning Quick Notes Series No. 25 (Washington, DC: The World Bank, 2010), p. 1.

24. El-Zoghbi, "Advancing Financial Access in the Arab World"; El-Zoghbi and Martinez, "Can Postal Networks Advance Financial Inclusion in the Arab World?"

25. Ala'a Abbassi, Mohammed Khaled, Klaus Prochaska, and Michael Tarazi, "Access to Finance: Microcredit and Branchless Banking in the Hashemite Kingdom of Jordan," CGAP, March 16, 2009, available at: http://fr.afraca.org/download/gener al_rural_finance_publications/Microcredit-and-Branchless-Banking-in-The-Has hemite-Kingdom-of-Jordan-Report-by-Mohammed-Khaled-et-al.pdf (accessed May 3, 2019).

26. Omar Imady and Hans Dieter Seibel, "SANDUQ: A Microfinance Innovation in Jabal Al-Hoss, Syria," *Nenaraca Newsletter* (2003): 1–12; Alexandra Frasca, "A Further NICHE MARKET: Islamic Microfinance in the Middle East and North Africa," Center for Middle Eastern Studies and McCombs School of Business University of Texas at Austin (2008).

27. All names in the chapter have been modified because of the permission requirements of the publisher.

28. This book addresses related issues in Khan, Cham, and Zaman's chapters: viz. 2, 5, and 8 respectively.

29. Shahid Muhammad Khan Ghauri and Amal Sabah Obaid Qambar, "Rewards in Faith-Based versus Conventional Banking," *Qualitative Research in Financial Markets* 4, no. 2/3 (2012): 176–196.

30. Sarah A. Tobin, "Is it Really Islamic?" Evaluating the "Islam" in Islamic Banking in Amman, Jordan," in *Production, Consumption, Business and the Economy: Structural Ideals and Moral Realities* (Bingley, UK: Emerald Group Publishing Limited, 2014), pp. 127–156.

31. Refer to Sonko and Sonko (chapter 2) and Cham (chapter 5) for definitions.

32. Also see Zaman's (chapter 8) criticisms in this book.

33. Mohammed Malley, "Jordan: A Case Study of the Relationship between Islamic Finance and Islamist Politics," in Clement M. Henry and Rodney Wilson (eds.), *The Politics of Islamic Finance* (Edinburgh: Edinburgh University Press, 2004), pp. 191–215, 210–212.

34. Ibid.

35. Emin Baki Adas, "The Making of Entrepreneurial Islam and the Islamic Spirit of Capitalism," *Journal for Cultural Research* 10, no. 2 (2006): 113–137; Mehmet Asutay, "A Political Economy Approach to Islamic Economics: Systemic Understanding for an Alternative Economic System," *Kyoto Bulletin of Islamic Area Studies* 1, no. 2 (2007): 3–18. Mehmet Asutay, "Conceptualising and Locating the Social Failure of Islamic Finance: Aspirations of Islamic Moral Economy vs. The Realities of Islamic Finance," *Asian and African Area Studies* 11, no. 2 (2012): 93–113; Mehmet Asutay and Nazim Zaman, "Divergence Between Aspirations and Realities of Islamic Economics: A Political Economy Approach to Bridging the Divide," *IIUM Journal of Economics and Management* 17, no. 1 (2009): 73–96; Samuel Bowles, *The Moral Economy: Why Good Incentives are No Substitute*

for Good Citizens (New Haven, CT: Yale University Press, 2016); Joshua D. Hendrick, *Gülen: The Ambiguous Politics of Market Islam in Turkey and The World* (New York, NY: NYU Press, 2013); Filippo Osella and Caroline Osella, "Muslim Entrepreneurs in Public Life between India and the Gulf: Making Good and Doing Good," *Journal of the Royal Anthropological Institute* 15, no. s1 (2009); Daromir Rudnyckyj, "Spiritual Economies: Islam and Neoliberalism in Contemporary Indonesia," *Cultural Anthropology* 24, no. 1 (2009): 104–141; James C. Scott, *The Moral Economy of the Peasant: Subsistence and Rebellion in Southeast Asia* (New Haven, CT: Yale University Press, 1976); Charles Tripp, *Islam and the Moral Economy: The Challenge of Capitalism* (Cambridge: Cambridge University Press, 2006).

36. Tobin, "Islamized Postal Savings."

37. Naser I. Faruqui, "Islam and Water Management: Overview and Principles," *Water Management in Islam* (2001): 1–32.

38. Martin Lings, *"Muhammad." His Life Based on the Earliest Sources* (Rochester, Vermont: Inner Traditions International, 1983), pp. 1–3.

39. Jami' Tirmidhi, Chapters on the description of the Day of Judgement, Ar-Riqaq, and Al-Wara'. Vol. 4, Book 11, Hadith 2421.

40. Faruqui, "Islam and Water Management," 1–32, 14.

41. Faruqui, "Islam and Water Management," 1–32, 15; Tobin, "Islamized Postal Savings."

42. Mohamad Nedal Alchaar and Abboud Sandra, *Islamic Finance Qualification (IFQ): The Official Workbook* (Securities & Investment Institute, 2009); Ibrahim Warde, *Islamic Finance in the Global Economy* (Edinburgh: Edinburgh University Press, 2000).

43. Adel Ahmed, "Global Financial Crisis: An Islamic Finance Perspective," *International Journal of Islamic and Middle Eastern Finance and Management* 3, no. 4 (2010): 306–320; Ulrich Derigs and Shehab Marzban, "Review and Analysis of Current Shariah-Compliant Equity Screening Practices," *International Journal of Islamic and Middle Eastern Finance and Management* 1, no. 4 (2008): 285–303; Sayd Farook, "On Corporate Social Responsibility of Islamic Financial Institutions," *Islamic Economic Studies* 15, no. 1 (2007): 31–46; Mohammed Husain Khatkhatay and Shariq Nisar, "Shariah Compliant Equity Investments: An Assessment of Current Screening Norms," *Islamic Economic Studies* 15, no. 1 (2007): 47–76.

44. "The Quran and the Prophet about Money Matters," *The Quran and the Prophet About Money Matters* | SoundVision.com. Accessed January 30, 2018. https ://www.soundvision.com/article/the-quran-and-theprophet-about-money-matters.

45. Robert W. Hefner, "Ambivalent Embrace: Islamic Economics and Global Capitalism," in Jonathan B. Imber (ed.), *Markets, Morals, and Religion* (Abingdon-on-Thames, UK: Routledge, 2006), pp. 141–155.

46. Gregory Starrett, "The Political Economy of Religious Commodities in Cairo," *American Anthropologist* 97, no. 1 (1995): 51–68; Gregory Starrett, "Muslim Identities and the Great Chain of Buying," in Dale Eickelman (ed.), *New Media in the Muslim World: The Emerging Public Sphere* (Bloomington: Indiana University Press, 2003).

47. Saba Mahmood, *Politics of Piety: The Islamic Revival and the Feminist Subject* (Princeton, NJ: Princeton University Press, 2005).
48. Robert W. Hefner, *Market Cultures: Society and Morality in the New Asian Capitalisms* (Boulder, CO: Westview Press, 1998).

BIBLIOGRAPHY

Abbassi, Ala'a, Mohammed Khaled, Klaus Prochaska, and Michael Tarazi. "Access to Finance: Microcredit and Branchless Banking in the Hashemite Kingdom of Jordan." *CGAP*, March 16, 2009, available at: http://fr.afraca.org/download/general_rural_f inance_publications/Microcredit-and-Branchless-Banking-in-The-Hashemite-Kin gdom-of-Jordan-Report-by-Mohammed-Khaled-et-al.pdf (accessed May 3, 2019).

Adas, Emin Baki. "The Making of Entrepreneurial Islam and the Islamic Spirit of Capitalism." *Journal for Cultural Research* 10, no. 2 (2006): 113–137.

Ahmad, Ziauddin. "The Theory of Riba." *Islamic Studies, Islamabad* 17, no. 4 (1978): 171–185.

Ahmed, Adel. "Global Financial Crisis: An Islamic Finance Perspective." *International Journal of Islamic and Middle Eastern Finance and Management* 3, no. 4 (2010): 306–320.

Akhtar, Shamshad and Douglas Pearce. *Microfinance in the Arab World: The Challenge of Financial Inclusion.* MENA Knowledge and Learning Quick Notes Series No. 25. Washington, DC: The World Bank, 2010.

Alchaar, Mohamad Nedal and Abboud Sandra. *Islamic Finance Qualification (IFQ): The Official Workbook.* London, UK: Securities & Investment Institute, 2009.

Anderson, Benedict. *Imagined Communities.* London and New York, NY: Verso, 1991.

Asutay, Mehmet. "A Political Economy Approach to Islamic Economics: Systemic Understanding for an Alternative Economic System." *Kyoto Bulletin of Islamic Area Studies* 1, no. 2 (2007): 3–18.

Asutay, Mehmet. "Conceptualising and Locating the Social Failure of Islamic Finance: Aspirations of Islamic Moral Economy vs. The Realities of Islamic Finance." *Asian and African Area Studies* 11, no. 2 (2012): 93–113.

Asutay, Mehmet and Nazim Zaman. "Divergence between Aspirations and Realities of Islamic Economics: A Political Economy Approach to Bridging the Divide." *IIUM Journal of Economics and Management* 17, no. 1 (2009): 73–76.

Ben Naceur, Sami, Adolfo Barajas, and Alexander Massara. "Can Islamic Banking Increase Financial Inclusion?" 2015. *IMF Working Paper* No. 15/31 (Posted March 24, 2015).

Benthall, Jonathan and Jérôme Bellion-Jourdan. *Charitable Crescent: Politics of Aid in the Muslim World.* London, UK: I.B. Tauris, 2003.

Bowles, Samuel. *The Moral Economy: Why Good Incentives are No Substitute for Good Citizens.* New Haven, CT: Yale University Press, 2016.

Derigs, Ulrich and Shehab Marzban. "Review and Analysis of Current Shariah-Compliant Equity Screening Practices." *International Journal of Islamic and Middle Eastern Finance and Management* 1, no. 4 (2008): 285–303.

Farook, Sayd. "On Corporate Social Responsibility of Islamic Financial Institutions." *Islamic Economic Studies* 15, no. 1 (2007): 32–46.

Faruqui, Naser I. "Islam and Water Management: Overview and Principles." In *Water Management in Islam.* Ottawa: IDRC and Tokyo: UNU Press, 2001.

Frasca, Alexandra. "A Further NICHE MARKET: Islamic Microfinance in the Middle East and North Africa." Center for Middle Eastern Studies and McCombs School of Business University of Texas at Austin, 2008.

Hefner, Robert W. "Islamic Economics and Global Capitalism." *Society* 44, no. 1 (2006): 16–22.

Hefner, Robert W. "Ambivalent Embrace: Islamic Economics and Global Capitalism." In Jonathan B. Imber (ed.), *Markets, Morals, and Religion.* Abingdon-on-Thames, UK: Routledge, 2006, pp. 141–155.

Hefner, Robert W. *Market Cultures: Society and Morality in the New Asian Capitalisms.* Boulder, CO: Westview Press, 1998.

Hendrick, Joshua D. Gülen. *The Ambiguous Politics of Market Islam in Turkey and The World.* New York, NY: NYU Press, 2013.

https://www.soundvision.com/article/the-quran-and-the-prophet-about-money-m atters.

Imady, Omar and Hans Dieter Seibel. "SANDUQ: A Microfinance Innovation in Jabal Al-Hoss, Syria." *Nenaraca Newsletter*, 2003.

Imber, Jonathan B., ed. *Markets, Morals, and Religion.* Abingdon-on-Thames, UK: Routledge, 2006.

Iqbal, Munawar and Philip Molyneux. *Thirty Years of Islamic Banking: History, Performance and Prospects.* New York, NY: Springer, 2016.

Khan, Feisal. "How 'Islamic' is Islamic Banking?" *Journal of Economic Behavior & Organization* 76, no. 3 (2010): 805–820.

Khatkhatay, Mohammed Husain and Shariq Nisar. "Shariah Compliant Equity Investments: An Assessment of Current Screening Norms." *Islamic Economic Studies* 15, no. 1 (2007): 47–76.

Kuran, Timur. "Islamic Economics and the Islamic Subeconomy." *Journal of Economic Perspectives* 9, no. 4 (1995): 155–173.

Kuran, Timur. *Islam and Mammon: The Economic Predicaments of Islamism.* Princeton, NJ: Princeton University Press, 2004.

Lings, Martin. *"Muhammad." His Life Based on the Earliest Sources.* Rochester, Vermont: Inner Traditions International, 1983, pp. 1–3.

Mahmood, Saba. *Politics of Piety: The Islamic Revival and the Feminist Subject.* Princeton, NJ: Princeton University Press, 2005.

Malley, Mohammed. "Jordan: A Case Study of the Relationship between Islamic Finance and Islamist Politics." In Clement M. Henry and Rodney Wilson (eds.), *The Politics of Islamic Finance.* Edinburgh: Edinburgh University Press, 2004, pp. 191–215, 210–212.

Maurer, Bill. "Re-Formatting the Economy: Islamic Banking and Finance in World Politics." *Islam in World Politics* 1 (2005): 62.

Meijer, Roel. *Cosmopolitanism, Identity and Authenticity in the Middle East.* Abingdon-on Thames, UK: Routledge, 2014.

Mohieldin, Mahmoud, Zamir Iqbal, Ahmed Rostom, and Xiaochen Fu. *The Role of Islamic Finance in Enhancing Financial Inclusion in Organization of Islamic Cooperation (OIC) Countries.* Washington, DC: The World Bank, 2011.

Muhammad Khan Ghauri, Shahid and Amal Sabah Obaid Qambar. "Rewards in Faith-Based versus Conventional Banking." *Qualitative Research in Financial Markets* 4, no. 2/3 (2012): 176–196.

Osella, Filippo and Caroline Osella. "Muslim Entrepreneurs in Public Life between India and the Gulf: Making Good and Doing Good." *Journal of the Royal Anthropological Institute* 15, no. s1 (2009): S202–S221.

Rudnyckyj, Daromir. "Spiritual Economies: Islam and Neoliberalism in Contemporary Indonesia." *Cultural Anthropology* 24, no. 1 (2009): 104–141.

Salamandra, Christa. *A New Old Damascus: Authenticity and Distinction in Urban Syria.* Bloomington, IN: Indiana University Press, 2004.

Scher, Mark J. and Naoyuki Yoshino, eds. *Small Savings Mobilization and Asian Economic Development: The Role of Postal Financial Services.* New York, NY: Routledge, 2015.

Scott, James C. *The Moral Economy of the Peasant: Subsistence and Rebellion in Southeast Asia.* New Haven, CT: Yale University Press, 1976.

SoundVision.com. "The Quran and the Prophet about Money Matters." Accessed January 30, 2018.

Starrett, Gregory "Muslim Identities and the Great Chain of Buying." In Dale Eickelman (ed.), *New Media in the Muslim World: The Emerging Public Sphere.* Bloomington: Indiana University Press, 2003.

Starrett, Gregory. "The Political Economy of Religious Commodities in Cairo." *American Anthropologist* 97, no. 1 (1995): 51–68.

Taylor, Charles. *The Ethics of Authenticity.* Cambridge, MA: Harvard University Press, 1992.

Tirmidhi, Jami'. Chapters on the description of the Day of Judgement, Ar-Riqaq, and Al-Wara'. Vol. 4, Book 11, Hadith 2421.

Tobin, Sarah A. "'Is it Really Islamic?' Evaluating the 'Islam' in Islamic Banking in Amman, Jordan." In *Production, Consumption, Business and the Economy: Structural Ideals and Moral Realities.* Bingley, UK: Emerald Group Publishing Limited, 2014, pp. 127–156.

Tobin, Sarah A. "Islamized Postal Savings: A Model for Risk-Sharing." In Luna Khirfan (ed.), *Order and Disorder: Urban Governance and the Making of Middle Eastern Cities.* Montréal: McGill-Queen's Press-MQUP, 2017.

Tobin, Sarah A. *Everyday Piety: Islam and Economy in Jordan.* Ithaca, NY: Cornell University Press, 2016.

Tripp, Charles. *Islam and the Moral Economy: The Challenge of Capitalism.* Cambridge: Cambridge University Press, 2006.

Warde, Ibrahim. *Islamic Finance in the Global Economy.* Edinburgh: Edinburgh University Press, 2000.

Zubaida, Sami. *Law and Power in the Muslim World.* London, UK: I.B. Tauris, 2003, p. 5.

Chapter 5

Islamic Banking and Price Stability

Evidence from the GCC, Iran, and the Sudan

Tamsir Cham

INTRODUCTION

Islamic banking is growing rapidly in recent years in terms of both assets and loans. Islamic financial institutions are spread around the world in both Muslim and non-Muslim countries. Although Islamic banks are heavily concentrated in the Middle East, the Islamic financial instruments are used in other countries such as Malaysia and Pakistan. It should be noted that these countries operate both Islamic and conventional banking systems.

Proponents of Islamic finance argued that Islamic finance and banking is directed mainly toward the real sector and hence it is noninflationary. It enhances economic growth through its effect on the real sector. However, Iran and the Sudan have been experiencing high inflation. These two countries have few things in common: The banking system purely operates under Shari'ah principles; Iran and the Sudan are under economic sanctions and both countries are oil-exporting countries.

Our analysis includes the Gulf Cooperation Council (GCC). We choose GCC countries as a comparator group because (i) with the exception of Malaysia, the GCC countries have the largest Islamic banking assets (see DCIBF [2014]) and (ii) the GCC countries, Iran and the Sudan are all members of the MENA region.[1] They are all oil-rich and oil-exporting countries. Although most of the GCC countries pegged their currencies to the US dollar, Iran and the Sudan are under a managed floating exchange rate regime. The rules and regulations governing the Islamic mode of finance and Islamic banking remain the same across the economies. However, different jurisdictions have their own Shari'ah boards that set the necessary guidelines for the effective functioning of Islamic banks.

Inflation in the GCC has remained relatively low in single digits. However, from 2007 to 2010 there was an uptick in inflation, which elevated to double digits for Kuwait, Oman, and Saudi Arabia. This period coincided with the global financial crisis. For Iran and the Sudan, inflation continues to remain high. Although inflation rates moderated during certain periods with inflation rates below 10 percent, Iran and the Sudan continue to register double digits inflation since September 2010. The highest inflation rates occurred in the Sudan and Iran during November 2012 and July 2013 with rates of 49 percent and 44 percent, respectively. However, inflation rates moderated during the global financial crisis (see figure 5.1).

There are a lot of studies that looked into the determinants of domestic prices in the GCC, Iran, and the Sudan, applying various methods. Many of these studies investigated the linkages in money demand, money supply, exchange rate, and inflation. Moriyama (2008) examined inflation dynamics in the Sudan using single, vector-auto regression and Vector Error Correction Models (VECM). The empirical results revealed monetary growth and changes in the nominal exchange rate affect inflation with a lag period of eighteen to twenty-four months.

Almounsor (2010) investigated inflation dynamics in Yemen using quarterly data from 2005 to 2007 applying single, structural vector-auto regression and VECM. The empirical findings revealed that international prices and exchange rate depreciation significantly affect domestic prices. Osorio and Unsal (2011) presented a quantitative analysis of inflation dynamics in Asia including the GCC, Iran, and the Sudan using a Global VAR (GVAR) model, which incorporated the role of regional and global spillovers in driving Asia's inflation. They found that the main drivers of inflation are monetary and supply shocks although the contributions of these shocks have declined. However, demand-side pressure has picked up in recent years.

Kandil and Morsy (2009) examined the determinants of inflation in the GCC using a model that includes both domestic and external factors. They found inflation in major trading partners with the GCC as the most important external factor. Oil revenue also reinforces inflationary pressure in the GCC. Hence, in the short run, an increase in government spending increases inflation.

Bonato (2007) studied the determinants of inflation in Iran. The study examined the relationship between nominal variables and inflation; it sought to explain the reasons for the decline in inflation that occurred up to the first

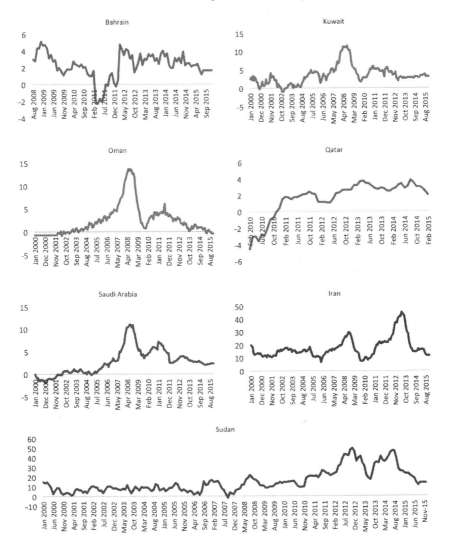

Figure 5.1   **Inflation.** *Source*: Author.

half of 2006. The empirical findings revealed a strong relationship between inflation and money supply. McCarthy (2007) examined the pass-through of external factors such as the effects of the exchange rates and import prices on domestic prices for several industrialized economies using a VAR model. According to his study, in the post-Bretton Woods era, impulse responses indicate that exchange rates have a modest effect on domestic price inflation.

In addition, while import prices have a stronger effect, the pass-through is greater in countries with larger import share and more persistent exchange rates and import prices.

In the GCC countries, studies have shown that higher government spending and credit growth have successfully targeted supply side constraints, slowing down price inflation (see Kandil and Morsy 2009). Similarly, a number of studies have looked into the relationship between Islamic banking, Islamic finance, and macroeconomic variables. Imam and Kpodar (2016) investigated whether the development of Islamic banking is good for growth using data covering the period 1990–2010. They found that Islamic banking is positively associated with growth after controlling other determinants of growth. They concluded that Islamic countries that suffer from low growth need to enhance their banking sector through modernizing the legislative, regulatory, and infrastructural environment.

Imam and Kpodar (2013) investigated the determinants of the pattern of Islamic bank expansion worldwide using country-level data spanning from 1992 to 2006. Their study revealed that Islamic banks complement conventional banks. Adedifar et al. (2015) reviewed recent empirical literature in Islamic banking and finance. The empirical findings revealed no major difference between Islamic and conventional banks in terms of their efficiency, competition, and risk features. They found that Islamic finance enhances inclusion and financial development. They also found that Islamic banks perform better than conventional banks in the areas of risk and return features of mutual funds.

Gheeraert and Weill (2015) investigated whether Islamic banking influences macroeconomic efficiency through total productivity by employing stochastic estimation technics with a sample of seventy countries, covering Islamic banks worldwide for the period 2000–2005. Their results support the view that Islamic banks enhance macroeconomic efficiency to a certain point. However, beyond that certain point, Islamic bank expansion adversely affects macroeconomic efficiency (total productivity).

Zeitun (2012) studied the impact of foreign ownership, bank-specific variables, and macroeconomic indicators on the performance of Islamic and conventional banks in the Gulf Cooperation Council (GCC) region employing annual data for the period 2002–2009. They found that GDP and inflation significantly affect bank performance. Cost to income ratio negatively impacts the performance of both Islamic and conventional banks, and foreign ownership does not have an impact on bank performance.

Hassan and Bashir (2003) examined the performance of Islamic banks using data for the period 1994–2001, taking into account both internal and external factors. Their findings revealed that while macroeconomic variables have a positive impact on bank performance, taxes negatively impact bank performance. Similarly, Bougatef (2015) examined the impact of correction in the health of Islamic banks using the GMM estimation method for sixty-nine Islamic banks with data series ranging from 2008 to 2010. Their empirical findings revealed that the corruption level significantly impacts financial soundness indicators. Cihak and Hesse (2010) looked into the financial stability of Islamic banks covering eighteen banking systems with a significant presence of Islamic banks. They found that small Islamic banks tend to be financially stronger than small conventional commercial banks. However, large conventional commercial banks tend to be financially stronger than large Islamic banks.

However, we have not come across any study that included Islamic finance as one of the determinants of inflation in the Middle East, despite the importance of the Islamic mode of finance in the demand for money in the region. According to the 2014 Dubai Center for Islamic Banking and Finance annual report, total assets for Islamic banks have increased by more than 40 percent from 2010 to 2013. As pointed out earlier, it has been widely claimed that Islamic finance and banking focuses on the real sector and does not have an impact on inflation. We have not found any empirical evidence for this though. Therefore, we investigate whether Islamic finance through its facility in extending credit could affect domestic price inflation. This research is aimed at addressing this empirical research gap and to provide an insight into the relationship between Islamic banking and inflation. We assess whether Islamic bank growth has been one of the contributing factors to high inflation in these countries.

The motivation for this study is the importance of Islamic banking and finance in the countries studied and the recent increased in Islamic banking growth and the high level of inflation in Iran and the Sudan.[2] The two countries have double digits inflation rates. We investigate whether the increases in domestic prices are due to increases in Islamic banking growth. This chapter is organized as follows: the second section provides an overview of the Islamic mode of finance. The third section discusses the model and estimation method used. The fourth section presents data and empirical results. Conclusions and recommendations are discussed in the last section.

BOX 5.1 THE ISLAMIC MODE OF
FINANCE: STYLIZED FACTS

There are three main categories of Islamic finance–sales-based mode of finance, finance-based contracts, and investment-based contracts.

A *sales-based mode of finance* is a financing mode include different types of *murabaha, salam, Istisna* and *Ijarah.*

Murabaha is a sale transaction in which a commodity is exchanged for the cost of the commodity and some profit margin above it.

Salam is a sale contract where a monetary transaction is made in exchange for a good(s), which is delivered in advance with certain payments. *Salam* serves the interest of both the buyer and seller. The seller gets the desired money in advance exchange of the promise to deliver the commodity which is sold. This facility helps to cover the seller's financial needs which include personal expenses and his productive activity.

Istisna is a sale transaction where the monetary payments are effected either in full, in part or promised to be settled in exchange for a commodity which will be delivered at an agreed-upon time.

Ijarah is a mode of leasing transaction where an agreement is undertaken between the Islamic bank and a client. The former finances the equipment or any facility on behalf of the latter with agreed terms, such as agreed rental plus additional fees which are paid by the client into an account. This will allow the latter to purchase the equipment or facility at the end of the lease period when all the payments are effected. In this leasing arrangement, Islamic banks buy and acquire the necessary asset as a result of a request from customers who prefer to own the leased asset at the end of the lease period.

A *finance-based contract* is a type of contract were the investor provides the capital and or expertise or management. There are five types - *Mudaraba* (partnership finance), *Muzara 'a* (offer land and share proceeds of the produce), *Musakah* (agriculture), *Muharasa* and *Musarakah* (provide finance and or management)

Mndharabah is a mode of finance where Islamic banks use depositors' money in exchange of specified ratios. The banks use the money and lend it to potential investors in exchange of agreed returns.

Muzara 'a is a contract agreement where one party presents the required resources, mainly land, to another party with the required technical expertise and the proceeds of the produce are shared between the two parties.

Investment-based contracts include mutual funds, *takaful* (solidarity, mutual support), and wealth management.

Source: Compiled by author.

MODEL

We develop a hybrid model by borrowing from an earlier work by Valdovinos (2008) and Moriyama (2008) with few modifications. The model is based on the following: the composition of inflation and the quantity theory of money (QTM). Firstly, an overall country's consumer price index consists of domestic price (Pd) and foreign ($P*$) components, given by the following equation:

$$P = P_d^\alpha \left(EP^* \right)^{1-\alpha} \tag{1}$$

Where α is the share of the domestic component, which is assumed to be constant and E is the exchange rate. From the quantity theorem of money,[3] domestic inflation is given by the following equation:

$$MV = P_d Y \tag{2}$$

$$P_d = MV / Y$$

Where M denotes the money supply, V is the velocity of money (the rate at which money changes hands), and Y is the level of output of the economy. Taking the natural logarithm of equations (1) and (2) yields equations (3) and (4) respectively:

$$p = \alpha p_d + \left(1 - \alpha \right) [e + p^*] \tag{3}$$

$$p_d = m - y + \mu t + \lambda \tag{4}$$

The lower-case letters represent percentage changes (growth rates) and the term $\mu t + \lambda$ presents the velocity component of equation (2).

With the expansion of Islamic finance and banking, credit could expand which could stimulate dom estic demand. In addition, the profit-risk sharing nature of Islamic finance could further increase spending expectations and increase the velocity of money which could feed into domestic prices. Taking these arguments as bases, we present an introduction of Islamic banking variable in the augmented QTM model. Hence, from substituting equation (4) into equation (3) and the introduction of the Islamic banking variable (Ib), we get a linear transformation of the quantity theory of money represented in equation (5):

$$p = F(e, m, y, wcpi, ib; X) = Z\beta + X\gamma + \varepsilon \tag{5}$$

Where $Z = F$ (e, m, y, $wcpi$, ib), X is a vector of other variables and ε is the disturbance term. The coefficients of the exchange rate and money supply capture the effects of the exchange rate and monetary developments on inflation respectively. Other things equal, the depreciation of the country's currency and an increase in the money supply will lead to an increase in inflation. In addition, an increase in foreign prices will be transmitted to domestic prices and subsequently lead to an increase in domestic prices. Islamic banking growth could increase output and enhance demand which could translate into higher prices since Islamic banking offers more resources to economic agents, in which depositors' money is offered in the form of credit on agreed terms. This arrangement increases economic agents' resources and income to some extent. The increased resources increase demand and, with unchanged supply, will lead to an increase in prices. In addition, an increase in international food and oil prices may positively affect domestic prices. We investigate the impact of Islamic banking growth on inflation using equation (5). We first use the single-equation model; second, we apply vector autoregression (VAR) and, finally, we use VECM to examine whether there is any long run relationship among the variables. In order to solidify our findings, we apply panel regression analysis as well.

In order to derive a single equation from equation (5), we need its linear transformation so we use the first difference of the variables,[4] which is given as:[5]

$$P_t = \alpha_0 + \alpha_1 MS_t + \alpha_2 ER_t + \alpha_3 WCPI_t + \alpha_4 Y_t + \alpha_5 IB_t$$

$$+ \alpha_6 Woil_t + \alpha_7 Wfood_t + \varepsilon_t \qquad (6)$$

Where,

P_t is the monthly inflation rate at time t;
MS_t is the monthly money and quasi growth rate at time t;
ER_t is the national currency per US dollar exchange rate at time t;
$WCPI_t$ is the monthly world consumer price index at time t;
Y_t is the monthly growth in imports (proxy for real economic activity) at time t;[6]
IB_t is the Islamic banking growth rate at time t;
$Woil_t$ is the world oil price growth rate at time t;
$Wfood_t$ is the world food price growth rate at time t; and
ε_t is the disturbance term.

Inflation depends on money supply growth, real GDP growth, nominal exchange rate, world consumer price index, world food prices, world oil prices, and Islamic banking growth. All the variables have been transformed into growth rates. Equation (6) comprises different models of inflation within which different hypothesis can be tested. Since macroeconomic variables do adjust instantaneously, we rewrite equation (6) in autoregressive lag form:

$$P_t = \alpha_0 + \sum_{i=1}^{k} \alpha_{1i} P_{t-1} + \sum_{i=0}^{k} \alpha_{2i} ER_{t-1} + \sum_{i=0}^{k} \alpha_{3i} WCPI_{t-i}$$

$$+ \sum_{i=0}^{k} \alpha_{4i} MS_{t-i} + \sum_{i=0}^{k} \alpha_{5i} Y_{t-i} + \sum_{i=0}^{k} \alpha_{6i} IB_{t-i}$$

$$+ \sum_{i=0}^{k} \alpha_{7i} WOIL_{t-i} + \sum_{i=1}^{k} \alpha_{8i} WFOOD_{t-i} + \varepsilon_t \tag{7}$$

Where k is the lag length.

Since the macroeconomic variables are nonstationary and integrated of order one, we reformulate equation (7) into an error-correction format as specified in equation (8):

$$\Delta P_t = \beta_0 + \sum_{i=1}^{k} \beta_{1i} P_{t-1} + \sum_{i=0}^{k} \beta_{2i} ER_{t-i} + \sum_{i=0}^{k} \beta_{3i} WCPI_{t-i} + \sum_{i=0}^{k} \beta_{4i} MS_{t-i}$$

$$+ \sum_{i=0}^{k} \beta_{5i} Y_{t-i} + \sum_{i=0}^{k} \beta_{6i} IB_{t-i} + \sum_{i=0}^{k} \beta_{7i} WOIL_{t-i}$$

$$+ \sum_{i=1}^{k} \beta_{8i} WFOOD_{t-i} + \beta_9 \left[P_t - \alpha_1 ER_t - \alpha_2 WCPI_t \right.$$

$$\left. - \alpha_3 M_t - \alpha_4 Y_t - \alpha_5 IB_t \right] + \varepsilon_t \tag{8}$$

The term in brackets represents the error-correction term and the coefficient, β_9, is the speed at which the economy adjusts for any disequilibrium. Likewise, the parameters of the variables in the log-difference $(\beta_{1i} - \beta_{8i})$ display the short response and α_s signify long-term responses. A substantial effect from a lagged to current prices β_{1i} would show inflation inertia which could be because of expectations.

DATA AND EMPIRICAL RESULTS

Data

The empirical analysis is conducted using monthly data from January 2001 to December 2015.[7] While data on money supply, consumer price index, exchange rates, world oil prices, world food prices, world oil prices are sourced from the International Money Fund (IMF), IFS database; imported value is sourced from IMF, DOT database. Islamic banking data are sourced from Bankscope. Since data on Islamic banking is annual and the rest of the data variables are monthly, we transform the data from low frequency to high frequency using Eviews. We admit the loss of data quality due to data transformation; however, this is the best option available to us. All variables are in growth rates. For money supply, we used money and quasi-money. The CPI variable used is the composite consumer price index. For foreign prices, we used the world consumer price index (WCPI). We used the nominal exchange rate of national currency per US dollar. Since GDP is available only on annual frequency, we used the volume of imports as a proxy for the economic activity.

Unit Root Tests

We applied both standard Augmented Dickey-Fuller (ADF) unit root test and panel unit root test. Both tests revealed that the series are nonstationary. The ADF unit root test for individual country series indicate nonstationary but stationary at first difference I(1). The results of the panel indicate the presence of unit root as LLC, IPS, and both Fisher tests fail to reject the null of unit root for the money supply, consumer price index, exchange rate, and import. However, all the series are stationary at I(1). Appendix 5D, Table D.1 and Table D.2 contain the ADF unit root and panel unit tests results respectively.

EMPIRICAL RESULTS AND ANALYSIS

Summary Statistics

We begin our empirical analysis by presenting summary statistics of inflation, Islamic banking growth, and other independent variables. Table 5.1 presents mean values, maximum, minimum, and standard deviation of the

Table 5.1   Descriptive Statistics

	CPI	MS	ER	IB	WCPI	WFOOD	WOIL
Mean	6.426	17.210	5.896	0.310	3.736	5.535	11.788
Median	3.217	14.955	0.000	0.135	3.618	3.564	6.294
Maximum	49.452	60.976	356.812	137.818	6.939	48.384	92.873
Minimum	-5.619	-7.110	-22.625	-52.934	1.363	-28.156	-55.455
Std. Dev.	8.899	11.157	36.322	4.363	0.862	14.616	31.502
Skewness	2.034	0.811	8.554	23.440	0.983	0.636	0.186
Kurtosis	7.954	3.343	80.197	803.769	5.743	3.544	2.774
Observations	1,260	1,260	1,260	1,260	1,260	1,260	1,260

Author generated.

variables used in the study. These statistics provide preliminary information regarding the distribution of the variables. All variables have positive means ranging from 0.310 to 17.210. The mean value of Islamic banking growth is 0.31 while the standard deviation is 4.363. The maximum and the minimum values of Islamic banking growth are -52.93 and 137.818 respectively, which is fairly distributed. The minimum and the maximum values of inflation are -5.619 and 49.452 respectively. The maximum value indicates that some countries are experiencing hyperinflation. The value of the standard deviation reveals that the exchange rate is more volatile compared to other variables. The mean value of money supply growth suggests that on average the monetary authorities have been implementing expansionary monetary policy.

Single Equation Results

From equation (6) inflation depends on money supply growth, real GDP growth, nominal exchange rate, world prices, oil prices, and Islamic banking growth. We include three dummies for the periods of the financial crisis, periods of oil prices hitting low, and high respectively. The estimated result of equation (6) is summarized in table 5.2. The coefficients represent elasticities and the standard deviations are in parenthesis. We perform regressions of inflation on a set of variables including Islamic banking growth, domestic and external factors. We check the correlations among the explanatory variables and conclude that the hypothesis of multicollinearity can be accepted. Only the external variables, which are international food and oil prices and world consumer price index, have correlations above 0.5, which makes us comfortable to introduce them simultaneously and in some instances one at a time in the models (see Appendix E).

The regression results from the single equation reveal the following: (i) Islamic banking growth significantly decreases inflation in Oman, Qatar, and Iran, (ii) money supply significantly increases inflation in Oman, (iii) exchange depreciation tends to increase inflation in Iran and the Sudan, (iv) high international food prices, on the one hand, raise domestic prices in Oman and Saudi Arabia[8] and, on the other hand, it dampens inflation in Bahrain and Qatar, (v) higher world consumer price index increases inflation in Kuwait and Iran but dampens inflation in Oman, and (vi) higher oil prices increase inflation in Qatar but decrease inflation in Bahrain, Kuwait, Saudi Arabia, Iran, and the Sudan. While the periods of the financial crisis reflect increased inflation in Bahrain, Kuwait, and Saudi Arabia, it dampens domestic prices in Oman, Qatar, Iran, and the Sudan. Furthermore, the periods of low oil prices reflect increases in inflation in Saudi Arabia and the Sudan, which is a reflection of subsidies due to low oil revenues. The periods of high oil prices increase inflation in Bahrain and Oman[9] but dampen inflation in Qatar.

Table 5.2 Single Equation Model Regressions

					Dependent Variable: DCPI		
Variable	Bahrain	Kuwait	Oman	Qatar	Saudi Arabia	Iran	Sudan
INTERCEPT	1.848	-4.033	0.556	1.183	-2.657***	5.074	9.837
	(0.455)	(0.705)	(0.263)	(1.316)	(0.711)	(3.301)	(4.524)
D(CPI(-1))	0.258**	0.189	0.165**	0.838***	-0.502	0.301	0.888***
	(0.120)	(0.188)	(0.083)	(0.247)	(0.331)	(0.433)	(0.264)
D(MS)	-0.002	0.033	0.065***	-0.001	-0.008	-0.001	-0.101
	(0.028)	(0.050)	(0.019)	(0.043)	(0.061)	(0.340)	(0.253)
D(ER)						0.001**	10.305**
						(0.001)	(5.006)
D(IMP)	0.233	0.188	-0.031	-1.149	0.336	0.467	0.300
	(0.535)	(0.450)	(0.172)	(6.009)	(0.666)	(3.037)	(2.496)
D(IB)	-0.002	-4.975	-4.885**	-11.267**	-0.132	-7.823*	2.213
	(0.005)	(6.200)	(2.00)	(5.106)	(0.600)	(4.380)	(5.318)
D(WCPI)	-0.076	1.882***	-0.174**	0.234	1.209***	4.050***	1.831
	(0.124)	(0.191)	(0.071)	(0.356)	(0.192)	(0.893)	(1.225)
D(WFOOD)	-3.36***	0.609	1.398***	-6.600***	5.956***	-3.467	-4.104
	(0.787)	(1.278)	(0.434)	(2.274)	(1.341)	(5.868)	(8.216)
D(OIL)	-1.048***	-2.082***	0.182	4.096**	-2.606***	-9.879***	-8.472**
	(0.396)	(0.630)	(0.239)	(1.151)	(0.643)	(2.840)	(4.143)
DUMFC	0.836***	3.103***	-0.225*	-6.173***	4.295***	-3.629**	-5.690**
	(0.246)	(0.382)	(0.134)	(0.711)	(10.990)	(1.771)	(2.502)
DUMOILL	0.250	0.839	-0.099	1.342	1.453**	-4.066	20.751***
	(0.282)	(0.654)	(0.227)	(1.204)	(0.662)	(2.988)	(4.284)
DUMOILH	0.909**	0.024	0.466*	-2.857**	0.352	3.594	6.143
	(0.450)	(0.693)	(0.239)	(1.271)	(0.721)	(3.205)	(4.541)

Adjusted R^2	0.40	0.64	0.38	0.56	0.69	0.24	0.27
F- Stats	11.03	25.37	7.85	19.52	31.92	4.45	5.31
DW	0.56	0.29	2.19	0.39	0.23	0.17	0.23
SE	1.05	1.61	0.54	2.98	1.65	7.45	10.58
AIC	3.00	3.86	1.66	5.08	3.91	6.92	7.63
SC	3.19	4.08	1.90	5.29	4.13	7.15	7.85

The coefficients of the variables are listed, and standard errors are in parentheses. *** 1 percent significance level, ** 5 percent significance level, and * 10 percent significance level.
Author generated.

It is also interesting to note that past inflation increases inflation in Bahrain, Oman, Qatar, and the Sudan.

The main drivers of inflation in Bahrain is past inflation, representing an indication of inflation inertia, periods of financial crisis and periods of high oil prices. However, an increase in international food prices and high oil prices tends to dampen domestic prices. This could be an indication of the presence of subsidies because of higher oil revenue receipts. In addition, the non-pass through of international prices on domestic prices could be a result of artificial control of domestic and hence international price developments as a result of which they are not transmitted to domestic prices. Our findings to a larger extent agree with the work of Kandila and Morsy (2009).

In Kuwait, in the short run, higher world consumer prices are transmitted to domestic prices. In addition, the periods of financial crisis result in the increases in domestic prices. However, the increase in world oil prices tends to dampen inflation which could be a reflection of subsidies. In Oman domestic prices are positively influenced by past inflation, increases in money growth, increases in international food prices, and periods of high oil prices. However, growth in Islamic banking, increase in world consumer prices, and the period of financial crisis decrease inflation. In Qatar, the increase in Islamic banking growth, increase in international food prices, and the periods of financial crisis and high oil prices ease inflationary pressure. This could be a reflection of subsidies and to some extent evidence of price controls. However, there is evidence of inflation inertia. In addition, the increase in international prices increases inflation, which could be due to demand pressure because of the increase in oil revenue. In Saudi Arabia domestic prices are driven mainly by world consumer prices and world food prices. Periods of the financial crisis and periods of low oil prices have shown increases in domestic prices. However, the increase in oil prices decreases domestic prices. This could also be a reflection of subsidies because of the increase in oil revenues as Saudi Arabia is a major oil exporter.

In Iran, a pure Islamic banking country, domestic prices dampen as a result of an increase in Islamic banking growth and an increase in oil prices. In addition, periods of financial crisis tend to dampen inflation in Iran. This could be due to the economic sanctions the country faces as it is disconnected financially from the rest of the world. However, the depreciation of the local currency vis-à-vis the US dollar increases inflation. Similarly, increases in world consumer prices lead to increases in domestic prices as well.

Inflation in the Sudan is positively influenced by past inflation, exchange rate depreciation, and periods of low oil prices. However, increase in world oil prices decreases inflation in the Sudan, which could be a reflection of subsidies from oil revenue. Similarly, the period of the last financial crisis tends to dampen domestic prices. This could be due to the sanctions, which make the country less connected to the world. Our empirical results show no indication that growth in Islamic banking increases inflation. In fact, our empirical results indicate that it dampens domestic prices. In the short run, an increase in Islamic banking growth significantly decreases domestic prices in Oman, Qatar, and Iran.

Given that the unit root tests reveal that the variables are nonstationary, we perform a co-integration test. The results of Johansen tests suggest the existence of co-integrating vectors. Appendix 5E, Table E.1 and Table E.2 summarize the co-integration and panel co-integration tests. Since there is an existence of co-integrating vectors, we perform a vector error correction estimate to determine the short and long-run dynamics of inflation across the countries under consideration.

In Bahrain, in the long run, the main drivers of inflation are the money supply and world consumer prices. However, Islamic banking growth dampens inflation in Bahrain in the long run. In the short run, inflation is driven by inflation inertia and international food prices. From the impulse response functions, persistent inflationary effects are attributed to a certain extent by world consumer prices and growth in economic activity. However, money supply growth, changes in the exchange rate, and Islamic banking growth show no persistent effects overtime. In Kuwait, the main drivers of inflation, in the long run, are money supply growth and exchange rate depreciation. The impulse response functions show that persistent inflationary effects are due to the pass-through channels of changes in the exchange rate and world consumer prices. The inflationary effects of money supply and Islamic banking growth appear to have the least persistent effects. In Oman, the main driver of inflation, in the long run, is money supply. In the short run, the main causes of inflation are money supply and international oil and food prices. The impulse response functions reveal persistent inflationary effects mainly due to growth in the money supply. However, there is no persistent inflation over time with the other determinants. In Qatar, money supply and the world consumer price index are the main drivers of inflation in the long run. The impulse response shows persistent inflationary effects attributed to growth in money supply and real economic growth. However, the world consumer price index and Islamic banking growth do not have long pronounced effects. In Saudi Arabia, the world consumer price index is the main driver of inflation in the long run. In the short run, money supply, past inflation, and the world consumer price index are the main causes of inflation. The impulse response shows persistent inflationary effects attributed to growth in Islamic banking and money supply. However, world consumer prices and real economic activity do not have long pronounced effects.

While in the long run, inflation in the Sudan is mainly determined by money supply and the world consumer price index. In the short run, however, past inflation is the main driver of inflation. To some extent, the impulse response functions illustrate persistent inflationary effects due to Islamic banking growth, money supply growth, and change in the exchange rate. However, changes in world consumer prices appear less persistent over time. In Iran, money supply, world consumer prices, and exchange rate depreciation are the main drivers of inflation in the long run. In the short run, past inflation and international food prices are some of the causes of inflation. The impulse response illustrates persistent inflationary effects attributed to change in the exchange rate and growth in Islamic banking. The pass-through channels of money supply growth and world consumer prices do not appear to last long. In Iran, Islamic banking growth significantly decreases domestic prices in the short and long run. In the Sudan, to a certain extent, Islamic banking growth decreases inflation in the short run.

From the VECM, we conclude that Islamic banking growth does not impose any inflationary pressure on domestic prices for the countries under study. In fact, it dampens domestic prices in certain countries, namely Iran, Bahrain, and, to some extent, Oman.

For robustness checks to strengthen our assessment, we perform a panel regression with fixed effect with different specifications. The outcome of the panel regression results reveals that the coefficient of the variable of interest, Islamic banking growth is negative, and insignificant in all specifications indicating that growth in Islamic bank does not exert any inflationary pressure in the selected countries. However, the regression results indicate that in the GCC countries, Iran, and the Sudan inflation is determined mainly by money supply growth and exchange rate depreciation vis-à-vis the US dollar. All results suggest the existence of the pass-through on inflation. In addition, lag (previous period) inflation positively affects current inflation, suggesting that inflation exhibits inflation inertia.

Furthermore, the world consumer price index and world food prices positively affect inflation in all specifications. While the coefficient for world food prices significantly affects prices in these economies, world consumer price index and world oil prices are significant in only one specification. The possible explanation is that these countries are mainly oil-exporting economies. Three dummies, DUMFC, DUMOILL, and DUMOILH, were introduced representing periods of the financial crisis, low oil prices, and high oil prices respectively. While the coefficients for DUMFC remain insignificant in all specifications, the coefficient for DUMOILH is positive and significant in two out of the four specifications. The intuition is that periods of high prices represent increases in oil revenue, which exerts demand pressure. Likewise, periods of low oil prices represent low oil revenues, which slow down demand.

The elasticities of inflation to the money supply, exchange rate, and world food prices based on the panel regression reveal that a percent increase in money supply, depreciation of the currency against the US dollar, and world food prices inflation raise inflation by 0.024 percent, 0.005 percent, and 0.01 percent respectively. In addition, a percentage point increase in world consumer price and high oil price increases inflation in by 0.11 percent and 0.486 percent respectively. However, a 1 percent decrease in the periods of low oil prices dampens inflation by 0.230 percent.

We run panel regression with fixed effect with four specifications. The regression results are presented in table 5.3. In the first model, we include all the variables together with three dummies, DUMMFC, DUMOILH, and DUMOILL namely periods of financial crisis, periods of low oil prices, and periods of high oil prices respectively.

Table 5.3   Panel Least Squares

Variable	Dependent Variable: D(CPI)			
	Model 1	*Model 2*	*Model 3*	*Model 4*
INTERCEPT	-0.143	-0.373	-0.001	-0.028
	(0.330)	(0.013)	(0.054)	(0.053)
D(MS)	0.024*	0.026**	0.022*	0.024*
	(0.013)	(0.013)	(0.013)	(0.013)
D(ER)	0.005*	0.005*	0.001*	0.005*
	(0.003)	(0.003)	(0.003)	(0.003)
D(IMP)	-0.001	-0.001	-0.001	-0.001
	(0.001)	(0.002)	(0.002)	(0.002)
D(IB)	-0.001	-0.001	0.000	-0.000
	(0.004)	(0.001)	(0.001)	(0.006)
WCPI	0.031	0.111**		
	(0.062)	(0.057)		
WOIL	0.001		0.004**	
	(0.002)		(0.002)	
WFOOD	0.010***			0.012***
	(0.004)			(0.003)
DUMFC	-0.142	-0.186	-0.145	-0.163
	(0.125)	(0.121)	(0.125)	(0.120)
DUMOILL	-0.137	-0.230*	-0.194	-0.162
	(0.144)	(0.139)	(0.142)	(0.139)
DUMOILH	0.297	0.486**	0.380*	0.369
	(0.227)	(0.204)	(0.219)	(0.196)
Adjusted R^2	0.034	0.026	0.027	0.033
F- Stats	4.30	2.34	2.47	3.05
DW	1.63	1.61	1.62	1.63
SE	1.42	1.43	1.43	1.42
AIC	3.55	3.56	3.56	3.55
SC	3.59	3.62	3.62	3.62

The coefficients of the variables are listed, and standard errors are in parentheses. *** 1 percent significance level, ** 5 percent significance level, and * 10 percent significance level.
Author generated.

The outcomes of the panel regression reveal that money supply growth, exchange rate depreciation, and increase in world food prices mainly determine inflation in Iran, the Sudan, and GCC countries. We introduce the world consumer price index, world oil price index, and world food price index in the regression equation one at a time. When world CPI is introduced in the regression, money supply growth, exchange rate depreciation, and increase in world CPI positively affect domestic prices in these economies. In addition, while periods of high oil prices positively influence inflation, low oil prices dampen inflation. This could be attributed to the fact that in periods of high oil prices, these economies get overheated due to the increase in demand.

Similarly, when the world oil price index is introduced, oil price, money supply, and exchange rate depreciation result in increases in the domestic price. Similarly, periods of high oil prices positively influence inflation. Given that these countries are oil-rich countries and are major exporters of oil, an increase in oil price enhances revenue and gives more room for fiscal spending.

Furthermore, when the world food index is introduced in the regression, its coefficient becomes positive and statistically significant. Since the region is a major food importer, an increase in the world food price index results in an increase in domestic prices.

However, in all specifications, the coefficients of the variable of interest, Islamic banking growth, remain negative, indicating Islamic banking growth in these countries does not increase domestic prices. Hence, the empirical findings offer conclusive evidence that growth in Islamic banking does not lead to an increase in domestic prices. Similarly, the coefficients for financial crisis, DUMFC, are insignificant in all the specifications of the model indicating that financial crisis does not have any impact on prices in these economies. Hence, the argument that Islamic banking and finance target the real sector and is noninflationary holds some ground. From the analysis, the main drivers of inflation in these economies are money supply, exchange depreciation, and the surge in international oil and food prices.

The variance decomposition indicates that the variance of inflation in the GCC countries, Iran, and the Sudan is dominated by its own lag, followed by international food and oil prices and monetary growth. Islamic banking growth and the exchange rate contribute the least in the variance of inflation in the region. The least variance by the exchange rate could be due to the fixed exchange rate regime in the GCC countries and economic sanctions on Iran and the Sudan.

The impulse response shows persistent inflationary effects attributed to international food and oil prices and growth in the money supply. However, the pass-through channels of Islamic banking growth and real economic activity do not last long. This reinforces the argument that growth in Islamic banking is not inflationary.

CONCLUSION

In this chapter, we examine the impact of Islamic banking growth on inflation dynamics in the GCC, Iran, and the Sudan using monthly time series and panel data from 2001 to 2015. These countries are among countries with the largest presence of Islamic banking. Our empirical analysis reveals that Islamic banking growth does not have any inflationary effects in the GCC, Iran, and the Sudan. In fact, the results show Islamic banking growth dampens inflation in the short run and long run. From the single regression results, Islamic banking growth significantly decreases domestic prices in Oman, Qatar, and Iran. From the error-correction model, Islamic banking dampens inflation in Bahrain, Iran, and the Sudan. The findings reveal Islamic banking growth dampens domestic prices in five out of seven countries under consideration. The results of panel regression with fixed effect reveal no indication that Islamic banking growth increases domestic prices. Hence, our findings support the hypothesis that Islamic banking and finance enhance price stability.

There is a strong impact of inflation inertia on inflation. Similarly, money supply and exchange rate depreciation do have a significant impact on domestic prices. The variance decomposition reveals that inflation is dominated by its own lag, international food and oil prices and monetary growth. Furthermore, the findings reveal persistent inflationary effects attributed to international food and oil prices and monetary growth. However, Islamic banking growth is the least relevant when it comes to inflation.

Given the above phenomena, it is recommended that central banks reiterate their assurance to maintain low and stable inflation. Hence, the monetary authorities should continue with tight monetary policies coupled with proper fiscal management in order to have conducive macroeconomic environments. Most of the GCC countries peg their currencies to the US dollar. In Iran and the Sudan, the depreciation of the local currency against the US dollar is passed on to domestic prices. The results reveal that revenues generated during periods of high oil prices need to be used wisely rather than engaging in extra-spending activities. Hence, there is a need to accumulate foreign exchange reserves in order to minimize external shocks particularly during the periods of low oil prices. The foreign exchange buffer scan helps countries when confronted with economic sanctions: namely Iran and the Sudan.

Given that most of these countries are food importers, increases in international food prices are transmitted to domestic prices. Hence, there is a need for these countries to diversify their economies and not to solely depend on oil. One possible option is to scale up financing in the non-oil sectors, particularly in the agricultural sector which minimizes food imports in the GCC countries. While our results are in line with the notion that Islamic finance is directed more toward supporting the real sector and, therefore, noninflationary, more work is needed to investigate the extent to which our estimates are robust. For instance, it would be of interest to disaggregate Islamic finance into different categories rather than using Islamic banking growth as a whole as a proxy for Islamic finance. However, empirical research in this area is subject to the availability of data. These findings are the first empirical work to shed light on the impact of Islamic banking on domestic prices. Hence, the empirical results can serve as a reference point for future research in the area.

NOTES

1. In our analysis, we exclude the United Arab Emirates due to incomplete data series.

2. The banking systems in these countries operate under Shari'ah principles.

3. Aggregate prices and total money supply are related according to equation (2). The intuition is that a change in the rate of money growth results in an equal change in inflation rate, which apparently led to the conclusion by Milton Friedman that "inflation is always and everywhere a monetary phenomenon." The reason for such a claim is the assumption that the velocity of money or its growth rate is constant. However, recent US data have claimed that the velocity of money is no longer constant. Hence, monetary forces may not be the only factors affecting inflation.

4. The unit root test indicated that all the variables are nonstationary at level but stationary at first difference. See table 5.1 for unit root results.

5. Note that M and MS denote the same variable (money supply growth); e and ER (exchange rate) and Y and IMP (output proxy by imports).

6. Real economic activity was approximated by the monthly volume of imports.

7. The data is sourced from the International Monetary Fund's International Financial Statistics.

8. Our results collaborate with that of Kandil and Morsy (2009).

9. Our findings are in line with that of Kandil and Morsy (2009).

BIBLIOGRAPHY

Abedifar, Pejman, Shahid M. Ebrahim, Philip Molyneux, and Amine Tarazi, "Islamic banking and finance: Recent empirical literature and directions for future research," *Journal of Economic Surveys*, 29, 4 (2015): 637–670.

Almounsor, A., "Inflation dynamic in Yemen: An empirical analysis," *International Monetary Fund Working paper*, WP 10/144 (2010).

Bonato, L., "Money and inflation in the Republic of Iran," *International Monetary Fund Working paper*, WP 07/119 (2007).

Bougatef, K., "The impact of corruption on the soundness of Islamic banks," *Borsa Istanbul Review*, 15, 4 (2015): 283–295.

Cihak, Martin and Heiko Hesse, "Islamic banks and financial stability: An empirical analysis," *Journal of Financial Services Research*, 38, 2 (2010): 95–113.

DCIBF, "Islamic banking growth, efficiency and stability," *Dubai Center for Islamic Banking and Finance Annual Report* (2014).

Gheeraert, L. and W. Laurent, "Does Islamic banking development favors macroeconomic efficiency. Evidence on the Islamic finance-growth nexus," *Economic Modelling*, 47 (2015): 32–39.

Hassan, M. Kabir and A.M. Bashir, "Determinants of Islamic banking profitability," In paper presented at the *Proceedings of the Economic Research Forum (ERF) 10th Annual Conference*, Marrakesh–Morocco, December 16–18 (2003).

Hassan, M. Kabir and Mervyn K. Lewis, *Handbook of Islamic Banking*. Cheltenham, UK and Northampton, MA, USA: Edward Elgar, 2007.

Imam, Patrick and Kangni Kpodar, "Islamic banking: Good for growth?" *Economic Modelling*, 59 (2016): 387–401.

Imam, Patrick and Kangni Kpodar, "Islamic banking: How has it expanded?" *Emerging Markets Finance and Trade*, 49, 6 (2013): 112–137.

Islamic Research and Training Institute, *Ibisonline.net*, IRTI, ISDB.

Kandil, Magda and Hanan Morsy, "Determinants of inflation in GCC," *International Monetary Fund Working paper*, WP 07/119 (2009).

Moriyama, K., "Investigating inflation dynamic in Sudan," *International Monetary Fund Working paper*, WP 08/189 (2008).

Osorio, Carolina and D. Filiz Unsal, "Inflation dynamics in Asia: Causes, changes, and spillovers from China," *International Monetary Fund Working paper*, WP 11/257 (2011).

Sacredoti, Emilio and Yuan Xiao, "Inflation dynamics in Madagascar 1971–2000," *International Monetary Fund Working paper*, WP 01/168 (2001).

Valdovinos, Carols G. Fernandez, "Inflation dynamics in The Gambia," *International Monetary Fund Working paper*, draft (2008).

Zeitum, R., "Determinants of Islamic and conventional banks performance in GCC countries using panel data analysis," *Global Economy and Finance Journal*, 5, 1 (2012): 53–72.

Chapter 6

The Sukuk Industry in Malaysia

Nursilah Ahmad

INTRODUCTION

Malaysia is seen as a success story of rapid growth and structural change with equity. The country has enjoyed a stable macroeconomic environment with low unemployment and inflation rates for decades. However, due to the 2008 global financial crisis, the economy has experienced a slowdown in the growth rate. The government has introduced the New Economic Model of 2010 (NEM2010) to shift the country from a middle-income economy to a high-income economy by 2020. In support of these goals, the government has taken steps to liberalize its financial sector and increase its position as one of the key players in Islamic finance. This chapter looks into the Islamic finance landscape of Malaysia by focusing on the Sukuk industry and prospects and challenges facing the industry. By examining the Sukuk market behavior, it is hoped that policymakers may utilize Sukuk as key financial tools to drive the domestic financial sector and demonstrate its bearings on equitable growth.

The Global Islamic Finance Report 2016/2017 crowned Malaysia as the global leader in Islamic banking and finance based on the Islamic Finance Country Index (IFCI). The IFCI was first introduced in 2011 to indicate government's commitment to using Islamic banking and finance as a policy tool in the economic agenda. It is not a small achievement for a small, open economy such as Malaysia, with a population of approximately 31.16 million people, which is equivalent to only about 0.42 percent of the total world population.

Domestically, the market share of Islamic banks in Malaysia quadrupled from 7.1 percent in 2010 to reach 28 percent in 2016 (Bank Negara Malaysia, 2017). However, the industry's annual growth rate slowed from 24.2 percent in 2011 to 8.2 percent in 2016. Hence, there is a need to explore for sustained growth given the rise of Islamic finance globally. Shari'ah-compliant financial products and services are now offered in fifty Muslim and non-Muslim jurisdictions worldwide (Thomson Reuters, 2017). Khalid Howlandar of Moody's rating agency expected 2018 to be "the landmark year" for Islamic finance propelled by a paradigm shift in the economics of Sukuk.

According to Thomson Reuters's State of the Global Islamic Economy Report 2016/2017, the existing Islamic finance market stood at an estimated US$2 trillion in assets in 2015 and of this US$2 trillion, Islamic banking was responsible for US$1.451 trillion, the *takaful* (Islamic insurance) sector for US$38 billion, Sukuk outstanding for US$342 billion, Islamic funds for US$66 billion, and other financial institutions for US$106 billion. The same report projected that the total Islamic finance assets are expected to reach US$3.5 trillion by 2021. Islamic banking would be the key driver of growth and is expected to reach US$2.7 trillion in assets by 2021.

In March 2017, Islamic banking comprised 25 percent share of the banking sector of the country. Recent observation pointed out, however, that the sector has been slow in capturing the market share from conventional banks. This might pose challenges to achieve the targeted 40 percent market share as outlined in the second Malaysian Financial Sector Masterplan. The goal in this chapter is to highlight the trend in Islamic finance in Malaysia with a special focus on the Sukuk industry.

In 2019, the RAM Rating Agency reported that Malaysia was the top Sukuk issuer in the world with 35.1 percent of US$39.5 billion issued in the first quarter of the year. Indonesia was in second place with a share of 17 percent followed by Saudi Arabia with 15.3 percent. Indonesia may become the frontliner in the industry in the future due to its sustainability agenda together, with Saudi Arabia, whose persistent budget deficits may increase government issuances in Sukuk. However, for now, Malaysia will continue to lead the industry and provide stability for the global issues (Ruslina Ramle, 2019). This was supported by the BNM Interbank Islamic Bills (BNIB-i) issuances which were introduced in early 2018 by the Financial Market Committee to support liquidity development for onshore financial markets (*The Star*, 2019). BNIB-i was recognized as a high-quality liquid asset (HQLA) (RAM, 2019). Similar to historical trends, the financial services and infrastructure and utility sectors were the key players of the domestic Sukuk market (RAM, 2019).

ISLAMIC BANKING AND FINANCE IN MALAYSIA

The evolution of Islamic banking in Malaysia could be traced to the establishment of the Pilgrims Fund Board in 1963. However, it was twenty years after

Table 6.1 Evolution of Islamic Banking and Sukuk Industry in Malaysia

Year	Milestones for Islamic Banking
1983	Malaysia passed the Islamic Banking Act; Bank Islam began operations in July 1983
1993	Interbank Money Market was established
1997	BNM (Bank Negara Malaysia) established Shari'ah Advisory Council
1999	The second Islamic bank was established, Bank Muamalat
2001	Establishment of International Islamic Financial Market (IIFM)
2003	Islamic Financial Services Board (IFSB) started operations in Malaysia
2006	The Malaysia International Islamic Financial Centre (MIFC) was established
2010	International Islamic Liquidity Management Corporation (IILM) was established
2013	Islamic Financial Services Act 2013 was passed by parliament
Year	*Milestones for Sukuk Industry*
Pre-1990s	Islamic investment issues/certificates were introduced in Jordan, Pakistan, Turkey and Malaysia. There was no active market for Sukuk
1990–2000	First corporate Sukuk issued by Shell MDS Malaysia in 1990. This is the period of theoretical development and model building for the industry
2001–Present	Emergence of Sukuk market with rated international Sukuk issuance. Growth of halal industry supported innovation in Sukuk market

Source: Adapted from Ahmad (2013).

that that the first Islamic bank (Bank Islam) was established in July 1983. Subsequently, numerous other events took place that boosted the development of Islamic banking in the country as shown in table 6.1.

According to the central bank of Malaysia, Bank Negara Malaysia (BNM), double-digit financing growth performance was expected for Islamic banking until 2020, which was higher than the single-digit forecasted for conventional banking growth. However, from 2018 until 2020, the growth rate was expected to be close to that of the year 2017.

In January 2017, Malaysia made headways in the Islamic finance market by introducing the world's first Shari'ah-compliant pension fund, *Simpanan Syariah*, which was launched with a total of RM59.03 billion and taken up by 635,037 members. The scheme was an alternative to the conventional Employment Provision Fund (EPF) for contributors who were interested in converting their savings to a fully Shari'ah-compliant status. By December 2017, there was a new requirement for Shari'ah committee members to have certified Shari'ah qualifications when they seek re-appointment at various financial institutions in Malaysia. The move was made to address Shari'ah risks that are complex in nature and might be difficult to discern except for trained professionals.

MALAYSIA'S FINANCIAL SECTOR BLUEPRINT, 2011–2020

The ten-year Malaysia Financial Sector Blueprint "charts the future direction of the financial system as Malaysia transitions towards becoming a high-value-added, high-income economy." According to the Blueprint, Malaysia's financial system has become less fragmented through consolidation and rationalization from 1980 to 2011. The recommendations in the Blueprint outlined the roadmap and strategies of the financial landscape in the next ten years (2011–2020) as shown in table 6.2.

Table 6.2 Malaysia's Blueprint Capital Market Plan 1 (CMP1) and Plan 2 (CMP2)

Capital Market Plan 1 (CPM1)	*Capital Market Plan 2 (CMP 2)*

• A ten-year plan (2001–2010) outlining strategic focus and actions, with 152 recommendations to address 4 key Malaysian capital-market challenges.
• Objectives:
  1. To be the preferred fund-raising center for Malaysian companies;
  2. To promote an effective investment-management industry and a more conducive environment for investors;
  3. To enhance the competitive position and efficiency of market institutions;
  4. To develop a strong and competitive environment for intermediation services;
  5. To ensure a stronger and more facilitate regulatory regime;
  6. To establish Malaysia as an international ICM.
• The three phases:
  ○ Phase 1: 2001–2003 (three years)—To strengthen domestic capacity and develop strategic and nascent sectors;
  ○ Phase 2: 2004–2005 (two years) —To further strengthen key sectors and gradually liberalize market access;
  ○ Phase 3: 2006–2010 (five years)—To further strengthen market processes and infrastructure toward becoming a fully developed capital market, and enhance international positioning in areas of comparative and competitive advantages.
	• The roadmap to transform the competitive dynamics of Malaysia's capital market over the next ten years (2010–2020). Outliners growth strategies to address structural challenges and critical linkages to foster a more diverse and innovative intermediation environment, and to nurture new growth opportunities.
	• (A) Growth strategies:
	  1. To promote capital information;
	  2. To expand intermediation efficiency and scope;
	  3. To deepen liquidity and risk intermediation;
	  4. To facilitate internalization;
	  5. To build capacity and strengthen information infrastructure.
	• B) Governance strategies:
	  1. To enhance product regulation to manage risks;
	  2. To expand accountabilities as intermediation scope widens.
	  3. To develop a robust regulatory framework for a changing market landscape;
	  4. To facilitate effective oversight of risks.
	  5. To strengthen corporate governance;
	  6. To broaden participation in governance.

Source: SC (Securities Commission Malaysia) website.

The Blueprint highlighted the financial sector developments from 2001 until 2011. During this period, the financial sector recorded an average annual growth rate of 7.3 percent to account for 11.7 percent of real GDP in 2010 (2001: 9.7%). The financial sector was expected to grow at the rate of 8 percent to 11 percent annually and contribute 10 percent to 12 percent of nominal GDP in 2020 (2010: 8.6%). The content of the Blueprint is briefly highlighted in the next paragraph.

Chapter One of the Blueprint covered the global and domestic landscapes and the expected financial landscape in 2020. It was projected that 60 percent of the global total world output will be produced by the emerging economies of Asia, the Middle East, Latin America, and Africa, hence increasing the significance of these economies. Two key trends were identified: first, the strengthening of the domestic sources of growth through private domestic demand; second, greater global and regional economic and financial integration. These trends would help achieved greater balance between domestic and external demand as sources of economic growth. By 2020, the share of private consumption is expected to be around 61 percent of GDP (2010: 53%).

Chapter Two continued with the topic of "The Financial Sector That Best Serves the Malaysian Economy." By 2010, the financial sector has accounted for 11.7 percent of real GDP (2001: 9.7%). After the first Financial Sector Masterplan in 2001, Malaysia was expected to create a financial sector that best served the Malaysian economy by 2020. Islamic banking and finance would be expected to contribute 40 percent share of total Islamic domestic financing by 2020 (2010: 29%).

Chapter Three was themed "Enhancing Regional and International Financial Linkages." The focus was on the internalization of Islamic finance and stronger cross-border linkages. According to the Asian Development Bank (IDB), Asia required an investment worth US$8 trillion from 2010 to 2020. Islamic finance contributed 2.1 percent share to GDP in 2009. This is in line with global ethical consumer demand for Socially Responsible Investment (SRI) as an important asset class in the future.[1]

Chapter Four was titled "Safeguarding the Stability of the Financial System." The focus was on the roles of Islamic finance. Governance and risk management, effective regulatory and supervisory regime, stability, integration, and cross-border linkages were the key areas discussed. Based on content analysis method, we investigated the presence of social capital in this particular chapter. In general, there was a strong emphasis on the structural organization and rules and regulations. The Blueprint emphasized the governmental component (effectiveness of formal institutions in facilitating collective action) of social capital. There were also quite a number of references to cooperation, integration, and cross-border networking among the Islamic banking institutions and other entities.

Chapter Five concluded with "Key Enablers for the Development of the Financial System." This chapter comprised of three sub-topics covering electronic payments, empowering consumers, and talent development. The plan was to increase e-payment transactions per capita to 200 transactions per capita by 2020 (2010: 44 transactions). At the same time, financial consumer education to gain financial literacy would also be promoted. Hence, there would be greater demand for high-quality talents by the financial sector. The Credit Counselling and Debt Management Agency will have an important role to educate adult consumers in financial literacy. Extensive institutional infrastructure has been put in place to ensure a sufficient pool of talent for a dynamic financial sector.

The new Basel III Accord has highlighted two long-standing concerns for Islamic banking. First, Islamic banks have ample liquidity but lack high-quality Shari'ah-compliant instruments. Second, Islamic banking lacked secondary interbank markets to trade these instruments. Market watchers believe that an alternative solution is to popularize the Sukuk market. Sovereign and quasi-sovereign Sukuk would help mop-up the excess liquidity problems of Islamic banks. However, for the Sukuk industry to reach a similar stage of the conventional bond cycle, standardized regulation is needed, and both value and volume of issuances should be increased. Sukuk should contribute to the real economy by promoting development, financing diversification, and mitigating financial decline.

AN OVERVIEW OF THE SUKUK INDUSTRY

The Sukuk market is the fastest growing and most promising segment of Islamic finance in the complex global economy outlined by Khan in chapter 2. It has become an important component of the global finance market. There is also an increase in the issuance of Sukuk by corporate and public sector entities due to the growing demand for alternative investments. Malaysia stands out in terms of domestic market issuance in Asia, followed by Indonesia. Bahrain and The Gambia both have more than 200 issues over the years since their first issuances in early 2000. The non-OIC Sukuk issuers include Singapore, United States, United Kingdom, China, Hong Kong, Germany, Japan, and France.

A reliance on sovereign issuances and the global economic slowdown have taken their toll on the Sukuk industry. Sukuk issuances fell 43 percent in 2015 and continued to fall by 18 percent for the first nine months of 2016 globally. The decline is due to several reasons: first, the global economic slow down after the 2008 financial crisis; second, the sharp fall in global commodity prices; third, the policy change by Malaysia whereby the central bank suspended sales of short-term ringgit denominated Sukuk due to the depreciating ringgit; and fourth, the possibility of interest rate hikes in the United States (Nikkei Asian Review, 2016). However, the Sukuk market is expected to continue to record issuances of more than US$100 billion and to expand into a wider variety of countries and sectors.

The development of the Sukuk market can be represented by four main phases. The first phase accounted for small local issuances by the Malaysian government from 1996 to 2001. The second phase, from 2002 to 2007, started with the Malaysian government issuing the first-rated international Sukuk, followed by other local and international issuances. The third phase, from 2008 to 2010, was marked by a series of defaulted events, global financial crisis, and Shari'ah-compliant issues raised by the Accounting and Auditing Organization for Islamic Financial Institutions (AAOIFI). The fourth phase, from 2011 to date, Sukuk remain competitive due to a wider range of investors (Thomson Reuters Zawya, 2013). The next challenge is for the industry to gain a greater market share.

What Is Sukuk?

"Sukuk" (plural of *sakk*) is the Arabic term for Islamic securities, which in economic terms is akin to conventional bonds. The literal meaning of "*sukuk*" is "certificate." Technically, Sukuk refer to securities, notes, papers, or investment certificates with features of liquidity and tradability. Sukuk have both bond and stock-like features issued to finance trade or the production of tangible assets. Unlike conventional bonds, Sukuk need to have an underlying tangible asset transaction either in ownership or in a master lease agreement. It represents ownership of underlying assets, usufructs (benefits), services, or investment. The money that a Sukuk holder gets represents a share in the profit of the underlying asset.

The Securities Commission Malaysia (SC) defines Sukuk as "a financial document or certificate which represents the value of an asset evidencing an undivided pro-rata ownership of an underlying asset." Sukuk must comply with Shari'ah, which must be free from interest (*riba*), excessive risks (*gharar*), or investments that promote vices or are discouraged by Shari'ah (such as alcohol and gambling). Sukuk financing activities are mostly for the infrastructure and utilities, financial services, property and real estate, oil and gas, and energy. Like conventional bonds, Sukuk can be traded, rated by credit agencies, and redeemed.

Origin of Sukuk

There is evidence to suggest that Sukuk structures were used within Muslim societies as early as the Middle Ages. The word "*sukuk*" can be traced back to classical commercial Islamic literature as the method of paying the salaries of government officers who would later redeem the certificate to buy goods or groceries (Clifford Chance Report, 2009). The contemporary Sukuk today is based on the decision of the Islamic Jurisprudence Council dated February 6–11, 1988, which stated that "any combination of assets (or the usufruct of such assets) can be represented in the form of written financial instruments which can be sold at a market price provided that the composition of the group of assets represented by the Sukuk consist of a majority of tangible assets."

The history of modern Sukuk started during the late 1980s. In February 1988, the Fiqh Academy of the OIC countries legitimized the concept of Sukuk. The first Sukuk was issued in 1990 in Malaysia by Shell MDS, valued at RM125 million (US$33 million) of *Bai'-Bithaman Ajil* type. Therefore the Sukuk market has been around for only about two decades. The industry has gone through the default, bankruptcies, and restructuring life-cycle. It has taken 400 years for the conventional bond market to get where it is today. A more recent development saw a larger number of non-Muslim entities joining the market due to increasing preferences for ethical financial solutions, especially in Europe. In addition, Sukuk appears to fit in well with Basel III principles. Financial institutions regulated by Basel III are required to invest in specified percentage of HQLA of fixed-income instruments.

There are five main phases of global Sukuk development starting from the early historical period until 2017 (ISRA, 2017). During the early classical use of Sukuk, Sukuk were issued as commodity grain coupons and financial certificates used to finance public debt. For the period before the 1990s, the Sukuk industry was considered as an ad hoc development, where no active market emerged. Besides Jordan, several attempts were made by other countries to issue Sukuk before 1990, notably Pakistan, Malaysia, and Turkey. Except for Malaysia, these issuances were, however, short-lived due to the unfavorable conditions at that time in those countries. The Sukuk market underwent a nascent stage in 1990–2010 when awareness was created for the industry players. The years 1990–2000 was considered as the period of theory and model building where there was no active market development. However, in Malaysia at the time, the Sukuk industry was gaining much recognition and interest (RAM, 2013). The year 2001–2016 was considered as the emergence of Sukuk market, where the market emerged with the issuance of the government of Bahrain's first sovereign Sukuk, Malaysia's issuance of first-rated international asset-based Sukuk and other more innovative product developments such as retail and perpetual Sukuk. Starting from 2017 onward, the Sukuk industry entered into an expansion stage, where more innovations are expected and there are strong investors' appetite for Sukuk (ISRA, 2017)

Sukuk, Shares, and Bonds

Bonds and shares are two basic capital-market instruments. Bonds represent debt capital while shares represent equity capital. With its fixed interest return and principal guaranteed, a bond is classified as a fixed-income security. Since bonds are loans, their returns are predetermined and have no relation to the actual performance of the firm. In contrast, shareholders, as owners of a firm, will earn a return based on the performance of a firm. Unlike interest which is set ex-ante (expected), dividends are determined ex-post (historical) and are not typically guaranteed.

Various Sukuk structures and contracts based on Shari'ah principles are available: namely *ijarah, salam, istisna', musharakah, mudarabah,* and *wakalah. Ijarah* and *musharakah* structures are the most popular Sukuk structures. There are also innovative various forms, concepts and hybrids of Sukuk, such as exchangeable and convertible and foreign currency Sukuk. These types of Sukuk can be further categorized into sale-based, lease-based, and equity- or agency-based, namely: sale-based Sukuk (*bay bithamin-ajil, murabahah, salam,* and *istisna*), lease-based Sukuk (*ijarah*), equity-based Sukuk (*musharakah and mudarabah*), and agency-based Sukuk (*wakalah*).

The Development of the Sukuk Industry

The Islamic capital market consists of the debt market and equity market. Sukuk, or Islamic bonds, are the most active Islamic debt market financial instrument to date. As mentioned earlier, the development of the Sukuk market was initiated in 1990 since the first Sukuk issued by Shell MDS Pvt. Ltd., a multinational corporation operating in Malaysia. Subsequently, after the 1997 financial crisis, there was growing importance of Sukuk financing. The first international sovereign Sukuk was issued by the government of Bahrain in 2001, followed by Indonesia in 2002. Since then, there has been increasing participation in Sukuk issuances from both Muslim and non-Muslim countries. The World Bank issued its first Sukuk from Malaysia in 2006. Germany was the first country to issue Sukuk in Europe in 2004. It was a €100 million quasi-government Sukuk ijarah issued in the federal state of Saxony-Anhalt in Germany. In November 2012, FWU, a Munich-based financial group, announced the first and the largest corporate issuance in Europe worth €55 million Sukuk ijarah. The underlying assets are a proprietary computer software system and associated property rights developed in-house by the FWU Group. It marks the first Sukuk to have intellectual property as underlying assets.

The global Islamic finance industry has grown from about US$10 billion worth of invested assets in 1975 to more than US$2 trillion in 2017. By the end of 2010, 5.5 percent of the US$2.2 trillion invested in Islamic instruments was held in dedicated Islamic funds, with 31.1 percent in broader-based assets (mainly in Shari'ah-compliant bank accounts and money-market vehicles). The rest was held in other Islamic instruments, particularly Sukuk, insurance packages (takaful), and equity products. Real growth in the Sukuk market started in 2003 when the AAOIFI issued a standard on investment Sukuk and listed fourteen different types of Sukuk.

Research suggests that there will be a need for trillions of dollars of Islamic assets (Sukuk and other instruments) in the near future to fulfill the liquidity surpluses of this growing market. The 2008 global financial crisis has contributed to the second wave of rising sovereign Sukuk issuers. In early 2013, the sovereign issuers contributed more than half in terms of the percentage in value contribution to the industry. However, in terms of the number of issues, the corporate sector dominates.

For the domestic market, the issuance is also sovereign-lead. This would insulate domestic investors from currency risk exposure and help develop a benchmark curve to facilitate the growth of the domestic market. It is expected that more countries will issue Sukuk in their home currencies to meet domestic funding needs. In another recent development for the Sukuk mutual funds market, a number of banks are setting up their own Sukuk funds to offer to their private clients. This would help diversify the investment portfolio of Sukuk investors.

The growth was affected by the 2007 financial crisis since there was a noticeable drop in the growth rates in the global market. To date, Malaysia and the United Arab Emirates (UAE) are the two leading countries in terms of Sukuk issuances. Due to the flight to safe havens of fixed-income investments after the 2007 crisis, sovereign and quasi-sovereign types of Sukuk issuances dominated the market. Sukuk are mostly issued either in Malaysian ringgit or US dollar. The US dollar continues to be the preferred international currency for issuance.

It is expected that with the rising importance of Bahrain and the Dubai International Financial Exchange (DIFX), there would be more issuances in riyals and Kuwaiti dinars (SC, 2010). For the period 2004 to 2006, the international Sukuk market was bigger than the domestic Sukuk market. However, the trend was reversed in 2007 when the domestic Sukuk market became bigger. The IIFM (2010) refers to the situation as the "currency effect," in which as a consequence of the financial crisis in 2007, that originated in the United States, there has been a shift away from dollar-denominated issues toward local currency-based issues arising from the Gulf Cooperation Council (GCC), Indonesia, and Pakistan.

The Asia and Far East region, the GCC, and the Middle East continue to dominate the issuances based on both the number of issues and the percentages of the total value. The more advanced economies that have issued Sukuk, besides the traditional Muslim economies, are Turkey, United States, United Kingdom, Germany, and France. The local currency domestic market is expected to develop further, spurred by Indonesia, Turkey, Pakistan, and the GCC countries. Sovereign or sovereign-linked entities continue to dominate issuances domestically and this would assist in the setting up of local benchmark curves.

Table 6.3 depicts the top Sukuk markets in 2016 and their global market share. Malaysia was still leading with 46.4 percent, followed by the GCC countries with 26.2 percent. Indonesia and Turkey each represented 9.9 percent and 5.5 percent, respectively. The top two sectors were financial services and government.

By 2016, global Sukuk outstanding was domiciled in over twenty countries with an investor base ranging from Europe to the Middle East and Asia. In 2015, at least thirteen jurisdictions have tapped the global sovereign Sukuk market. Ten countries that were voted as having the best developed ecosystems for Islamic finance based on selected Islamic finance indicators, arranged from highest to lowest, were Malaysia, UAE, Bahrain, Saudi Arabia, Oman, Kuwait, Pakistan, Qatar, Indonesia, and Jordan.[2] Of late, some countries outside the key markets have launched some pioneering Sukuk issues reflecting the positive market momentum.

Malaysia once again leads this indicator ranking, followed by these countries in descending order: the UAE, Bahrain, Saudi Arabia, Oman, Kuwait, Pakistan, Qatar, Indonesia and Jordan (State of the Global Islamic Economy

Table 6.3 Top Sukuk Markets and Global Market Share in 2016

Jurisdiction	Issues Amount (US$ billion)	Global Market Share (%)	Top Sectors
Malaysia	34.7	46.4	Financial Services Government Power and Utilities Transportation
GCC Countries	19.6	26.2	Financial Services Government Oil and Gas
Indonesia	7.4	9.9	Government Financial Services Industrial and Manufacturing
Turkey	4.1	5.5	Financial Services Government

Source: MIFC (2010), Thomson Reuters (2017).

2016/2017 Report). To take advantage of this strong footing, the government has set the targets for the industry to achieve by 2020. These include increasing the global share of Islamic banking assets from 8 percent in 2009 to 13 percent in 2020, increasing the global share of takaful contribution from 11 percent in 2009 to 20 percent in 2020, increasing Islamic financing's share of total financing in Malaysia from 29 percent in 2010 to 40 percent in 2020, and targeting at least one Islamic financial institution to become one of the global top ten players by asset size by 2020.

Sukuk Issuance by Structure

What are the preferred types of Sukuk issued domestically and internationally? For the domestic issuances, there were ten different Sukuk structures issued, ranging from *al-Murabahah* to *al-Salam* from 2001 to January 2013. The pattern seemed to be consistent across time. The four top domestic issuances based on structure, from the highest to lowest, were al-Murabahah, al-Musharakah, al-Ijarah, and Bai-Bithamin Ajil.

At the international level, Sukuk ijarah, Sukuk al-musharakah, Islamic exchangeable Sukuk, and Sukuk al-mudarabah were the top four Sukuk structures issued from 2001 to 2010. The more recent years showed a slightly changing composition where the top four issuances, from highest to lowest, are Sukuk ijarah, wakalah, hybrid, and musharakah. There was no Sukuk hybrid issued domestically. In addition, Islamic exchangeable Sukuk, al-mudharabah, and al-salam were not issued in recent years.

Sukuk Issuance by Issuer Status

The same analysis is conducted to examine the issuer status of Sukuk issuances from 2001 to early 2013. The issuers were categorized into either corporate, sovereign, or quasi-sovereign. Before 2011, corporate and sovereign issuers were almost at par in terms of percentages. By 2011, due to the 2008 financial crisis and the consequent flight of investors to safe havens, the number of sovereign and quasi-sovereign Sukuk issuers increased due to lack of confidence and stability.

Looking at the situation from the international perspective, prior to 2011, the corporate sector was very active with 68 percent of total issuances. However, by 2011, there was an almost similar number of issuances by the corporate sector (45%) and the sovereign sector (41%). The issuance by the quasi-sovereign sector remained at the same level over the years at 14 percent. Another noticeable trend indicated that financial institutions were no longer the majority of investors in Sukuk as fund managers, takaful operators, high net worth individuals (HNWIs), and others were now investing in Sukuk.

Sukuk Issuance by Sector

The global aggregate Sukuk issued by sector for the period 1996 until 2012 was dominated by the governmental and financial services sectors, followed by transport, power and utilities, real estate, telecommunications, and another category. The construction sector has good potential to be developed. Global demand for investment in infrastructure is growing as existing infrastructure needs to cope with growing population and urbanization rates. The Organization for Economic Cooperation and Development (OECD) estimates that globally US$71 trillion is needed for investment in infrastructure by 2030 (Mardam-Bey et al., 2013).

THE SUKUK MARKET IN MALAYSIA

In Malaysia, as of December 2009, 57 percent of outstanding corporate bonds in the Malaysian bond market were Shari'ah-compliant (SC, 2009). From a macroeconomic perspective, the overall share of Sukuk in GDP increased each year from 2000 until 2009. In 2009, the percentage share of domestic Sukuk to GDP was 6.2 percent, corporate Sukuk represented 0.73 percent of GDP, and sovereign Sukuk represented 5.47 percent of GDP in 2009 (IFIS and BNM). During earlier years, Malaysia dominated the Sukuk market in terms of both number and volume (IFIS Report, 2010).

There were 323 Sukuk issuers for the period between 2001 and 2009 of which 92 firms were listed on the Main Board, Second Board, MESDAQ, or ACE Market of Bursa Malaysia and the rest were financial and non-financial firms. Three major industries dominated the corporate Sukuk market of Malaysia. Financial firms, including banks, accounted for the biggest share of 28 percent. Companies involved in transportation, logistics, and telecommunications industries came second with 26 percent. The energy and utility companies (electricity, oil, gas, and water) constituted an aggregate share of 20 percent.

By domicile, Malaysia's secondary Sukuk market stood at US$183.8 billion, representing a share of 52.6 percent of total Sukuk outstanding. This was followed by Saudi Arabia and the UAE with a market share of 16.3 percent and 8.9 percent, respectively. The Securities Commission Malaysia (SC) has estimated the total size of Malaysia's capital market (comprising stock market capitalization and debt securities) to more than double from RM2 trillion in 2010 to RM4.5 trillion by 2020. It is estimated that the internationalization of the Malaysian stock market can increase the potential size of the Malaysian capital market by another 30 percent to RM5.8 trillion in 2020. In order to achieve the target, the facilitation of volume strategies and higher efficiency of increased economies of scale are required (Asian Development Bank, 2011).

PROSPECTS AND CHALLENGES IN ISLAMIC FINANCE

There are challenges ahead facing Islamic banking and finance globally. The market watchers cited two possible reasons. First is the low banking penetration rate, and the second is costly financial services. Banking penetration is defined as the percentage of adults with an account at a formal financial institution. It remains low within the Organization of Islamic Cooperation (OIC) member countries and in the world's Muslim population as a whole, with an average of around 32 percent and 29 percent, compared with the global average of 62 percent.

The market analysts also suggest that if pricing policy does not differ greatly between conventional and Islamic banking products, Muslims are more likely to opt for Shari'ah-compliant products due to the risk-sharing and the ethical nature of its business model. However, at the moment the pricing of Sukuk instruments are considered higher due to the Shari'ah-compliant requirements. Costs of issuing Islamic bonds in Asia are still significantly higher than the costs of issuing conventional bonds. Other potential challenges facing the industry include the legislative framework, tax framework, Shari'ah standardization, the development of sustainable supply of corporate Sukuk, and the level of financial intermediation provided by non-banking financial institutions and diversification of investor bases (ISRA, 2017).

To turn challenges into opportunities, AllianceDBS Research believes that the growing Muslim population and an in-depth understanding of financial behavior among Muslims are factors that would drive growth. According to them, Islamic economies represented about 9.5 percent of the global GDP in 2014. Approximately one-sixth of the world's population is Muslim, most of whom are based in the Middle East and Asia. Hence, a careful study of the financial behavior of the users of financial services, based on different geographical regions and demographic groups, is needed. Reliance on the supply side alone, according to Say's Law, will not be a sustainable approach in the long run for the industry.

Sukuk are structured to generate the same economic effects as conventional bonds, but in a Shari'ah-compliant manner. This is achieved by using assets and various contractual techniques acceptable under Shari'ah. The industry could benefit from economies of scale which would help to sustain it over the longer term. Pricing policies and awareness are two important factors to capture the non-Muslim market share. It was reported that about 80 percent of the Sukuk issued have been subscribed by conventional international investors (Aziz, 2007). Issuance of Islamic debt by non-Muslim countries is increasing recently due to the perception of less volatile market conditions and an improving regulatory backdrop (The Express Tribune, 2017). This trend could be exported worldwide in order to capture a bigger global market share.

Additionally, the industry lacks consistency in product structures and investment practices that might adversely affect its credibility and reputation. The industry players need to study market behavior and focus on risk-return characteristics of the products rather than concentrating on the Shari'ah-compliant aspect only. Harmonization of standards across different geographical locations and different schools of thought can reduce uncertainty due to Shari'ah concerns.

There is also an accusation that Islamic banking is operating in a similar fashion as its conventional counterpart: that is, profit-oriented rather than serving the real needs of the society.[3] Khaliq Ahmad raises two issues pertaining to the profit-maximizing behavior of Islamic banks. First, form over substance. Second, are the *maqasid al-shariah* requirements (objectives of the Shari'ah). As for the former, based on legal perspectives, Islamic banking and financial products are unique and distinct but, operationally, the practice is similar to conventional banking in terms of pricing, adopting interest-based benchmarks, the treatment of late payments, and so on. As for the *maqasid shariah*, profit maximization should not be the sole objective of financial institutions. But a genuine concern for society should involve risk-sharing contracts based on profit and loss sharing equity financing. However, Islamic banks are more interested in debt-based products and services such as *murabahah* and *tawarruq* while equity-based financing such as *mudharabah* and *musharakah* are least popular. Khaliq Ahmad ended with a suggestion to ensure sustainable development by adopting Islamic financing as a tool. *Maqasid al-shariah* should be the overriding objective of any economic decision making. Islamic banks should work on maximizing profit in a welfare-enhancing manner. This could be achieved through risk-sharing and wealth redistribution policies embedded in Islamic financing contracts. One alternative is to adopt an asset-light business model. For example, the latest issuance of sovereign Sukuk by the Malaysian government in 2016 was not backed by any tangible assets. The Sukuk was backed by equity and transportation vouchers instead. As a role model of other countries, the challenge for Malaysia now is to continue to be the leader in the development of Islamic finance. Table 6.4 highlights some of the key issues and challenges facing the Malaysian Sukuk market, with some recommended solutions.

There is also an argument that the Sukuk industry has failed to secure a greater market share post-2008 financial crisis. Could it be that the market players are unable to either identify or address the key challenges to the industry? The State of the Global Islamic Economy Report, 2016/17 (Thomson Reuters, 2017) summarizes the key challenges as follows:

- Lack of awareness and understanding of Islamic finance products and services among the public;

Table 6.4   Issues and Challenges Facing Malaysian Sukuk Market

Recommendations	Issues and Challenges	Opportunities
To improve demand (buy side)—medium-term solutions	• Greater awareness of impact investing (e.g., achieving social objectives without compromising commercial returns) is required;	• SRI is a US$60 trillion industry that is still expanding. The common shared values between Sukuk and SRI can foster greater linkages between Islamic finance and conventional SRI investors. Ongoing efforts by the Islamic finance community to build awareness and promote a shift in mindset to consider social impact objectives.
	• Lack of participation by retail investors despite a few retail issues under GLCs;	• Increase awareness among members of the public to invest in retail Sukuk.
	• Shortage of liquidity-management instruments for Islamic banks;	• Develop new products or promote innovation to enable Islamic banks to compete effectively against their conventional counterparts;
To improve demand (sell side)—medium-term solutions	• Strengthen value-based intermediation (VBI)—in July 2017, BNM released guidelines on Value-based intermediation: strengthening the roles and impact of Islamic finance.	• VBI has been identified as the next market mover for Islamic finance. Similar initiatives (e.g., peer-to-peer crowd funding) devoted to achieving social justice will heighten Malaysia' appeal in light of the United Nations' Sustainable Development Goals (SDGs).

Source: ISRA (International Shari'ah Research Academy for Islamic Finance), 2017; RAM (Rating Agency Malaysia), 2019.

- Few Shari'ah-compliant monetary policy instruments;
- Complex financial products and corporate structures in some countries;
- Underdeveloped safety nets and resolution frameworks;
- Regulators who do not have the capacity or unwilling to ensure Shari'ah compliance.

SUKUK AND THE WAY FORWARD

To ensure sustainable growth, the Sukuk industry has to consider several issues. Among them are greater transparency, standardization, Shari'ah-compliant risk, and risk associated with the structure of Sukuk. Efforts are being made to resolve the issues as evident in the recent development of the Sukuk industry, for example, cross-border Sukuk issuance and hybrid Sukuk. Thomson Reuters in their "Sukuk Perceptions and Forecast Study 2013" suggest that the Sukuk industry might learn from the Eurobond market that took off in just two decades after it was launched, supported by changes in the macroeconomic environment and the use of cross-currency swaps. The report details out reasons for and against Sukuk to become the next Eurobond. Among factors that would hinder growth are weak trading infrastructure, inability to standardize and Shari'ah-compliant requirements. However, Basel III requirements and global appeal for Shari'ah-compliant instruments would support the industry. There is also good prospect due to populous and diverse markets like Indonesia, Egypt, and Pakistan. In addition, the Shari'ah-compliance process adds to additional disclosure and greater transparency requirements.

One of the ways to ensure the success of recent efforts to get economies out of their fiscal imbalances would be introducing Sukuk to manage the infrastructure needs of these economies. In addition to that, with the growing awareness of green technology and climate preserving growth, Sukuk provides another innovative solution for large-scale infrastructure requirements. As the global economy is transitioning toward a more sustainable energy use, the Islamic finance industry has the potential to contribute to climate-resilient economies. Sukuk could mobilize essential finance needed to fund the rising number of clean energy initiatives since the majority of clean energy projects will rely on large, long-term infrastructure spending. For instance, bank financing for long-term infrastructure projects is becoming less attractive under the Basel III rules, shifting the financing of infrastructure to capital markets, which used to tap resources from long-term institutional investors such as pension funds and insurance companies. Since these projects are based on tangible assets to generate revenues, which are consistent with the Islamic finance norm of creating economic value, they are therefore suitable for Sukuk financing.

The new Basel III Accord has highlighted two long-standing concerns about Islamic banking. First, Islamic banks have ample liquidity but lack of high-quality Shari'ah-compliant instruments. Second, Islamic banking lacked secondary interbank markets to trade these instruments. Market watchers believe that an alternative solution is to popularize the Sukuk market. Sovereign and quasi-sovereign Sukuk would help mop-up the excess liquidity problems of Islamic banks. Some suggest that for Sukuk to reach a similar stage of the conventional bond cycle, standardized regulation is needed, and both value and volume of issuances should be increased. Sukuk should contribute to the real economy by promoting development, financing diversification, and mitigating financial decline.

CONCLUSION

Sukuk has become the barometer of the Islamic finance industry. The biggest challenge for the industry, according to some, is in managing Shari'ah non-compliance risk and the realization of *maqasid al-shariah* in all Sukuk transactions. Therefore, understanding Sukuk market behavior is critical to the sustainability of the future growth of the industry. This will further facilitate faster Sukuk issuances and monitoring of the secondary market and help the industry achieve the desired equitable economic development. In conclusion, the critical success factors for the establishment of the global Sukuk market include the following:

i. Identify key market stakeholders—the development of a country's economic growth is the responsibility of all market players. Specific roadmap and blueprint for the inclusion of an Islamic capital market in the existing fiscal and monetary policy objectives will highlight the contribution and participation of Sukuk as effective monetary and fiscal policy instruments.

ii. Conducive environment and ecosystem—a strong legal and regulatory regime, with a conducive tax environment will help sustain long-term capital-market growth. Strong support from the related bodies will create a more dynamic and resilient Sukuk industry.

iii. Intermediation of domestic financial resources—an effective mobilization of domestic financial resources can help sustain the financial environment. The wealth of a nation depends on a country's robust macroeconomic factors, government stability, competitive financial system, productive investment, and value creation and innovation.

iv. Sustainable supply from the private sector—the private sector has important roles to play in promoting economic growth and the Sukuk industry. Sukuk industry players should reap the benefits of digital technologies to achieve increased productivity through Islamic Financial Technology (fintech), which has emerged to offer Shari'ah-compliant financial products, services, and investments. This technology has increased the potential for Islamic finance penetration and for Islamic finance to compete with its conventional counterpart.

v. Harmonized and standardized Shari'ah governance framework—A unified and standardized Shari'ah governance process blended into the existing financial system can promote the harmonization and interpretation of Shari'ah principles, add clarity to product development, build market confidence, and create awareness of the benefits of Islamic finance.

NOTES

1. See Diagana (chapter 7) for Islamic finance from an ethical point of view.
2. State of the Global Islamic Economy 2016/2017 Report.
3. See Sonko (chapter 3) and Zaman (chapter 8) for more on the criticisms.

BIBLIOGRAPHY

AAOIFI. *Investment Islamic Bonds* (Shari'ah Standard No. 18). Accounting and Auditing Organization for Islamic Financial Institutions (AAOIFI): Manama (2008). Available at: <http://www.aaoifi.com>.

Ahmad, Nursilah. "Are Basel III Reforms Punitive to OIC Economies?" *Muamalat, The Newsletter of the Faculty of Economics and Muamalat*, vol. 1, no. 1, pp. 3–5 (2014).

Ahmad, Nursilah. "Financing Social Change Through Social Capital: Malaysia's Financial Sector Blueprint 2011–2020." Chap. 4, 123–148, in Mohammed Obaidullah and Nurul Aini Muhamed (eds.), *Critical Readings in Islamic Social Finance*, vol. 2, YTI Lecture Series, USIM Press: Negeri Sembilan (2016).

Ahmad, Nursilah. "The State of Global Sukuk Market with Special Reference to Sukuk Issuing OIC Member Countries." Research Report prepared for the Statistical Economic and Social Research and Training Centre for Islamic Countries (SESRIC), Ankara, Turkey (December 2013).

Ahmad, Nursilah. "The Thriving Sukuk Industry." *Muamalat, The Newsletter of the Faculty of Economics and Muamalat*, vol. 11, no. 1, pp. 10–13 (2012).

Ahmad, Nursilah & Abd. Rahim, S. "Dow Jones Sukuk Index (DJSI) and Dow Jones Sukuk Total Return Index (DJTR) Volatility Behavior." *Proceeding of the National Conference on the Sciences and Social Sciences (NACOSS)*, Open University Seremban, Malaysia (2017).

Ahmad, Nursilah & Abdul Rahim, S. "Sukuk Ijarah vs. Sukuk Musyarakah: Investigating Post-Crisis Stock Market Reactions." *International Journal of Humanities and Management Sciences*, vol. 1, no. 1, pp. 87–91 (2013).

Ahmad, Nursilah & Ab. Wahab, N. "Growth and Development of Sukuk Market in Malaysia." *Proceedings of the Annual Conference on Global Economy, Business and Finance*, Beijing, China (2012).

Ahmad, Nursilah, Hashim, N. & Johari, F. "Measuring the Size of Output Gap in Sukuk Issuing OIC Member Countries." *Mediterranean Journal of Social Sciences*, vol. 6, no. 2S5, pp. 249–254 (2015).

Ahmad, Nursilah, Mohd Daud, S.N., & Kefeli, Z. "Economic Forces and the Sukuk Market." *Procedia—Social and Behavioral Sciences*, vol. 65, no. 3, pp. 127–133 (2012).

Al-Maglauth, A.K. *Sukuk: An Inside Study and its Background, Structures, Challenges and Cases*. Master thesis, Open University of Malaysia (OUM): Bahrain Branch (2009).

Asian Development Bank. *Annual Report 2011 of the Asian Development Bank* (2011). Available at: http://www.adb.org/sites/default/files/adb-ar2011-v1.pdf.

Aziz, Z.A. "Islamic Finance In Southeast Asia: Local Practices, Global Impact: Enhancing Interlinkages and Opportunities—The Role of Islamic Finance." *Governor's Speech at the Islamic Finance Conference*, Georgetown University, Washington, DC (2007). Available at: <http://www.bnm.gov.my/index.php?ch =en_speech&pg=en_speech&ac=259&lang=bm.

Bank Negara Malaysia (BNM). "Funds Raised in the Capital Market." *Monthly Statistical Bulletin*. Bank Negara Malaysia: Kuala Lumpur (2010).

Bank Negara Malaysia (BNM) & Securities Commission Malaysia (SC). *Malaysian Debt Securities and Sukuk Market*. Bank Negara Malaysia: Kuala Lumpur (2009).

Bloomberg. *Dow Jones Sukuk Index Methodology* (2015). Available at: https://www.djindexes.com/mdsidx/downloads/meth_info/Dow_Jones_Sukuk_Index_Metho dology.pdf>.

CIMA FM Magazine. *CIMA: Chartered Institute of Management Accountant*. Clifford Chance Report (2012). Available at: http://www.cliffordchance.com/publi cationviews/publications/2013/04/introduction_to_sukuk.html.

Eikon Thomson Reuters 2017. (2017). Available at: https://eikon.thomsonreuters.c om/index.html.

Ernst & Young. *Ernst & Young Islamic Funds and Investments Report 2009. Surviving and Adapting in a Downturn* (2009). http://www.asaif.org/content/ download/4885/44574/file.

Ernst & Young. "Growing Beyond DNA of Successful Transformation." *World Islamic Banking Competitiveness Report for 2013* (2012). Available at: http: //www.ey.com/Publication/vwLUAssets/Jan__Bank_2._World_Islamic_Briefin g/$FILE/2.%20World%20Islamic%20Briefing.pdf.

Financial Sector Blueprint, 2011–2020. *Strengthening Our Future: Strong, Stable, Sustainable*. Government of Malaysia: Kuala Lumpur (2011).

Garg, S. "Sukuk and its Growth Across Major Islamic Financial Markets." *Perspective*, Finacle Inforsys (2013). Available at: www.infosys.com/financial.

https://www.researchgate.net/publication/317950429_The_Pitfalls_of_the_Mala ysian_Sukuk_Industry_Issues_and_Challenges_in_practice.

https://www.thestar.com.my/business/business-news/2019/05/13/malaysia-takes-top-spot-in-global-sukuk-issuance-in-q1/.

htpps://www.sukuk.com.

IFIS (Islamic Finance Information Service). *Global Sukuk Market H2-2010 Report* (2010). http://www.iefpedia.com/english/wp-content/uploads/2011/04/ IFIS-Global-Sukuk-Market-H2-2010-Report-%E2%80%93-Islamic-Finance-Information-Service.pdf.

IIFM (International Islamic Financial Market). *IIFM Sukuk Report 2nd Edition: A Comprehensive Study of Global Sukuk Market*. IIFM: Bahrain (2011).

IIFM (International Islamic Financial Market). *IIFM Sukuk Report 3rd Edition: A Comprehensive Study of Global Sukuk Market*. IIFM: Bahrain (2013).

ISRA (International Shariah Research Academy for Islamic Finance). *Sukuk: Principles & Practices*. International Shariah Research Academy for Islamic Finance and Securities Commission Malaysia: Kuala Lumpur (2017).

Mardam-Bey, I., Berenjforoush, P., & Peter, M. "Sukuk: Bridging the Gap." *Islamic Finance and Infrastructure*. EMEA Finance (April/May 2013). Available at: www. taylor-dejongh.com/.../uploads/2013/05/Sukuk-Bridging-the-Gap.

MIFC (Malaysia International Islamic Financial Centre). "The Rise of Islamic Finance." Special advertising section reprinted from July 26, 2010 issue of Fortune (2010).

Mohamad, N.E.A., & Mohd Saad, N. "Sukuk in Malaysian Capital Market." *Proceedings of the 3rd International Conference on Business and Economic Research*. Bandung, Indonesia (2012).

Mohammad Sidek, N.Z., & Ahmad, N. "Social Capital in Islamic Finance: The Case of Sukuk." *International Business Management*, vol. 10, no. 19, pp. 4670–4678 (2016).

Oman Tribune. "Sukuk Issuance Falls 18% This Year, May Hit $54b in '17" (December 6, 2016). Available at: <http://omantribune.com/details/20628/>.

RAM (Rating Agency Malaysia). "Malaysia's Sukuk Issuance in 1Q 2019 Shored Up Global Performance." *Sukuk Snapshot*, May 2019. RAM Rating Services Berhad: Kuala Lumpur (2019). Available at: https://www.ram.com.my/pressrelease/?prv iewid=4961.

RAM Ratings. *2009 Corporate-Default & Ratings-Performance Study (1992–2009)*. RAM Rating Services Berhad: Kuala Lumpur (2010a).

RAM Ratings. *Sukuk Focus*. RAM Rating Services Berhad: Kuala Lumpur (2010b).

Rusgianto, Sulistya, & Ahmad, N. "Volatility Behavior of Sukuk Market: An Empirical Analysis of the Dow Jones Citigroup Sukuk Index." *Middle East Journal of Scientific Research*, vol. 13 (Research in Contemporary Islamic Finance and Wealth Management), pp. 93–97 (2013).

Ruslina, Ramle. "Malaysia's Sukuk Issuance in 1Q 2019 Shored Up Global Performance." *Sukuk Snapshot*. RAM Rating Services (May 2019). Available at: https://www.ram.com.my/pressrelease/?prviewid=4961.

SC (Securities Commission Malaysia). "Islamic Securities Guidelines (Sukuk Guidelines)." Securities Commission Malaysia: Kuala Lumpur (2011). Available at: http://www.sc.com.my/.

SC (Securities Commission Malaysia). *Malaysia's Capital Market Plan 1 (CMP1)*. Available at: https://www.sc.com.my/capital-market-masterplan-1/.

SC (Securities Commission Malaysia). *Malaysia's Capital Market Plan 2 (CMP2)*. Available at: https://www.sc.com.my/wp-content/uploads/eng/html/cmp2/cmp2_ final.pdf.

SC (Securities Commission Malaysia). *Quarterly Bulletin for the Malaysian Islamic Capital Market*. Securities Commission Malaysia: Kuala Lumpur (2009).

Shen, N.M. "Islamic Finance Sector in Malaysia is Yet to Reach its Full Potential." *The Malaysian Reserve* (2017). Available at: https://themalaysianreserve.com/201 7/08/07/islamic-finance-sector-malaysia-yet-reach-full-potential/.

Tan, C.K. "Global Sukuk Issuance Slides 43% in 2015." *Nikkei Asian Review* (2016). http://asia.nikkei.com/Markets/Capital-Markets/Global-sukuk-issuance-slides-43-in2015?page=2.

The Express Tribune. "Islamic Finance Attract non-Muslim Countries" (2017). Available at: https://tribune.com.pk/story/1588519/3-islamic-finance-attracts-non-muslim-countries/.

Thomson Reuters. *State of the Global Islamic Economy Report 2016/17* (2017). https://ceif.iba.edu.pk/pdf/ThomsonReutersstateoftheGlobalIslamicEconomyReport201617.pdf.

Thomson Reuters. *Thomson Reuters Zawya Sukuk Perceptions and Forecast Study 2013*. Islamic Finance Gateway: Thomson Reuters (2012).

Tuah, Y. "Islamic Finance: The Unconventional but Nascent Financial System." *Borneo Post Online* (2017).

Vishwanath, S.R., & Azmi, S. "An Overview of Islamic Sukuk Bonds." *Journal of Structured Finance*, vol. 14, no. 4, pp. 58–67 (2009).

Whitely, P. "Economic Growth and Social Capital" (2002). http://www.shef.ac.uk/uni/academic/n-q/perc/polpas/pp5.html.

Chapter 7

Islamic Finance as a Contributor to Development Finance

Some Views from the World Bank Group

Ousmane Diagana

INTRODUCTION

As a citizen of West Africa, I spent many years working on the ground in the region and I know how important it is to secure as many sources of finance as possible for our countries to accompany their progress toward economic and social development.[1] The effectiveness of development financing relies, in substantial part, on the ethics of the contributing organizations. This is true of the World Bank Group; this is also true of Islamic finance.

The ethics of organizations, and most especially of international organizations, must be focused on what the organization has to contribute to the world. In recent years, ethics has sometimes been seen as a sort of byproduct of compliance, a way of avoiding the worst in organizations. I have a different view: ethics must first bring out the best in people and therefore in the organizations where they are active; ethics must show the way; it must inspire staff to care deeply for the ultimate objectives of the organization. For international organizations, this means that ethics must promote a culture of active altruism. Ethics must have a seat at the table in the discussions of development strategies, in the framework of public policy definition, and of course in the evaluation of their impact. At the same time, organizations need to establish ethics departments that can put in place control and corrective mechanism to avoid that, in exceptional cases, individuals drift away from the moral of the organization and affect the morale of staff members. This is essential for international organizations, such as the World Bank, that are committed to building a better world. I would argue that this is equally

149

essential for organizations that are involved in Islamic finance. This is especially relevant since Islamic finance is by definition and by essence ethical.

The ethics of Islamic finance is a well-researched topic which I will not delve into. I would like to focus on two aspects: the significant common ground between different forms of ethical finance and the diversification of the offer of financial products that derive from the technical differences that are introduced by Islamic finance.

The World Bank has insisted on the necessity of expanding investment in developing countries. The new sustainable development goals (SDGs) that bring together economic social and environmental priorities require to turn the billions of available development finance into trillions in investments. The international financial institutions have made outstanding efforts to contribute. During the fifteen-year effort to reach the Millennium Development Goals (MDGs), MDB support has grown from $50 billion to $127 billion annually in grants, concessional and non-concessional loans, risk-sharing instruments, guarantees, and equity investment. Yet, much more is needed. The World Bank has estimated in 2013[2] that the undersupply of infrastructure in developing economies is at around US$1 trillion per year, through 2020, with an additional US$200 to US$300 billion required annually to ensure that infrastructure investments are low emitting and climate-resilient. The Africa Progress Report, 2015, reminded us that 620 million people in Africa have no access to electricity and the report estimates that $55 billion per year is needed, until 2030, in order to meet demand and provide universal access to electricity in the region[3].

In this context all forms of financial contributions are more than welcome: they are necessary. In particular, the international community is grateful for the excellent contribution that Islamic finance is providing. The World Bank has created the global Islamic finance development center as a knowledge hub for developing Islamic finance globally, conducting research and training, and providing technical assistance and advisory services to World Bank Group client countries interested in developing Islamic financial institutions and markets. As our colleagues from the center put it: "Islamic finance is equity-based, asset-backed, ethical, sustainable, environmentally- and socially-responsible finance. It promotes risk sharing, connects the financial sector with the real economy, and emphasizes financial inclusion and social welfare."[4]

The World Bank shares with Islamic finance a focus on social justice, fair processes, and concern for financial impact. This is an essential aspect of any form of ethical finance and one which is present in Islamic finance. Islamic finance is often better known for a form and activities that are compatible with religious norms. The approach that is taken by ESG-conscious[5] investments is similar although the resulting selection of projects is not exactly identical. Ethics and rules of conduct intersect and overlap while taking into account traditions, culture, principles, and norms. The World Bank Group is one of the places in the world that combines these traditions. For instance, in 2016, the World Bank arranged for the International Finance Facility for Immunization, two $700-million vaccine Sukuk issuances that combine the requirements of ESG investors with those of Islamic finance.

SHORTCOMINGS OF GLOBAL FINANCE

It is impossible to list all the ways in which finance can transcend profits to take into account the social, economic, or environmental impact of investments and operations. Let me give an example of that that still exists in creating access to finance. The Global Findex database created by the World Bank shows that in 2014, 62 percent of the world adult population had a bank account or an account with mobile banking services compared to only 51 percent in 2011.[6] Nevertheless, there are still 2 billion people in the world who are unbanked. Access to finance is a particular problem for the Muslim world, as it is estimated that less than 20 percent of its population use conventional banks.[7] This is important because financial inclusion helps families become more resilient in the face of emergencies. Finance is not necessarily a tool for the very rich: it is also an important instrument to lift the poor out of poverty.

The financial world also has its storms and its furors. The financial crisis ten years ago highlighted once again the excesses that can exist in the financial sector. Once again, this led to new regulations in the sector but also to renewed calls for better ethics in finance. Excessive risk-bearing played a role in the demise of a number of financial institutions and financial instruments. In such a context, the diversity of the offer of financial services increases the financial market's resilience.

ISLAMIC BANKING

A 2010 IMF study compared the performance of Islamic banks with conventional banks[8] during the financial crisis and found that Islamic banks, on average, showed stronger resilience to financial fluctuations in 2007 and 2008 and less resilience to economic fluctuations, in particular in 2009.[9] This shows that Islamic banking and conventional banking have different strengths and weaknesses and benefit from coexisting. In 2011, Kenneth Rogoff, one of the leading economists on the analysis of financial crises, said: "Perhaps scholars who argue that Islamic financial systems' prohibition of interest generates massive inefficiencies ought to be looking at these systems for positive ideas that Western policymakers might adopt."[10]

For instance, Hasan and Dridi (2010) point out that the share of consumer loans (and thus of associated risks) was markedly different in conventional banking and in Islamic banking in 2008, at least in several of the countries they studied (see table 7.1).

Hasan and Dridi (2010) concluded that the change in profitability between 2007 and 2008, for the sample of banks they analyzed, showed differences between Islamic banks and conventional banks. On average, the profitability of their sample of conventional banks dropped by 34.1 percent between 2007 and 2008, while the profitability of their sample of Islamic banks was reduced by only 8.3 percent over the same period. When the sample of banks is segmented by countries, large differences between countries emerge, but in each country, there is a discrepancy between the change in profitability of conventional banks and of Islamic banks (see table 7.2).

When comparing 2009 with 2007, Hasan and Dridi (2010) found that the profitability of conventional banks fell by 13.4 percent on average, while it was reduced by 47.9 percent for the Islamic banks in their sample. A segmentation by country reveals, as before, large differences between countries, but every country displays a discrepancy between the change in profitability of conventional banks and the change in profitability of Islamic banks (see table 7.3).

Faye et al. (2013)[11] in a comparative study of 279 conventional banks and 11 Islamic banks in Africa over the period 2005–2010 also identify differences in resilience and conclude that, within their sample, "Islamic banks are more stable as they report lower insolvency risk and higher return on average assets."

The diversity that Islamic finance brings to the market adds stability to it but it also adds complexity to global and individual market regulation. It requires a global dialogue and the determination of principles common to all forms of finance.

CONCLUSION

Beyond these few ideas, I want to illustrate how ethical questions integrate with economic and financial realities. Ethical questions are not abstract, floating in thin air. They emerge from flesh, tears, numbers, statistics, prices, and the structure of financial deals. They turn experience into knowledge, knowledge into investments, investment into growth, growth into development, and development into peace and stability. They turn the world we live in into the world we want to live in. I form the wish that Islamic finance, alongside other

Table 7.1 Share of Consumer Loans in the Sectoral Distribution of Credit in 2008, in Percent

	Saudi Arabia	Kuwait	UAE	Bahrain	Qatar	Jordan	Malaysia	Turkey
Conventional banking	18.9	12.8	24.2	32.0	25.0	15.6	11.6	28.1
Islamic banking	35.1	12.0	31.0	22.8	26.0	16.9	22.6	15.1

Source: Maher Hasan and Jemma Dridi, "The Effects of the Global Crisis on Islamic and Conventional Banks: A Comparative Study," *IMF Working Paper* (September, 2010).

Ousmane Diagana

Table 7.2 Average Change in Profitability between 2007 and 2008 for a Sample of Banks in Each Country, in Percent

	Saudi Arabia	Kuwait	UAE	Qatar	Jordan	Malaysia	Turkey	Bahrain off-shore
Conventional banking	-31.1	- 82.3	5.7	31.4	6.4	10.1	-31.9	-292.9
Islamic banking	2.0	-46.5	1.1	23.5	27.1	-2.6	-4.5	-19.2

Source: Maher Hasan and Jemma Dridi, "The Effects of the Global Crisis on Islamic and Conventional Banks: A Comparative Study," *IMF Working Paper* (September, 2010).

Table 7.3 Average Change in Profitability between 2007 and 2009 for a Sample of Banks in Each Country, in Percent

	Saudi Arabia	Kuwait	UAE	Qatar	Jordan	Malaysia	Turkey	Bahrain off-shore
Conventional banking	-19.2	-60.1	-7.6	38.4	-20.4	17.4	-0.6	-129.7
Islamic banking	-0.1	-78.3	-42.2	5.6	22.7	39.2	1.9	-197.5

Source: Maher Hasan and Jemma Dridi, "The Effects of the Global Crisis on Islamic and Conventional Banks: A Comparative Study," *IMF Working Paper* (September, 2010).

forms of ethical finance, especially global international public finance such as the World Bank Group, will be one of the vehicles of change in the world, of development, of social justice, and of elimination of poverty.

NOTES

1. This chapter was originally presented at the Africa Islamic Finance Forum in Abidjan on October 17, 2016, when Ousmane Diagana was chief ethics officer for the World Bank Group and vice president of Ethics and Business Conduct. He is currently vice president of Human Resources for the World Bank Group.

2. World Bank, IFC and World Economic Forum, *Tackling the Infrastructure Finance Deficit* (Washington, DC: The World Bank, January 2013).

3. Africa Progress Panel, *Africa Progress Report: Power, People, Planet* (Geneva: APP, 2015).

4. http://www.worldbank.org/en/topic/financialsector/brief/islamic-finance.

5. That is, paying attention to environmental, social, and governance issues.

6. Source: Findex data on World Bank website: http://www.worldbank.org/en/programs/globalfindex.

7. Source: Arunma Oteh, "How Islamic Finance can Contribute to the Achievement of Sustainable Development Goals" (Communication of September 29, 2016).

8. In Bahrain, Jordan, Kuwait, Malaysia, Qatar, Saudi Arabia, Turkey, and the United Arab Emirates, that is, over 80 percent of Islamic banking markets excluding Iran.

9. https://www.imf.org/en/News/Articles/2015/09/28/04/53/sores100410a and Maher Hasan and Jemma Dridi, "The Effects of the Global Crisis on Islamic and Conventional Banks: A Comparative Study," *IMF Working Paper* WP/10/201 (September 2010).

10. Kenneth Rogoff, *Global Imbalances without Tears,* Project Syndicate (March 1), 2011, cited in Usman Hayat and Adeel Malkik, *Islamic Finance: Ethics, Concepts, Practice* (Charlottesville: Literature review by CFA Institute Research Foundation, 2014).

11. Issa Faye, Thouraya Triki and Thierry Kangoye, "The Islamic Finance Promises: Evidence from Africa," *Review of Development Finance* 3, no. 3 (2013): 136–151.

BIBLIOGRAPHY

Africa Progress Panel. *Africa Progress Report: Power, People, Planet.* Geneva: APP, 2015.

Faye, Issa, Thouraya Triki, and Thierry Kangoye. "The Islamic Finance Promises: Evidence from Africa." *Review of Development Finance* 3, no. 3 (2013): 136–151.

Hayat, Usman, and Adeel Malkik. *Islamic Finance: Ethics, Concepts, Practice.* Charlottesville, VA: Literature review by CFA Institute Research Foundation, 2014.

http://www.worldbank.org/en/topic/financialsector/brief/islamic-finance.

http://www.worldbank.org/en/programs/globalfindex.

https://www.imf.org/en/News/Articles/2015/09/28/04/53/sores100410a.

Maher, Hasan, and Jemma Dridi. "The Effects of the Global Crisis on Islamic and Conventional Banks: A Comparative Study." *IMF Working Paper* WP/10/201 (September 2010).

Oteh, Arunma, "How Islamic Finance can Contribute to the Achievement of Sustainable Development Goals" (Communication of September 29, 2016).

Rogoff, Kenneth. "Global Imbalances without Tears." Project Syndicate (1 March, 2011).

World Bank, IFC and World Economic Forum. *Tackling the Infrastructure Finance Deficit.* Washington, DC: The World Bank, January 2013.

Chapter 8

Islamic Banking after Financial Crises

A Version of the Iceland Plan for Monetary Reform

Asad Zaman

INTRODUCTION

This chapter deals with the complexities and inequities of money creation in the interest-based modern economy. In this respect, the chapter pursues the unifying theme of Islamic finance as a complex adaptive system by extending and applying the arguments of Khan's chapter and Sonko and Sonko's chapter, applying them to the case of the economic analysis of endogenous money and the policy implications flowing from such analysis for setting up an alternative and truly Islamic financial system.

Throughout the Islamic world, there has been an effort to eliminate the interest-based financial system currently dominant in the West. Unfortunately, some crucial aspects of how money is created, and how private banks function, have been missing from the discussion. This is not surprising, because standard accounts of money creation taught in universities throughout the world are fundamentally wrong. Economists absorb these myths of money creation and carry out discussions about interest within a fundamentally flawed theoretical framework. Islamic economists have followed suit.

Our goal in this chapter is to show that, contrary to standard economic theory, money is created by private banks. Furthermore, the creation of money, which is vital to the economy, is intimately connected with the creation of interest-based debt. This system of private money creation, which also creates high levels of debt, is extremely harmful to the economy for many reasons. It is necessary to replace this system by a government-controlled creation of money. Because the topic is quite complex, we will only be able to provide a summary of some essential issues. A fuller discussion of many related aspects is available in "The Nature of Modern Money" by Zaman (forth-coming). Awareness of the issues under discussion is gradually increasing. Recently, the Iceland government has formulated a plan for monetary reform (Sigurjonsson 2015) along the lines under discussion here. The Iceland Plan centers around replacing private creation of money by Sovereign Money, to be only issued by the government. This is very much in line with Islamic teachings, which prohibit private creation of money. However, Islam focuses on the elimination of interest, which leads to more far-reaching changes.

MYTHS OF MONEY CREATION

What students are almost universally taught about money creation is almost the opposite of the truth. The standard monetary theory course teaches that the government creates high powered money or the monetary base. This is called M0 or M1, or narrow money. Loans made by private banks in a frac-tional reserve banking system multiply this monetary base to create broad money or M2. This discussion implies that the government is in control of the process of money creation. Furthermore, no distinction is made between narrow money, which is created by the government, and broad money, which is created by the private banks. As we will show, these two types of money are very different from each other and have different effects on the economic system. Furthermore, the private sector can create any amount of money, and the government has no control over this process. Sigurjonsson (2015) provides a detailed discussion and explanation of this issue.

In financially advanced economies, the monetary base is often less than 5 percent of broad money. Thus more than 95 percent of the money in existence is created by private banks. The controversy between endogenous and exog-enous theories of money lies in how much control private banks have in this process. According to the dominant exogenous theories, the process of money creation by banks is mechanical and automatic, which means that if the gov-ernments set the monetary base to be MB, then the amount of broad money which comes into existence is $M2 = k \times MB$, where k is the deposit multiplier. The endogenous money theories say, quite sensibly, that banks and borrow-ers exercise a lot of discretion and, therefore, k is very much dependent on what they choose to do. This means that 95 percent of the stock is created at the discretion of the private sector. Thus, the amount of money in circulation is not determined by the government but rather depends on choices made by banks and borrowers.

There is strong evidence that the endogenous money view is correct. Mcleay et al. (2014) of the Bank of England explain in detail the private creation of money by banks. Benes and Kumhof (2012) of IMF write, "The deposit multiplier is simply, in the words of Kydland and Prescott (1990), a myth. And because of this, private banks are almost fully in control of the money creation process." Mian and Sufi (2014) provide evidence that the quantitative easing regime adopted in the recent past, in which central banks created huge amounts of high powered money, had *no* effect on the stock of broad money. In effect, the central bank was powerless to change the money supply, contrary to the conventional theory of exogenous money. Similarly, the Iceland Plan for monetary reform (Sigurjonsson, March 2015) is based on the experience of the central bank, that it was unable to control money supply in the postcrisis era. This same problem was noted by the creators of the Chicago Plan, in the aftermath of the Great Depression of 1929.[1]

THE TRUTHS OF MONEY CREATION

A small portion of money is created by the government. This is called narrow money or M0. Nearly all over the world, the government is legally barred from printing money to fulfill its budgetary requirements. Instead, this responsibility is given to central banks, and considerable efforts are made to ensure that the central banks operate independently, without interference from the government. The money created by central banks only forms a small fraction of the total amount of money in the economy. The ratio of narrow money to broad money can vary from 3 percent to 30 percent or higher depending on the financial depth of the economy. Typically, a huge portion of money is created by private banks. We will call this portion "credit" to differentiate it from narrow money. In Pakistan, narrow money was around 8 trillion rupees, while broad money was around 13 trillion, according to SBP data for February 2015. Thus 5 trillion rupees were created as credit by the private sector. This credit is created by the private banks in response to demand for loans. That is, when anyone asks for a loan from the bank, the bank opens an account in his name and creates the amount of money as a book-keeping entry in his account. No actual money is transferred to the borrower's account; rather, money equal in value to the loan is created in the process of granting the loan. When the loan is repaid, this money is destroyed.

To summarize this discussion, there are two types of money. One is money created by central bank, which is called narrow money or the monetary base. The second type of money is created by private sector banks; we will call this "credit." When the bank makes a loan, it creates an account for the borrower and creates money as an accounting entry in the bank account. There is nothing behind this money, which is created out of nowhere. In the fractional reserve system, the amount of money created cannot be larger than a specified multiple of the reserves. It is thought that this restricts the money creation power of private banks and allows the central bank to control the amount of money in the economy. In fact, the central bank has the obligation to provide necessary reserves to private banks. Thus, the bank can make loans (and create money) in any amount, and then borrow the reserves necessary to fulfill the reserve requirements. Sigurjonsson (2015) provides a detailed explanation of why the central bank cannot control the total amount of money created in an economy.

A third type of money has become very prominent in recent times. There are many financial instruments which are created by financial institutions. These are highly liquid. There are huge markets for trading these instruments, which can be freely converted into money. Thus these are close substitutes for money and pure creation of financial institutions. Because these institutions and instruments can operate outside the ambit of regulations, this is called the shadow banking system, and the extension of money generated in the process is called shadow money. Although this is a very important part of the modern economy, we will not discuss this issue in this short note. For the issues under discussion in this chapter, it is enough to think of this as just another kind of credit money which is privately created by banks.

THE CLOSE RELATION BETWEEN MONEY AND INTEREST-BASED DEBT

Vast amount of money in the economy is created by private banks in the process of extending credit to private and public sectors. When banks extend credit, this is always in the form of an interest-based loan. Thus, when money is created, interest-based debt is also created at the same time. For the purposes of this discussion, Islamic banks do not differ in any significant way from conventional banks. Both create money in the process of making loans. Although the loans of Islamic banks are nominally interest-free, in practice the differences with commercial banks are negligible. If the bank were to make genuine *musharka* loans, where return to the bank would be closely tied to the performance of the loan, there is a potential for a significant difference. However, as Islamic banking is practiced today, *musharka* loans form a negligible portion of the portfolio. The *murabaha* loans are functionally equivalent (in terms of economic effects) to interest-based loans.

In principle, governments can create money just by printing money. Thus, money creation by the government need not give rise to interest-based debt. In practice, this is not true, and most money created by government is by borrowing on interest. We now explain why this is the case. In most economies around the world, the government is not permitted to print money to finance government operations. Sometimes this prohibition is formal and written into the law, while in other cases there are informal mechanisms to prevent the government from printing money. The theory is that if governments were allowed to do so, they would print massive amounts of money, causing huge inflation and a collapse of the monetary economy. With the correct understanding of money creation, this argument becomes puzzling and paradoxical. This is because when the government borrows money from banks, the banks create the money which is provided to the government. Thus whatever harms come from government creation of money, the same harms would result from the private creation of money. Ellen Brown (2011) presents historical evidence that governments entrusted with printing money have behaved responsibly, avoiding excessive money creation. On the other hand, the current system of private creation of money has led to excess money creation leading to severe economic problems such as increasing inequality and recurrent banking crises.

"Fiscal Responsibility" is the idea that the government should try to reduce or minimize budget deficits, keeping their expenditures in line with their revenues raised from taxes and other means. This makes intuitive sense—governments are known for profligate spending on supporters, useless projects as well as to buy votes. At the same time, fiscal responsibility should not prevent the government from borrowing to spend on essentials like food, health, and education. Ensuring adequate government spending on essentials and preventing wasteful expenditures are two of the central economic problems, which are inadequately addressed by conventional economic theories. On the other hand, this problem has received a lot of attention in the early literature on Islamic economics. Unfortunately, current Islamic economists have not paid much attention to this rich heritage.

In order to ensure fiscal responsibility, nearly all governments have formal or informal mechanisms that restrict their ability to print money to finance expenditures. When more money is needed, governments can raise this money by borrowing. This is done by issuing treasury bonds, which generates interest-based debt. The treasury bonds may be sold to the central bank, which can finance the purchase by printing money. Alternatively, they may be sold to domestic banks, which finance the purchase by issuing credit, adding to the stock of broad money. In all these cases, government borrowing creates interest-based debt and *also* increases the money supply. According to conventional multiplier theories debunked earlier, central bank printing of money generates high powered money M0 and therefore leads to a much larger increase in total money supply through the multiplier effect. Therefore, the preferred alternative is selling treasury bonds to commercial banks, since this should be less inflationary.

However, endogenous theories of money creation lead to different conclusions. As far as inflationary effects are concerned, all three transactions lead to the same amount of money creation—whether the government prints money, or the central bank prints money, or the private banks create credit to buy treasury bills. In the latter two scenarios, the government gets saddled with a burden of debt. When the debt is to the central bank, this is harmless. However, in the case of borrowing from private banks, private banks get a windfall in terms of unearned profits for no useful activity. Furthermore, they have less incentive to engage in their primary useful activity of seeking out and financing useful productive economic activity. This is called the "crowding out effect."

The proposal for Sovereign Money made as a recommendation to the government of Iceland (Sigurjonsson 2015) takes these considerations into account. Fiscal responsibility is used as an argument to prevent government creation of money and to give this responsibility to the private sector. However, as we will discuss later, the private sector has not done a good job. The power of money creation in the hands of the private sector has caused a tremendous amount of economic damage. It seems likely that giving this power to the government is also not a good solution. Left to their own devices, the government is likely to use the power to create money in harmful ways as well. The Iceland Plan envisions the separation of the two powers: creation of money and the spending of the money created. The creation should be done via a transparent and nonpartisan process, which takes into account the amount of money needed economically. From the Islamic point of view, a major advantage of the proposal is that this method will separate the creation of money from the creation of interest-bearing debt. Thus, such a proposal is fundamental to the elimination of *riba* from an economy.

THE HARMS OF DEBT-BASED AND PRIVATE MONEY CREATION

There are a large number of problems which result from the private creation of money by banks and borrowers. We mention only a few of them in separate sections below.

Injustice

Banks have the power to manufacture money by the stroke of a pen, but only in response to requests for loans. This power to create money gives them a tremendous advantage over all other segments of society. This is inherently unjust. Why should one particular class of the wealthy be granted this privilege when others are not? Money is a social good and the power to create it should belong to society as a whole. If the government is not representative or is subject to capture by powerful elites, or special interest groups, then it can also abuse the power of money creation, and cause harm and injustice.

A related problem with the present system is that banks will profit from the power of creation of money only if they can make loans. Therefore, it is in the interest of banks to create the desire for credit. This can be done and has been done in many ways. Facilitating installment sales, use of credit cards, encouraging consumers to borrow money to gamble on stocks, and so on have all been used to increase the demand for loans. As Mian and Sufi (2014) have pointed out, the interest-based debt is a highly unjust contract. If a home-owner loses his income, or if an investment project fails, the poor borrower loses all his money. However, the wealthy creditor retains all his money, and can even profit from the failure. Considerations of justice and equity would require that the wealthy party should at least share the risk. This is precisely what Islamic Law ensures.

The private sector banks make money by making loans. So, it is in their interest to encourage the taking of loans. Therefore, they devise schemes to make loans attractive to the public. One of these schemes is the credit card, which takes advantage of the psychological tendencies of consumers—whereas people are reluctant to part with hard-earned cash, they find it much easier to swipe a plastic card through the machine, which is just a promise to pay later. Many other schemes of a more damaging nature have been devised by bankers to make the public borrow heavily. The product of the banks is "virtual" money which they sell as loans, and banks go to great lengths to make sales of this product by providing loans to the public. The unjust and economically harmful nature of interest-based debt is discussed at book-length in *House of Debt* by Mian and Sufi (2014). A detailed and lengthy historical account of changing attitudes toward the morality of interest-based debt is given by Graeber (2011). A key argument of Graeber is that current institutions of rigidly enforceable debt impoverish societies. This reinforces the point made by Mian and Sufi (2014).

Increasing Inequality

Clearly, if one segment of society can create money at will, they will acquire an increasing share of the wealth produced. Following the Great Depression in 1929, a large number of rules and regulations were made to restrict the power of banks. The financial sector and the wealthiest segment of society lost out while the bottom 90 percent increased their income shares for the next fifty years. This state of affairs, declining wealth shares due to the regulation of the financial sector, did not please the wealthy elites. How they plotted a comeback is detailed in many sources, notably Klein (2008) and Alkire and Ritchie (2007).

The Reagan-Thatcher era represents the political success of the wealthy elites, through an ideological success in promoting the idea that the governments and regulations are harmful, and free markets achieve best results. Since the 1980s, there has been increasing de-regulation of the financial sector. As a result, the share of wealth of the top 0.1 percent started increasing and has continued its upward trend until it recently overtook the bottom 90 percent. There is now a huge amount of empirical evidence documenting the stark increase in inequality that has resulted from the financial deregulation.[2]

Not only has inequality increased within countries, but also among countries. This is because of interest-based finance is the basis for the neo-colonial system currently dominating the globe. What was previously accomplished by conquest and warfare is now being done by the use of interest-based loans. Financiers from wealthy countries provide loans to poor countries. The theory is that this is used to finance investments and projects which will create productivity and growth. The repayment would be financed out of the additional production created by the investment. This is what would happen if the Islamic principles of *musharka* finance were used. However, current practices lead to the financing of a huge number of nonviable projects. The lenders have no interest in whether or not the projects are completed, and whether or not they can produce financial returns. The loans made are considered as payments to corrupt leaders within the governments. The loan repayments come by increasing tax burdens on an already poor public. In effect, the loans are payments by the wealthy imperialist countries to the corrupt elite, in return for the service of taxing the public and providing tribute to the imperialists.

Hickel (2013) documents that about 136 billion dollars in foreign aid flow from the rich to the poor countries. At the same time, about 600 billion dollars in interest payments (often financed by additional loans at high interest) flow from the poor countries to the rich. In addition, rich countries acquire about a trillion dollars of capital flight from the poor; this included repatriations of capital by multinationals, as well as Swiss accounts of corrupt rulers. This massive exploitation of the poor by the rich is supported by the current monetary system and could not occur without our (Muslims) agreement to accept this as a permissible system for use within Islamic countries.

Speculation, Fraud, and Crises

What is done with money created by banks? If this money is used for highly productive investments, this is beneficial to society. If it is used for wasteful luxuries, speculation, and gambling, this is harmful to society. For many reasons, private creation of money leads to highly inefficient investments. One of the arguments made in favor of the current system of private money creation is exactly the opposite: it is argued that this system provides loans for the most profitable investments, the ones that are the most beneficial for society. As against this argument, Keynes wrote in *The General Theory of Employment, Interest and Money*: "Speculators may do no harm as bubbles on a steady stream of enterprise. But the position is serious when enterprise becomes the bubble on a whirlpool of speculation. When the capital development of a country becomes a byproduct of the activities of a casino, the job is likely to be ill-done." Keynes argued that instead of investing in productive enterprise, investors borrow from the banks to gamble on the stock market—these gambles determine the investment activities of the economy. For example, the global financial crisis was caused by gamblers who bet on ever-increasing house prices in the United States. The stock market channeled money to this market, which was perhaps the most destructive investment, eventually resulting in the blow-up of the global economy.

The documentary "Inside Job" shows how financial institutions caused the global financial crisis of 2008. These institutions were "too big to fail." That is, their collapse would have caused a collapse of the entire financial system. Thus, they could count on government support in case of collapse. Therefore, they could gamble with other people's money in a risk-free fashion. If they won, they would make huge gains. If they lost, the public would pay for their losses. This has become known as the "privatizing gains and socializing losses" strategy. It is so common and so widely used that hundreds of crises have occurred due to the current unregulated financial system. Laeven and Valencia (2008) date the start of systemic banking crises from 1970 and provide a database of 124 banking crises from 1970 to 2007.

Taxation and Fiscal Constraints

Government debt is harmful to the economy because the government must pay interest on what it borrows. To finance this, the government needs to tax productive sectors of the economy. These taxes lower productivity and reduce the capacity of the economy to produce goods and services. If the government were to print money directly (instead of having the central bank print it and loan it to the government), it would not need to raise taxes to finance it. This would lead to increased productivity.

Currently, the annual budget for Pakistan has 1.4 trillion rupees in payment of interest on debt, and only 0.5 trillion for development projects. It is impossible to generate growth without investing in development. All of these interest payments are going as unearned profits (i.e., profits provided without any social service, or anything of value) for the private financial sector. If the system of Sovereign Money is implemented, these interest payments could be eliminated. That would create vast amounts of fiscal space for financing social services. These could create rapid growth.

THE CHICAGO PLAN

In the aftermath of the Great Depression, several economists came to the realization that the source of the problem was the private creation of money by banks. They created the Chicago Plan which was designed to provide an orderly transition from the private system to a system where the government would have 100 percent control of the process of money creation. A key feature of the system is that banks would be required to have 100 percent reserves—they would no longer be able to give loans by creating money as accounting entries not backed by cash. There is strong support for this position from the Shari'ah—the action of coining currency by individuals is considered as hostility to the nation. This has also been the secular position, where many nations have used the forging of foreign currencies as acts of economic warfare against the foreign country. We turn to a discussion of some of the benefits of the Chicago Plan. Benes and Kumhoff (2012) created a model to evaluate the claims made for the Chicago Plan by its authors, in the context of the current US economic situation. They found support for all of the central benefits claimed for the Chicago Plan:

- *Elimination of Business Cycles:* Because banks can create or destroy money nearly at will, the stock of money fluctuates erratically. As Keynesian economic theory demonstrates, the quantity of money has very important economic effects. Too little leads to recession, while too much can cause inflation. The Chicago Plan gives control of the money supply to the government, which can use it to smooth out economic fluctuations caused by erratic changes in money supply. Government should use counter-cyclical monetary policy—in a booming economy, the money supply should be restricted to prevent inflation. In a slack economy, money supply should be expanded to increase employment and production. Private sector creation of money does the opposite since the demand for loans is high in a boom and low in a slack economy. Thus, the current system of private money production creates or exacerbates the business cycles.
- *Complete Elimination of Bank Runs:* There have been more than a hundred banking crises over the past century. The fractional reserve system is prone to runs because it routinely issues loans for a lot more money than is actually in the possession of the banks. The 100 percent reserve requirement eliminates the possibility of bank runs.
- *Dramatic Reduction of Public Debt:* In the current system, government sells treasury bills and goes into debt to finance expenditures. The central bank is authorized to print money and buy the treasury bills from the government. Instead of incurring debt, the Chicago Plan allows the government to directly print money to finance its expenditures. The government's

need for financing is reduced, leading to a reduction in taxation. This also increases productivity since taxes dampen productive efforts of both laborers and firms.

- *Dramatic Reduction of Private Debt:* The current system links the creation of money to the creation of debt on a one-to-one basis in the private sector. Money is created when banks give loans. As a large amount of money is necessary for the functioning of the system, so a large amount of interest-based debt is equally necessary for the functioning of the system. When government issues money directly, without creating debt, all of this private debt will be wiped out. The threats to an economy posed by excessive debt have been documented by many authors, notably Mian and Sufi in *House of Debt*.

- *Increased Efficiency of Production:* The private banking system creates money to finance investment, which is crucial for the future of the nation. This investment is directed toward the most privately profitable activity, which may be speculative rather than productive. There are many cases where socially profitable investments are not equally profitable on a private basis—most notably education and health. Public creation of money can be used to direct the investments toward the socially most beneficial activities. In addition, reduction or elimination of taxes leads to substantially improved incentives for firms and laborers, enhancing efficient production of goods and services.

- *More Efficient and Productive Investments in the Real Sector:* As we have seen, the private sector tends to make nonproductive investments. For example, in land, stocks, or financial gambles in derivatives. These generate quick money, but do not add value to the economy. Quite often, financial gains become so large that real investments do not take place. People can make more money by using financial instruments than they can be doing real productive activity. Two changes would substantially change this harmful scenario. One of them is the Sovereign Money idea, which prevents the private sector from creating money at will. With huge funds available at will, gambling becomes attractive. The second is elimination of interest. Investments should be made on the basis of *Musharka*—share in the profits earned. This ensures incentive compatibility and is exactly in line with Islamic teachings. Earnings should be made for providing a service. The investor provides the service of looking for attractive investments, and in sharing the inevitable risks of business. This would provide substantially superior real productive investments and lead to increased growth potential.

Recently, an advisory committee to the government of Iceland has created a draft for a proposal to implement development of the Chicago Plan, precisely to avoid the difficulties of private money creation and to gain the advantages of Sovereign Money creation by the state.[3]

POLITICAL OBSTACLES TO IMPLEMENTING THE CHICAGO PLAN

If the Chicago Plan has all of these benefits claimed, why has it not been implemented? The simple answer is that it is harmful to the interests of a very powerful segment of the wealthy elites. In the wake of the Great Depression, banking regulations and Keynesian economics created substantial constraints on the power of the rich. Nonetheless, they succeeded in blocking the Chicago Plan, which was even more radical. The effects of the regulation of the banking sector is clearly reflected in the graph of the wealth share of the top 0.1 percent. This shows a declining trend from 1930 to 1980, after which it starts increasing again, due to financial liberalization starting from the Reagan-Thatcher era. The global financial crisis of 2007 was engineered by these super-rich elites.[4] The collapse of the housing market led to houses worth more than $100,000 being available for fire-sale prices like $5,000. A huge amount of wealth was transferred from the public to these wealthy elites. Also, in the aftermath of the crisis, the wealthy were much better prepared. Whereas the Great Depression had led to heavy regulation of banking, all such regulation has been effectively blocked in the Congress. For example, to prevent speculation by banks, the Dodd-Frank Act was proposed as an equivalent for the Glass-Steagall Act which was repealed in 1999. However, while Glass-Steagall was only 30 pages and clearly banned banks from all kinds of speculation, Dodd-Frank is 300 pages and monstrosity full of loopholes. There is agreement among experts that any competent lawyer can find many ways to permit banks to speculate within the bounds of Dodd-Frank. This is just an illustration of the general picture that none of the problems that led to the financial collapse have been rectified. The Chicago Plan was discussed briefly and buried quietly without much discussion. Similarly, while there has been a lot of hue and cry, conferences and papers, on macro-prudential regulation, nothing has been done to prevent a new crisis of the same type. In other words, the top 0.1 percent who benefit vastly from the private creation of money are firmly in control and have blocked even a discussion of the merits of the Chicago Plan. As Shiller (2015) writes:

> One might think that years after the bursting of the speculative bubbles that led to the 2007–9 world financial crisis, we should be living in a distinctly different post-bubble world. One might think people would have "learned their lesson" and would not again pile into expanding markets, as so many did before the

crisis, thereby worsening incipient bubbles. But evidence of bubbles has accelerated since the crisis.

Why have no lessons been learned from the massively bad effects of the global financial crisis of 2008? It is because the lessons are different for different classes of people. A tiny percentage of the top elite have actually benefited greatly from the crisis, and have managed the aftermath to prevent the learning of lessons and the creation of regulations necessary to prevent future crises. Nonetheless, there is a growing awareness of these problems, and the Iceland Plan for monetary reform (Sigurjonsson 2015) shows how it may be possible to solve them.

AN ISLAMIC ICELAND PLAN

The Iceland Plan for monetary reform focuses on the private creation of money and proposes Sovereign Money as a solution. This is an update of the Chicago Plan designed for implementation in modern times. The plan for Sovereign Money is completely in accordance with Islamic Law but does not go far enough. In fact, one of the central problems is interest-based debt. As discussed briefly earlier, this system has been used to create massive transfer of monies from the poorer countries to the wealthiest ones. In the words of Ellen Brown (2011), wealthy investors

> crack open foreign markets in the name of "free trade," take down the local currency, and put the nation's assets on the block at fire-sale prices. The first step in this process is to induce the country to accept foreign loans and investments. The loan money gets dissipated but the loans must be repaid. In the poignant words of (former) Brazilian President Luiz Inacio Lula da Silva: The Third World War has already started. . . . The war is tearing down Brazil, Latin America, and practically all the Third World. Instead of soldiers dying, there are children. It is a war over the Third World debt, one which has as its main weapon, interest, a weapon more deadly than the atom bomb, more shattering than a laser beam.

Using the Iceland Plan as a basis, but also combining it with several other elements from Islamic Law, we create an Islamic version, which addresses many other shortcomings of the present financial architecture. A brief outline of some of the changes required is presented below.[5]

The process of development has two key elements. One is finding resources to finance investment. The second is to use the resources wisely. Even if a nation has huge resources and production, if these are not used wastefully, then the nation will decline. Islamic principles exist to take care of all of these aspects. In the first place, Islamic laws are clear on the principle of Sovereign Money.

SOVEREIGN MONEY

The principle that only the state has the right to mint coins is generally agreed upon. The general public does not hold these rights and attempting to do otherwise is considered illegal and punishable by law. This is also a principle of Islamic Law. Moulana Asmatullah (2014) writes that "the consensus of Islamic scholars is unanimous; as per Shari'ah only governments have the legal rights pertaining to minting. Individuals cannot produce coins equivalent to or different from the ones produced by the government. If a person attempts any such act, it will be considered an unlawful act and a display of hostility against the nation (Fasad fil Arz)." Evidence based on historical incidents and rulings by scholars is presented in support of this view. The Shari'ah view that printing of money by nongovernment sources is an act of hostility to the nation is also supported by historical evidence provided by Cooley (2014). He provided extensive details on how nations at war have forged the currencies of the other nation in large quantities in an attempt to destroy their economies.

On the surface, it appears that our current system of money creation does not violate this principle. Only the state is authorized to print money. However, the banks are authorized to issue credit to customers who apply for a loan. The fractional reserve banking system allows the banks to issue far greater credit than the amount of cash money they possess as reserves. This ability to issue credit, which is equivalent to money in circulation, is further enhanced by the central bank. The central bank provides loans to serve as reserves in whatever amount is needed by the private sector. The stability of the financial system is also guaranteed by the central bank, so that big banks enjoy implicit or explicit guarantees against failure. That is, they can create large amounts of money without risk—in case of demands which exceed the money in their possession, the central bank must act as a lender of the last resort.

This system of private money creation is supported by a web of deceit. It is taught in universities all over the world that private banks do not create money. It is also taught that governments are in control of the money supply. No distinction is made between bank-issued credit which is not backed by any asset, and the monies printed by the government. This collection of misconceptions serves to conceal the crucially important fact that the current system is based on private creation of money, in the form of credit, by banks. This gives banks and financial institutions an extraordinary amount of power. They use this power to influence educational systems and researchers to spread myths about money creation which conceal this source of power.

PRICE STABILITY

Adopting the Sovereign Money plan gives the state the sole right to create money, taking it away from private banks. Some of the adverse consequences of private creation of money have already been described. It is especially important to note that, since banks create money as interest-based loans, inflation is built into the system. Because of interest, money tomorrow must be worth less than money today. Private banks have devised many strategies to induce people to borrow, creating debt burdens that cause economic damage. One important consequence of switching to Sovereign Money will be a dramatic reduction in both public and private debt, as noted by Benes and Kumhof (2012).

By itself, switching to Sovereign Money is not a complete solution to the problem of how to handle money creation. Just as the abuse of this privilege by banks has caused tremendous damage, the government can also cause tremendous damage by abusing this privilege. Fortunately, Islamic Law has many provisions to prevent such abuse. There are no direct rules about money creation, but many principles of the Shari'ah do apply indirectly. Since money is a public good, the government must ensure that the production of money is socially beneficial and utilized for public benefit. Thus, ensuring that prices remain stable can be considered as a responsibility of the government. The Iceland Plan envisions a nonpartisan board that decides on how much money should be created. The decision to create money is completely separate from the decision on how this money is to be spent. The creation of money should focus on "inflation targeting" principles, while the decisions to spend should focus on creating full employment.

Currently, inflation targeting policy aims for low inflation, because zero inflation is basically impossible when interest rates are above zero. However, in a zero-interest economy, it does become possible to target zero inflation. Islamic conceptions of money suggest that this is the ideal policy goal. Imam Al-Ghazali has argued that the main function of money is a "measure of value." Thus, money is a yardstick used to measure the value of different objects, in order to make comparisons on a common scale, as is required by the market. Thus, he argues interest defeats the purpose of money by making its value variable across time. Extending this argument, we can say that money creation should also be done in a way to ensure that the prices remain stable across time. Failing this objective would create changes in the value of money, which would be harmful to the public. Thus, the government would not be allowed to earn seigniorage revenues by printing excess money to cause inflation.

The demonstration that in an interest-free Islamic economy, zero inflation rates can be achieved is technical and requires an elaborate economic model. This is the technical possibility demonstrated by Khan chapter 2. For the present, our goal is to indicate that complete price stability is possible in an Islamic economy, whereas it is impossible in any interest-based system.

ELIMINATION OF NONPRODUCTIVE INVESTMENTS

A major problem with the current system of private money creation is that the money created is used for nonproductive investments. This is a fundamental flaw of interest-based systems: it allows the rentier class to flourish. The rentier class is one which makes profits and earnings without making any productive contributions to the economy. Interest-based loans are one of the principal means by which the rentier class earns risk-free returns merely because they are owners of wealth, and not because of any productive activity. Keynes noted that rentiers exert a depressing influence on the economy and called for setting the interest rate to zero, so as to lead to the "euthanasia of the rentier." Islamic Law strongly supports this principle. Those who own wealth can earn a return on it by doing business with it, as long as they participate in the risks of the business. This risk-taking is considered as a contribution, as it allows for entrepreneurship. Interest is banned because it insulates owners of wealth from risk, leading to extreme injustice: even when the business runs a loss, the owner of wealth is compensated in full. It is this insulation of the wealthy from consequences of loss that has led to numerous financial crises, big and small, over the past century.

Currently, leading economists are debating over the causes of "secular stagnation" experienced throughout the globe in the past few decades. The period of low and declining economic growth coincides with the period of financial deregulation initiated in the 1980s in the Reagan-Thatcher era. Investors shifted from making investments in the real sector to investments in the financial sector. The prices of land, stocks, and other speculative assets increased, making these investments increasingly attractive and leading to bubbles in the price. For many years, financial sector investments have exceeded those of the real sector in returns—one can earn more from stocks or land than one can from running a factory, or a farm. This has led to decline in real investments, and hence long and persistent stagnation in growth.

An Islamic economy takes a multipronged approach to avoid this problem. Banning interest-based loans is a major step forward in preventing nonproductive investment. Banning gambling on stocks is another essential step. So far, Islamic economists have been content to follow the lead of the West; if they allow gambling on stocks, we also allow it. Following Islamic principles, we can think of many ways to prevent it, by deviating from Western patterns. For example, we could tie stock price to some fundamental valuations and not allow trading at prices deviating very far from this value. Also, we could impose costs or taxes on trades to prevent rapid trading. Very similar proposals have been floated by secular economists who have become cognizant of the costs of gambling in the stock market. Similar action needs to be taken to prevent speculation on land prices. All of this will be very much facilitated by Sovereign Money, since this step will prevent creation of money for gambling by the private sector.

One crucial element in eliminating nonproductive investments is the replacement of interest-based loans by *musharka*. This is closely tied to the Islamic rules for *halal* earnings—in general, earnings should be based on, and proportional to, the services provided. Today wealthy individuals have earnings that exceed those of many populous nations. This is due to the interest-based system which rewards the mere possession of wealth. In the Islamic system, wealth can be used to earn more, provided that the wealthy participate in the risks of business. When they do so, as in the *musharka* system, they provide an essential service necessary to sustain entrepreneurship. This entitles them to make a profit on their wealth. *Musharka* finance has the potential of achieving what is claimed for the interest-based system—investors will seek out the most profitable investments, because their returns will be tied to the profit of the enterprise. The interest-based system earns a fixed return, and obtains it from collaterals, and hence has no direct concern with success or failure of the investment. This makes it highly inefficient.

ENCOURAGING PRODUCTIVE
INVESTMENTS AND EMPLOYMENT

Although economic theory suggests that the private sector will automatically find and finance the most productive investments, reality is strongly in conflict with this idea. It is often the case that private returns diverge vastly from social returns. Private profits from pollution, deforestation, over-fishing, killing off rare species of animals and plants may be large, while social costs are much larger. Furthermore, investments that are hugely profitable socially, such as providing education and healthcare to the poor, may not be privately profitable. The system of Sovereign Money creation increases the fiscal space for the government to allow it to undertake vastly more projects for social welfare. For instance, the government of Pakistan's budget for 2014 has 1.4

trillion rupees for interest payments on debt, 0.7 trillion for defense expenditures, and only 0.5 for development. A system of Sovereign Money would eliminate the interest payments, which are also revenues of the rentier class, and allow nearly four times as much expenditure on development. This would substantially accelerate the process of growth.

Even a quadrupling of development expenditure would not lead to rapid growth if it is spent on wasteful or useless projects. Thus, it is essential to identify the highest priority investments and ensure spending in those areas. Evidence from a variety of different sources shows that our best investments are in human beings—this differs from conventional economic theories of growth, which emphasize physical capital over humans. For example, the World Bank (2006) in the *Where Is the Wealth of Nations?* finds that most of the wealth is human: "The wealth estimates suggest that the preponderant form of wealth worldwide is intangible capital—human capital and the quality of formal and informal institutions." Investing in humans, and in institutions, is the bedrock for future success. As many authors have noted, the quality of institutions depends on the quality of human beings running them.[6] Economic theory has ignored the software of development and therefore has not had much success in creating development. On the other hand, Islamic history shows clearly the importance of developing human beings. The advent of our Prophet Mohammad *ṣallā Allāhu 'alayhi wa-sallam* led to the most remarkable episode of development in human history, where the ignorant and backward Arabs rose to the position of world leadership solely as a result of the human development created by the teachings of Islam.

The focus of government efforts should be on human and institutional development—where institutions must be considered as including the development of social norms taught by Islam. Conventional economists have raised a valid objection: the government is not well placed to carry out many types of developmental efforts. For example, in Pakistan, despite having better educated and better-paid teachers, government schools remain inefficient compared to private schools. Examination of Islamic teachings and history provides an answer to this puzzle. Islamic teachings place extreme importance on the development of neighborhood communities. Building institutions and norms are work that is most efficiently carried out by communities. The government must play an enabling role in encouraging the development of communities, and enabling them to carry out tasks required for social and economic development. By transferring responsibilities to communities, the government will be able to develop thousands of engines for growth, making up for capabilities that the government lacks.

An essential element of the community-driven approach is microfinance, which provides communities with the resources required to carry out developmental projects. This requires local community banks which can create a savings pool and provide money on the basis of trust. This has been a secret of all successful microfinance projects. Community banking has also been the secret of the success of Germany's rise to European leadership starting from complete ruin. The German community banking model was also used as a pilot for the highly successful Islamic bank Mit Ghamr.[7] Unfortunately, this was shut down by Gamal Abdul Nasser as a part of the crackdown on the Islamic Brotherhood. This experiment needs to be revived and replicated. An essential element of a new, fair, and just system for the creation of money will be a shift from large impersonal banks to small community-based banks which work with the trust relations available at the community level. In addition to money, Islam also provides additional mechanisms for expanding the supply of credit to communities. Atiq-ur-Rahman and Shahzad (2017) have shown how *Bai Salam* and *Bai Istisna* can be parts of an Islamic strategy of microfinance.

A community-based approach focusing on multidimensional human development and creating Islamic social norms of generosity and cooperation would lead to the provision of essential social services at a local level. This was the norm throughout Islamic history, where social services were provided by communities through the financial institutions of *Awqaf*—trusts for provision of a wide variety of different types of services. The government itself did not play a direct role but did play an important role as an enabler.[8]

CONCLUSION

We have started out by explaining that the current financial system leaves the creation of money to the private sector banks and financial institutions. This system has gained strength since the 1980s financial deregulation. The system has caused many different types of harm, including multiple major financial crises, increasing inequality, and high degrees of injustice in economic outcomes. Sustaining the system has required the propagation of several myths, designed to cover up the workings of the system. One important pair of myths is that the government is in control of the money supply, and the private banks do not create money. Both of these are false, as detailed in Sigurjonsson (2015). A third myth is that financial depth leads to increases in wealth through the process of financial intermediation. This myth of "wealth creation" by finance has been designed to cover the fact that rentiers earn money without doing any productive activity, as was widely recognized in an earlier era. If speculation leads to a boom in prices of land and stocks, this is not a wealth-creating activity; rather it is a wealth-destroying activity as it takes away from real productive activities, and provides excessive rewards to financiers and speculators.

Seeing through these myths leads to the understanding that private sector banks and financial institutions control the creation of money. To avoid serious injustice and multiple severe financial crises generated by the system, it is necessary to switch to a system of Sovereign Money, where the state has the sole right to create money. Plans for doing so were created following the Great Depression of 1929, and have recently been revived and updated in the Iceland Plan for monetary reform (Sigurjonsson 2015). These plans do not focus on the elimination of interest, but rather on the elimination of private money creation. Islam offers us the deeper insight that it is actually the interest-based system that is at the root of economic problems caused by private money creation. The goal of this chapter was to extend the Iceland Plan and to use it as a basis for creating a model for an interest-free economic system.

A multiplicity of coordinated reforms on different fronts are required to create a system in conformity with Islamic laws. Making isolated changes on a few fronts could easily lead to failure, with outcomes worse than current ones. One of the key changes required is taking away the power of private banks to create credit, and giving the state the sole authority to issue Sovereign Money. The second is to eliminate interest-based loans, replacing them with *musharka* for investment loans. After making these two changes, it would be possible to create money in an inflation-free fashion. Keeping prices stable would be a responsibility of the government, in a system that would be largely free of debt. Making these changes would create substantial amounts of money released from exploitative uses by rentiers. It would be important to ensure that this money is used wisely, making the best investments for the future. The role of human beings and institutions, the software, is crucial and under-emphasized in conventional economic theory. Governments are not well equipped to provide many social services. Islamic social structures leave this task to neighborhood communities, with the government playing a facilitating and enabling role. Financial organizations like *Awqaf*, and local community banks are more suited to providing the microfinance needed to energize communities to partner in the growth process. Current financial systems remove all surplus from communities and concentrate wealth in the hands of a tiny rentier class. Making the reforms suggested would create and empower the communities generating thousands of engines of growth and revolutionary changes.

NOTES

1. See Benes and Kumhof (2012).
2. See, for example, Piketty (2014) and Stiglitz (2012).
3. For details, see Sigurjonsson (2015).

4. See the documentary movie "Inside Job."

5. Some more details are available in Zaman (2015, On the Nature of Modern Money).

6. For example, see Glaeser et al. (2004).

7. See Alonso (2015).

8. For more details and references to the central role of Awqaf in social service provision, see Zaman (2015, Islamic Economics: A Survey of the Literature).

BIBLIOGRAPHY

Alkire, Sabina, & Ritchie, Angus. "Winning Ideas: Lessons from Free Market Economics," University of Oxford, *OPHI Working Paper* No. 6 (2007).

Alonso, Inmaculada Macias. "Mit Ghamr: Pioneer in Islamic Banking," Paper presented at 10th International Conference on Islamic Economics and Finance, Doha, Qatar (March 30–31, 2015).

Asmatullah, Moulana. *Money and its Usage: An Analysis in the Light of the Sharia'*, translated by Omar Javaid. Karachi: Darul Ishaat, 2014.

Atiq-ur-Rehman, & Asghar Shehzad. "Eradicating Poverty through Salam and Istisna: A Strategy for Poverty Reduction in Rural Pakistan," *Ma'arif Research Journal*, 3, January–June (2017): 29–38.

Benes, J., & Kumhof, M. "The Chicago Plan Revisited," *International Monetary Fund Working Paper*, WP 12/202 (2012).

Brown, Ellen. *Web of Debt: The Shocking Truth About Our Money System and How We Can Break Free*, 4th Edition. Chippenham, UK: Third Millenium Press, 2011.

Cooley, John. *Currency Wars: How Forged Money is the New Weapon of Mass Destruction*. New York, NY: Skyhorse Publishing, 2008.

Glaeser, Edward L., Rafael La Porta, Florencio Lopez de-Silanes, & Andrei Shleifer. "Do Institutions Cause Growth?" *Journal of Economic Growth*, 9, no. 3 (2004): 271–303.

Graeber, David. *Debt: The First 5,000 Years*. Brooklyn, NY: Melville House Publishing, 2011.

Hickel, Jason. "Aid in Reverse: How Poor Countries Develop Rich Countries," The New Left Project, 18 December 2013.

Klein, Naomi. *The Shock Doctrine: The Rise of Disaster Capitalism*. New York, NY: Metropolitan Books, 2008.

Laeven, Luc, & Valencia, Fabian. "Systematic Banking Crises: A New Database," *IMF Working Paper* WP/08/224 (2008).

McLeay, M., Radia, A., & Thomas, R. "Money Creation in the Modern Economy," *Quarterly Bulletin*, 54, no. 1 (2014): 14–27.

Mian, Atif, & Amir Sufi. *House of Debt: How They (and You) Caused the Great Recession, and How We Can Prevent it from Happening Again*. Chicago: University of Chicago Press, 2014.

Piketty, Thomas. *Capitalism in the Twenty-First Century*. Cambridge, MA: Belknap Press, 2014.

Shiller, Robert. *Irrational Exuberance*, Revised and Expanded Third Edition. Princeton: Princeton University Press, 2015.

Sigurjonsson, Frosti. *Monetary Reform—A Better Monetary System for Iceland*, report commissioned by Prime Minister of Iceland, Reykjavik, Iceland, March 2015.

Stiglitz, Joseph. *The Price of Inequality*. London: Penguin UK, 2012.

World Bank. *Where is the Wealth of Nations?* The International Bank for Reconstruction and Development. Washington: The World Bank, 2006.

Zaman, Asad. "The Nature of Modern Money," *Islamic Economic Perspectives and Theoretical Models*. Jeddah: IRTI, Forthcoming. Pre-publication draft available from SSRN: https://ssrn.com/abstract=2535697.

Appendix A

Chapter 3

Answers to follow-up/secondary questions. All except figure A.6 are from the Population Survey. Total population sample equals 2,500.

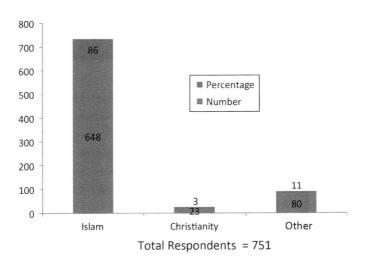

Appendix A.1   Religion. *Source*: Author's Survey.

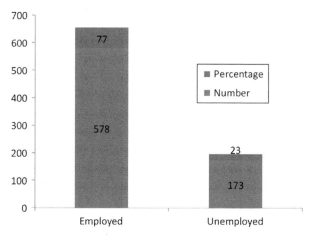

Appendix A.2   Employment Status. *Source*: Author's Survey.

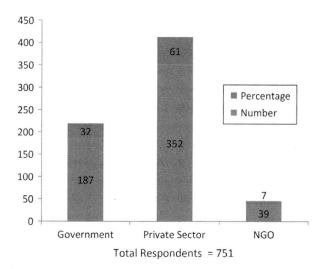

Appendix A.3   Employer. *Source*: Author's Survey.

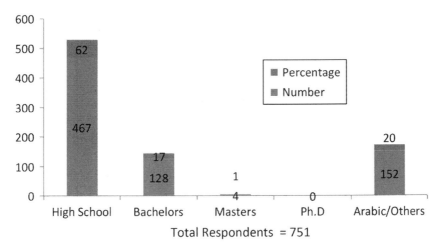

Appendix A.4 Educational Qualification. *Source*: Author's Survey.

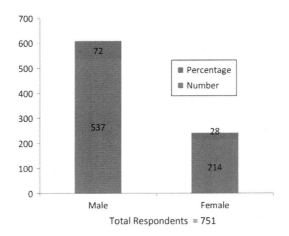

Appendix A.5 Gender (Population). *Source*: Author's Survey.

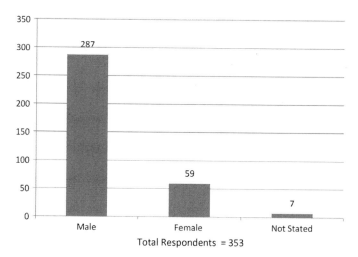

Total Respondents = 353

Appendix A.6   Gender (Business Community). Total number of respondents equals 346; that is, the total sample of the business community minus the seven not stated. *Source:* Author's survey.

Appendix B

Chapter 3

Questionnaires

SURVEY OF ISLAMIC BANKING IN
THE GAMBIA: THE POPULACE

General Questions

1. How much do you know about Islamic banking?
   - ☐ Very much
   - ☐ Little
   - ☐ Nothing

   If very much, please very briefly explain the following:
   MURABAHA
   _____

   MUDARABA
   _____

   MUSHARAKA
   _____

   SUKUK
   _____

2. Have you ever had an account in an Islamic bank?
   - ☐ Yes
   - ☐ No

   If yes, name of the bank and where?
   (optional)_____

3. If yes to question 3, were you satisfied with the bank?
   - ☐ Yes
   - ☐ No
   - ☐ Indecisive

   If yes, why?_____

   If no, why?_____
4. Do you believe that Islamic banking is different from conventional banking?

   If yes, why?

   _____

   If no, why?

   _____
5. Would you open an account in an Islamic bank if you have access to a new one?

   If yes, why?_____

   If no, why?_____
6. Does it matter to you whether your bank is Islamic or conventional?
   - ☐ Yes
   - ☐ No
7. Please rank the following according to their importance to you in choosing a bank:
   - ☐ Ease of getting loans
   - ☐ Rate of interest
   - ☐ Quality of service
   - ☐ Other, please state what _____

PERSONAL QUESTIONS

Your name (optional): _____

Sex: _____Age: _____Religion:_____

- ☐ Employed
- ☐ Unemployed

   If employed, where:

- ☐ Government
- ☐ Private sector (business)

▫ Nonprofit NGO
▫ Total estimated income from all sources

City/town of residence, email/telephone number
(optional):_____
  Highest formal qualification attained:
  ▫   High school
  ▫   Bachelor's
  ▫   Master's
  ▫   PhD
  ▫   Other

ANY OTHER COMMENTS?

THANK YOU VERY MUCH FOR YOUR TIME

SURVEY OF ISLAMIC BANKING IN THE GAMBIA: The Gambian
Business Community

1. How much do you know about Islamic banking?
   ▫   Very much
   ▫   Little
   ▫   Nothing

   If very much, please very briefly explain the following:
   MURABAHA
   _____

   MUDARABA
   _____

   MUSHARAKA
   _____

   SUKUK
   _____

2. Do you believe that Islamic banking is different from conventional
   banking?
   If yes, why? _____

   If no, why?_____

3. Have you ever had an account in an Islamic bank?
   ▫   Yes
   ▫   No

If yes, name of the bank and where (optional)?_____

If yes to question 3, were you satisfied with the bank?
- ☐   Yes
- ☐   No

If yes, why?_____

If no, why?_____

4. Would you open an account in an Islamic bank if you have access to a new one?

    If yes, why?_____

    If no, why? _____

5. Does it matter to you whether your bank is Islamic or conventional?
   - ☐   Yes
   - ☐   No

6. Any other comments?

PERSONAL QUESTIONS

Your position:_____Gender:_____

Member of GCC: _____Name, age, and contact (optional)?_____

Turnover of your company (optional): _____No. of employees: _____

THANK YOU VERY MUCH FOR YOUR TIME

Appendix C

Chapter 3

List of Islamic Financial Institutions in Africa

Algeria
Al Baraka Bank Algeria
Al Salam Bank Algeria
Takaful
Salama Assurances Algerie
Botswana
First National Bank of Botswana (Islamic window)
Cameroon
Afriland First Bank (Islamic window announced)
Chad
Ecobank (Islamic window)
Djibouti
Dahabshiil Bank International
Saba Islamic Bank
Salaam African Bank
Shoura Bank
Egypt
Al Baraka Bank Egypt
AT. Asset Management
A.T Brokerage
Faisal Islamic Bank
Ridge Islamic Capital
National Bank of Development
Takaful

Arab Orient Takaful Insurance Co. (Egypt)
Egyptian Saudi Insurance House (Egypt)
Egyptian Takaful (Life) (Egypt)
Egyptian Takaful (Non-Life) (Egypt)
Nile Family Takaful (Egypt)
Nile General Takaful (Egypt)
Solidarity for Family Takaful Insurance (Egypt)
Wethaq Takaful Insurance Co. (Egypt)
Ethiopia
Zamzam Bank International (under formation)
The Gambia
Arab Gambian Islamic Bank
Takaful Gambia Limited (Gambia)
Ghana
Ghana Islamic Microfinance
Guinea
Banque Islamique de Guinée
Kenya
First Community Bank
Gulf African Bank
Islamic Windows
Barclay's Bank Kenya (Islamic window)
Chase Bank
African Banking Corporation
Imperial bank
Diamond Trust Bank
Standard Chartered
Takaful
Takaful Insurance of Africa (TIA) (Kenya)
Liberia
African Arabian Islamic Bank
Libya
Takaful Insurance Company (Libya)
Mauritania
Banque Al Wafa Mauritanienne Islamique (BAMIS)
Islamic Bank of Mauritania (BIM)
Bank Mouamelat Sahiha (BMS)
Bank for Islamic Finance (BFI)
Mauritanian Bank of Investment (BMI)
Takaful
SMAI Islamique (Mauritania)
Taamin Assurances Islamiques

Mauritius
Century Banking Corporation
BAI (Takaful) (inactive)
Nigeria
Jaiz Bank
Lotus Capital
Senegal
Banque Islamique du Sénégal
SALAMA Senegal (Sosar Al Amane, Takaful)
South Africa
Absa Islamic Banking (Islamic window)
Al-Baraka Bank
Reliance Takaful
Habib Bank
Sudan
Abu Dhabi National Bank
African Bank for Trade and Development
Agricultural Bank
Animal Resources' Bank
Aljazeera Sudanese Jordanian Bank
Al Salam Bank - Sudan
Al-Shamal Islamic Bank
Arab Sudanese Bank
Bank of Khartoum
Baraka Bank (Sudan)
Blue Nile Mashreq Bank
Byblos Bank (Africa)
El-Nilien Bank
Emirates and Sudan Bank
Export Development Bank (previously El-Gharb Islamic Bank)
Faisal Islamic Bank
Family Bank
Farmer's Commercial Bank
Financial Investment Bank
Industrial Development Bank
Islamic Co-operative Development Bank
National Bank of EGYPT (Khartoum)
National Bank of Sudan
Omdurman National Bank
Qatar National Bank
Real Estates Commercial Bank
Savings and Social Development Bank

Saudi Sudanese Bank
Sudanese Egyptian Bank
Sudanese French Bank
Sudanese Islamic Bank
Tadamon Islamic Bank
United Capital Bank
Workers' National Bank
Takaful
Al Salama Insurance Co
Al-Ta'awuniya Insurance Co.
Al-Baraka
Blue Nile Insurance Co.
El Nilein Insurance Co.
General Insurance Co.
Islamic Insurance Co.
JUBA Insurance Co.
Middle East Insurance Co.
National reinsurance Co.
Red Sea Insurance Company Limited
Savana Insurance Co. Ltd
Shiekan Insurance & Reinsurance
The Sudanese Insurance and Reinsurance Company Ltd (SUDINRECO)
The United Insurance Co.
Tanzania
Amana Bank Ltd.
Tunisia
Al Baraka Bank, Tunisia
Zitouna Bank
Takaful
Assurance At Takafulia
El Amana Takaful
Zitouna Takaful
Source: Authors' field research and Islamic finance Wiki.

Appendix D

Chapter 5

Appendix 5D, Table D.1   Augmented Dicky-Fuller Unit Root Test

Bahrain			
Dependent Variable: DCPI			
Variable	Level	1st difference	2nd difference
CPI	0.009	0.000	Not needed
MS	0.430	0.000	Not needed
ER	0.992	0.98	0.000
LIMP	0.081	0.000	Not needed
IB	0.000	Not needed	Not needed
WCPI	0.006	0.000	Not needed
WFOOD	0.003	0.000	Not needed
WOIL	0.003	0.000	Not needed
Kuwait			
Dependent Variable: DCPI			
Variable	Level	1st difference	2nd difference
CPI	0.322	0.000	Not needed
MS	0.474	0.000	Not needed
ER	0.289	0.000	Not needed
LIMP	0.047	0.000	Not needed
IB	0.639	0.024	0.000
Oman			
Dependent Variable: DCPI			
Variable	Level	1st difference	2nd difference
CPI	0.603	0.000	Not needed
MS	0.212	0.004	Not needed
ER			
LIMP	0.052	0.000	Not needed
IB	0.159	0.000	Not needed
Qatar			
Dependent Variable: DCPI			
Variable	Level	1st difference	2nd difference
CPI	0.501	0.000	Not needed

(Continued)

MS	0.139	0.000	Not needed
ER			
LIMP			
IB	0.717	0.000	Not needed

Saudi Arabia
Dependent Variable: DCPI

Variable	Level	1st difference	2nd difference
CPI	0.745	0.000	Not needed
MS	0.135	0.000	Not needed
ER	0.091	0.000	Not needed
LIMP	0.000	Not needed	Not needed
IB	0.086	0.000	Not needed

Iran
Dependent Variable: DCPI

Variable	Level	1st difference	2nd difference
CPI	0.195	0.001	Not needed
MS	0.145	0.000	Not needed
ER	0.038	0.000	Not needed
LIMP	0.340	0.000	Not needed
IB	0.003	0.015	Not needed

Sudan
Dependent Variable: DCPI

Variable	Level	1st difference	2nd difference
CPI	0.745	0.000	Not needed
MS	0.023	0.000	Not needed
ER	0.624	0.000	Not needed
LIMP	0.009	0.000	Not needed
IB	0.086	0.000	Not needed

Appendix 5D, Table D.2   Panel Unit Root Test

Variable	Level	(Prob)	I(1) (Prob)
	Panel Unit Root Test		
MS	Levin, Lin, and Chu t*LC	0.5895	0.000
	Im, Peasaran, and Shin W-stat	0.013	
	ADF—Fisher Chi-square	0.0269	
	PP—Fisher Chi-square	0.0078	
CPI	Levin, Lin, and Chu t*LC	0.9238	0.000
	Im, Peasaran, and Shin W-stat	0.091	
	ADF—Fisher Chi-square	0.099	
	PP—Fisher Chi-square	0.0167	
ER	Levin, Lin and Chu t*LC	0.999	0.000
	Im, Peasaran, and Shin W-stat	0.336	
	ADF—Fisher Chi-square	0.141	
	PP—Fisher Chi-square	0.003	
IB	Levin, Lin, and Chu t*LC	0.927	0.000
	Im, Peasaran and Shin W-stat	0.000	
	ADF—Fisher Chi-square	0.000	
	PP—Fisher Chi-square	0.000	
WCPI	Levin, Lin, and Chu t*LC	0.1273	0.000
	Im, Peasaran, and Shin W-stat	0.000	
	ADF—Fisher Chi-square	0.000	
	PP—Fisher Chi-square	0.000	
WOIL	Levin, Lin, and Chu t*LC	0.2066	0.000
	Im, Peasaran and Shin W-stat	0.000	
	ADF—Fisher Chi-square	0.000	
	PP—Fisher Chi-square	0.000	
WFOOD	Levin, Lin, and Chu t*LC	0.0725	0.000
	Im, Peasaran, and Shin W-stat	0.000	
	ADF—Fisher Chi-square	0.000	
	PP—Fisher Chi-square	0.000	
IMP	Levin, Lin, and Chu t*LC 0.4701		0.000
	Im, Peasaran, and Shin W-stat 0.000		
	ADF—Fisher Chi-square 0.000		
	PP—Fisher Chi-square 0.000		

Appendix E

Chapter 5

Appendix 5E, Table E.1 Co-integration Test for Inflation Equation[i]

	Null Hypothesis[ii]					
	r = 0		r ≤ 1		r ≤ 2	
	Trace Stat. (95% C.V.)	Max Stat. (95% C.V.)	Trace Stat. (95% C.V.)	Max Stat. (95% C.V.)	Trace Stat. (95% C.V.)	Max Stat. (95% C.V.)
Bahrain	190.06*	53.50*	136.55*	47.23*	89.32*	32.59
	(125.61)	(46.23)	(95.75)	(40.08)	(69.82)	(33.89)
Kuwait	208.33*	59.90*	148.44*	46.18*	102.26*	41.36*
	(125.62)	(46.23)	(95.75)	(40.08)	(69.82)	(33.88)
Oman	194.83*	51.20*	143.63*	46.54*	97.08*	40.98*
	(125.62)	(46.23)	(95.75)	(40.08)	(69.82)	(33.88)
Qatar	178.14*	69.31*	108.83*	46.79*	62.04*	22.68*
	(125.62)	(46.23)	(95.75)	(40.08)	(69.82)	(33.88)
Saudi Arabia	185.81*	54.42*	108.83*	46.79*	62.04*	22.68
	(125.62)	(46.23)	(95.75)	(40.08)	(69.82)	(33.88)
Iran	169.38*	55.24*	114.15*	43.12*	71.03*	32.03
	(125.62)	(46.23)	(95.75)	(40.08)	(69.82)	(33.88)
Sudan	168.48*	60.36*	108.11*	47.47*	60.64	25.74
	(125.62)	(46.23)	(95.75)	(40.08)	(69.82)	(33.88)

[i] r is the number of co-integrating vectors.
[ii] Asterisks (*) indicate rejection of the hypothesis at 95 percent C. V. Critical values in parentheses.

Appendix 5E, Table E.2   Panel Co-integration Test[i]

Pedroni Residual Co-integration Test
Null Hypothesis: No co-integration
Variables CPI, MS, ER, IB, WCPI, and WOIL
Alternative hypothesis: common AR coefs. (within-dimension)

	Statistic	Prob	Weighted Statistic	Prob
Panel v-Statistic	0.564806	0.2861	-0.517246	0.6975
Panel rho-Statistic	0.425277	0.6647	1.306111	0.9042
Panel PP-Statistic	0.003645	0.5015	0.646971	0.7412
Panel ADF-Statistic	0.263121	0.6038	0.553739	0.7101

Alternative hypothesis: common AR coefs. (between-dimension)

	Statistic	Prob
Panel rho-Statistic	1.486293	0.9314
Panel PP-Statistic	0.789255	0.7850
Panel ADF-Statistic	0.743135	0.7713

---

[i] The panel co-integration test, all the eleven statistics do not reject the null hypothesis of no co-integration at the conventional level of 0.05.

Appendix F

Chapter 5

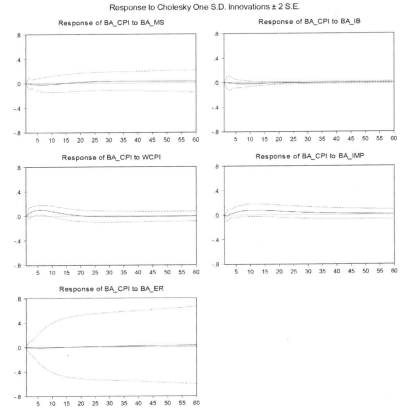

Response to Cholesky One S.D. Innovations ± 2 S.E.

Appendix 5F, Figure F.1   Impulse Response. *Source*: Author sourced from the International Monetary Fund's International Financial Statistics.

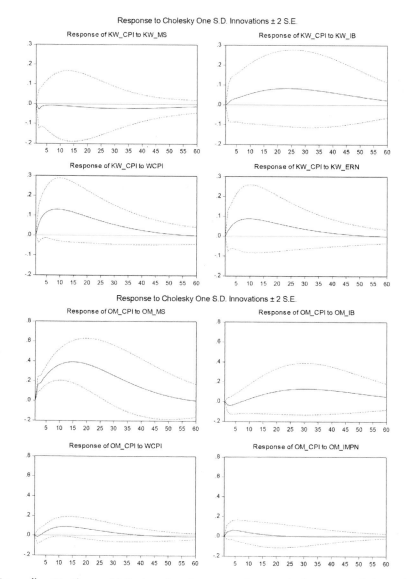

Appendix 5F, Figure F.1.2 Impulse Response. *Source*: Author sourced from the International Monetary Fund's International Financial Statistics.

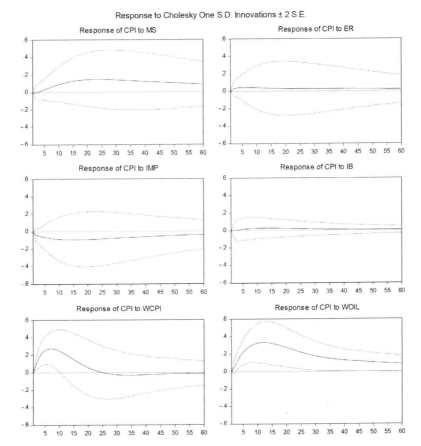

Appendix 5F, Figure F.2   Panel-Impulse Response of Inflation. *Source*: Author sourced from the International Monetary Fund's International Financial Statistics.

Appendix G

Chapter 5

Appendix 5G, Figure G.1   Correlation Matrix

Period	CPI	MS	ER	IMP	WCPI	IB
\multicolumn{7}{c}{Variance Decomposition of CPI}						
\multicolumn{7}{c}{Bahrain}						
1	100.00	0.00	0.00	0.00	0.00	0.00
6	97.97	0.07	0.01	0.17	1.35	0.42
12	88.90	0.09	0.04	0.24	8.55	2.19
18	84.77	0.28	0.06	0.68	10.31	3.90
24	83.18	0.51	0.07	1.26	10.25	4.74
30	81.56	0.62	0.07	1.68	11.00	5.07
36	80.66	0.65	0.07	1.91	11.45	5.27
\multicolumn{7}{c}{Kuwait}						
1	100.00	0.00	0.00	0.00	0.00	0.00
6	74.25	5.10	4.14	1.08	12.21	3.21
12	51.49	10.28	8.79	0.82	19.70	8.92
18	43.23	11.75	12.86	1.05	19.45	11.66
24	39.94	12.29	15.25	1.47	18.18	12.87
30	38.47	12.63	16.13	1.88	17.39	13.50
36	37.73	12.90	16.27	2.21	17.02	13.88
\multicolumn{7}{c}{Oman}						
1	100.00	0.00		0.00	0.00	0.00
6	70.78	14.77		0.28	14.11	0.06
12	54.43	27.29		0.30	17.92	0.06
18	44.98	37.36		0.24	17.38	0.05
24	38.94	44.48		0.20	16.25	0.13
30	35.19	49.04		0.18	15.21	0.37
36	32.98	51.67		0.17	14.41	0.77
\multicolumn{7}{c}{Qatar}						
1	100.00	0.00		0.00	0.00	0.00
6	71.27	6.22		0.07	0.64	21.80
12	60.66	14.63		0.30	1.76	22.64
18	54.31	20.17		0.54	3.67	21.31
24	50.43	23.09		0.76	5.69	20.03
30	48.12	24.47		0.96	7.31	19.15
36	46.77	25.05		1.16	8.42	18.61
\multicolumn{7}{c}{Saudi Arabia}						
1	100.00	0.00	0.00	0.00	0.00	0.00
6	86.93	1.10	1.29	0.60	9.62	0.46
12	87.72	2.61	1.56	0.36	6.92	0.83
18	88.21	3.79	1.33	0.36	5.18	1.13
24	88.35	4.59	1.12	0.38	4.32	1.23
30	88.39	5.17	1.01	0.38	3.83	1.23
36	88.35	5.59	0.97	0.36	3.53	1.20
\multicolumn{7}{c}{Iran}						
1	100.00	0.00	0.00	0.00	0.00	0.00
6	90.62	1.38	0.57	2.28	2.27	2.88
12	87.54	1.94	0.63	5.20	1.40	3.29
18	74.86	2.07	2.82	5.43	0.98	13.84
24	62.27	2.27	6.94	4.61	0.88	23.03
30	58.75	2.23	8.09	4.74	1.45	24.73
36	57.90	2.15	7.84	5.39	2.97	23.74
\multicolumn{7}{c}{Sudan}						
1	100.00	0.00	0.00	0.00	0.00	0.00
6	92.43	0.01	3.62	0.09	2.80	1.06
12	89.06	0.03	4.31	0.87	4.81	0.92
18	86.15	0.09	4.71	2.13	5.23	1.69
24	83.30	0.19	5.02	3.45	5.17	2.87
30	80.64	0.30	5.31	4.63	5.01	4.11
36	78.28	0.42	5.61	5.61	4.84	5.25

Source: Author sourced from the International Monetary Fund's International Financial Statistics.

Appendix 5G, Table G.1   Variance Decomposition of CPI

				Panel				
Period	CPI	MS	ER	IMP	IB	WCPI	WOIL	WFOOD
Panel								
1	100.00	0.00	0.00	0.00	0.00	0.00	0.00	0.00
6	96.48	0.04	0.05	0.10	0.00	0.53	0.46	2.34
12	93.12	0.20	0.06	0.17	0.01	0.50	1.06	4.88
18	91.89	0.39	0.08	0.21	0.01	0.38	1.39	5.65
24	91.80	0.53	0.10	0.23	0.01	0.39	1.53	5.40
30	92.00	0.63	0.11	0.25	0.01	0.42	1.59	4.99
36	92.19	0.69	0.12	0.27	0.01	0.41	1.62	4.69
42	92.30	0.74	0.13	0.28	0.01	0.40	1.65	4.50
48	92.34	0.78	0.13	0.29	0.01	0.38	1.67	4.39
54	92.36	0.81	0.13	0.30	0.01	0.38	1.69	4.32
60	92.37	0.84	0.13	0.31	0.00	0.37	1.71	4.26

Appendix H

Chapter 5

Appendix H

Appendix 5H, Figure H.1   Variance Decomposition

Correlation Matrix							
Bahrain							
	WOIL	WFOOD	IB	ER	IMP	WCPI	MS	CPI
WOIL	1.00	0.69	-0.07	0.03	0.52	0.55	0.31	-0.41
WFOOD	0.69	1.00	0.02	0.05	0.34	0.57	0.47	-0.46
IB	-0.07	0.02	1.00	0.01	-0.06	-0.03	-0.04	-0.03
ER	0.03	0.05	0.01	1.00	0.05	0.13	0.10	-0.01
IMP	0.52	0.34	-0.06	0.05	1.00	0.14	0.18	-0.37
WCPI	0.55	0.57	-0.03	0.13	0.14	1.00	0.50	-0.27
MS	0.31	0.47	-0.04	0.10	0.18	0.50	1.00	-0.04
CPI	-0.41	-0.46	-0.03	-0.01	-0.37	-0.27	-0.04	1.00
Kuwait							
	WOIL	WFOOD	IB	ER	IMP	WCPI	MS	CPI
WOIL	1.00	0.69	0.28	-0.69	0.35	0.55	0.03	0.16
WFOOD	0.69	1.00	0.15	-0.77	0.08	0.57	0.10	0.30
IB	0.28	0.15	1.00	-0.33	0.58	0.09	0.45	0.06
ER	-0.69	-0.77	-0.33	1.00	-0.22	-0.72	-0.13	-0.26
IMP	0.35	0.08	0.58	-0.22	1.00	0.17	0.25	0.17
WCPI	0.55	0.57	0.09	-0.72	0.17	1.00	0.10	0.57
MS	0.03	0.10	0.45	-0.13	0.25	0.10	1.00	0.42
CPI	0.16	0.30	0.06	-0.26	0.17	0.57	0.42	1.00
Oman							
	WOIL	WFOOD	IB	ER	IMP	WCPI	MS	CPI
WOIL	1.00	0.69	-0.07		0.25	0.55	0.10	0.25
WFOOD	0.69	1.00	-0.05		0.48	0.57	0.28	0.41
IB	-0.07	-0.05	1.00		-0.29	-0.17	-0.16	-0.20
ER								
IMP	0.25	0.48	-0.29		1.00	0.49	0.43	0.43
WCPI	0.55	0.57	-0.17		0.49	1.00	0.43	0.61
MS	0.10	0.28	-0.16		0.43	0.43	1.00	0.75
CPI	0.25	0.41	-0.20		0.43	0.61	0.75	1.00
Qatar							
	WOIL	WFOOD	IB	ER	IMP	WCPI	MS	CPI
WOIL	1.00	0.69	0.10		-0.32	0.55	0.56	0.01
WFOOD	0.69	1.00	0.28		-0.30	0.57	0.57	-0.16
IB	0.10	0.28	1.00		-0.31	0.08	0.43	-0.75
ER								
IMP	-0.32	-0.30	-0.31		1.00	-0.26	-0.25	0.14
WCPI	0.55	0.57	0.08		-0.26	1.00	0.52	-0.09
MS	0.56	0.57	0.43		-0.25	0.52	1.00	-0.39
CPI	0.01	-0.16	-0.75		0.14	-0.09	-0.39	1.00
Saudi Arabia							
	WOIL	WFOOD	IB	ER	IMP	WCPI	MS	CPI
WOIL	1.00	0.69	0.18	0.06	0.26	0.55	0.28	0.17
WFOOD	0.69	1.00	0.23	0.32	0.34	0.57	0.24	0.37
IB	0.18	0.23	1.00	0.03	0.28	0.00	0.03	-0.16
ER	0.06	0.32	0.03	1.00	0.06	0.28	0.23	0.40
IMP	0.26	0.34	0.28	0.06	1.00	0.37	0.26	0.10
WCPI	0.55	0.57	0.00	0.28	0.37	1.00	0.32	0.44
MS	0.28	0.24	0.03	0.23	0.26	0.32	1.00	0.40
CPI	0.17	0.37	-0.16	0.40	0.10	0.44	0.40	1.00
Iran							
	WOIL	WFOOD	IB	ER	IMP	WCPI	MS	CPI
WOIL	1.00	0.69	-0.06	0.04	-0.10	0.55	0.29	-0.07
WFOOD	0.69	1.00	-0.09	-0.07	0.00	0.57	0.32	0.03
IB	-0.06	-0.09	1.00	0.24	0.01	-0.26	-0.07	-0.35
ER	0.04	-0.07	0.24	1.00	0.21	-0.15	0.02	0.02
IMP	-0.10	0.00	0.01	0.21	1.00	-0.06	0.14	-0.16
WCPI	0.55	0.57	-0.26	-0.15	-0.06	1.00	-0.01	0.29
MS	0.29	0.32	-0.07	0.02	0.14	-0.01	1.00	-0.48
CPI	-0.07	0.03	-0.35	0.02	-0.16	0.29	-0.48	1.00
Sudan							
	WOIL	WFOOD	IB	ER	IMP	WCPI	MS	CPI
WOIL	1.00	0.69	0.08	-0.23	0.05	0.55	0.15	-0.18
WFOOD	0.69	1.00	-0.03	-0.10	-0.02	0.57	0.04	-0.15
IB	0.08	-0.03	1.00	-0.33	0.08	-0.09	0.28	-0.25
ER	-0.23	-0.10	-0.33	1.00	-0.07	-0.04	0.03	0.78
IMP	0.05	-0.02	0.08	-0.07	1.00	-0.14	0.01	-0.16
WCPI	0.55	0.57	-0.09	-0.04	-0.14	1.00	-0.04	-0.02
MS	0.15	0.04	0.28	0.03	0.01	-0.04	1.00	-0.11
CPI	-0.18	-0.15	-0.25	0.78	-0.16	-0.02	-0.11	1.00

Source: Author sourced from the International Monetary Fund's International Financial Statistics.

Index

Page references for figures are italicized.

About the Contributors

Haider Ali Khan is John Evans Distinguished University Professor at the Joseph Korbel School of International Studies, University of Denver. He was the chief international adviser to Arab Trade and Human Development in Cairo, and a senior economic adviser to the Secretary General of UNCTAD in Geneva, president of the Asian Development Bank, to UNDP, and several governments. He has published twenty-five books—some of which have been translated into other languages—and over two hundred articles in professional journals spanning several areas of global political economy and security—including Islamic economics and finance—particularly on issues of war, peace, and human well-being. He has received many international awards. Professor Khan is also an award-winning poet, translator, and literary, music, and art critic. He has written on global poetry, fiction, and art. His critical works are also on specific global writers and artists, including Rabindranath Tagore, Nazrul Islam, Shamsur Rahman, Baul poetry and music, Mirza Ghalib, Allama Iqbal, Faiz Ahmed Faiz, Nazim Hikmet, Octavio Paz, Pablo Neruda, Pablo Picasso, surrealism, Asian and Islamic Art, Guillaume Apollinaire, James Joyce, and the Japanese haiku master Basho as well as many modern and postmodern Japanese poets. His 2016 book in Bangla *Muktijuddher Dingulo: Probashe Alor Gaan* (The Days of Our Liberation War: Songs of Light Abroad) is an analytical memoir in haibun (an organic synthesis of haiku and complementary prose) form. His poems "War Sonata" and "Radioactive Man" in English and "Mandro Shaptok" (The Lowest Octave) and "Manush" (Humans) in Bangla have been anthologized widely.

Karamo N. M. Sonko (B.A. [Swaziland], MPhil [Cambridge], PhD [Denver]) is a trustee of international water organization (WellBoring) in

213

Chippenham, UK, and chairman of the West African affiliate (WellBoring West Africa), which he co-founded; chairman, Taf Africa Global property developers; chairman and founder of Heeno International foundation, Banjul, The Gambia; president and CEO of Jula Consultancy, Sharjah, UAE; and chief strategist for Africa, Orca Gold Inc., Vancouver, Canada. Dr Sonko has worked for a number of international institutions (including the IMF and the UN) and taught at five universities in Canada, France, and the United States. He has written and published extensively in academic journals, international magazines, and books on various subjects, especially with regard to Africa. Dr Sonko is a recipient of the 2017/18 Competitive Research Awards in Islamic Economics and Finance of the IRTI of the Islamic Development Bank (IsDB) in Jeddah, Saudi Arabia. He has advised many African and foreign multinationals on their business strategies and has developed his own version of PESTLE Analysis referred to as the "African PESTLE."

Nursilah Ahmad is currently a senior lecturer at the Faculty of Economics and Muamalat, Universiti Sains Islam Malaysia (USIM). She has occupied several other positions at USIM, such as deputy dean (Student Development and Performance Management), faculty of economics and Muamalat, Universiti Sains Islam Malaysia (USIM) (March 2013–April 2015); post-graduate coordinator, Faculty of Economics and Muamalat (2009); head of program, Bachelor of Corporate Administration and Relations (Honours); faculty of Economics and Muamalat, USIM (November 2009–March 2013); and postgraduate coordinator, Faculty of Economics and Muamalat, USIM (April – Nov. 2009). Dr Ahmad has numerous publications on international macroeconomics (exchange Rates and inflation), Islamic financial economics (*Sukuk*) and social economics (Ijtimai Sector – waqf). She has four years' experience as a research fellow at the Islamic Finance and Wealth Management Institute (IFWMI), Universiti Sains Islam Malaysia (2009–2013). She has a PhD (Economics), International Islamic University Malaysia (2009); MEc (Economics), International Islamic University Malaysia (2001); and BSBA (Economics), University of Denver, Colorado, USA (1992). She is an Asian resource person on Islamic finance, especially *Sukuk*, and international macroeconomics.

Tamsir Cham has a PhD in economics, Howard University; a master's in computer science, Howard University; and a bachelor's in mathematics and economics, Saint Mary's University; and certificate in public financial management, Harvard University. He is currently a Mason Fellow at the John F. Kennedy School of Government, Harvard University. He served as a research economist at the Islamic Research and Training Institute (IRTI), Islamic Development Bank (IDB) (2015–2019), where the research for this chapter was done. He had earlier served as an economist, International Monetary Fund (2010–2015); director of Macroeconomics, The Gambia Ministry of Finance and Economic Affairs (2009–2010); and analyst, Key Bank, Cleveland, Ohio, USA (2007–2008). He has taught business statistics and introductory macro-economics at Howard University, Cleveland State University, and University of The Gambia. He has authored a book on currency union and published papers on exchange rates, competitiveness, trade, and FDI.

Ousmane Diagana is vice president, Human Resources of the World Bank Group in Washington, D.C. At the time of writing this chapter he was chief ethics officer for the World Bank Group and vice president of Ethics and Business Conduct. Diagana became the vice president of World Bank Group Human Resources in February 2018. In this role, he provides overall strategic leadership on human resource matters to the entire World Bank Group and oversees the development and implementation of the World Bank Group People Strategy, and HR policies, programs, and services. Diagana is recognized as an organizational leader, personal mentor, and a professional role model. He brings to this role a deep knowledge of Bank Group opera-tions, a reputation for innovative and strategic thinking, recognized manage-rial skills, and country office perspective. Previously, he was World Bank country director for Côte d'Ivoire, Burkina Faso, Benin, Guinea, and Togo, based in Abidjan and prior to that he held the position of country director for Mali, Niger, Chad, and Guinea, based in Bamako. Between 2006 and 2009, Diagana was country manager in Niger, and from 2004 to 2006, he was pro-gram leader in Morocco. In these capacities, he effectively led diverse, multi-disciplinary teams to deliver innovative strategies and operations—including in fragile and conflict-affected countries. In 2009, Diagana received the Good Manager Award from the World Bank Group Staff Association in recognition of his leadership skills. He has degrees in economics, finance, and planning, as well as a certificate in education policies and analysis.

Mariama Sonko has a master of science degree in finance with Distinction from Heriot-Watt University. She has a *License* in economics and man-agement from Paris-Sorbonne University. She is executive assistant at Jula Consultancy in Sharjah, UAE, and has done internships in compa-nies in Mauritania and the Sudan. She is currently co-authoring a book on "Environmental, Social and Corporate Governance (ESG) in South Africa."

Sarah A. Tobin (PhD Boston University, 2011) is a senior researcher at the Chr. Michelsen Institute in Bergen, Norway. Her work explores transfor-mations in religious and economic life, identity construction, and personal piety. Ethnographically, Dr. Tobin focuses on Islamic piety in the economy, especially Islamic banking and finance, and in times of economic shifts, such as during Ramadan, in contested fields of consumption such as the hijab, and the Arab Spring. Her latest projects research these questions with Syrian refugees in Jordanian camps of Za`atari, Azraq, and Cyber City, and in urban areas throughout Jordan. Dr. Tobin's recent books are *Everyday Piety: Islam and Economy in Jordan* (Cornell University Press, 2016) and *The Politics of the Headscarf in the United States* (Cornell University Press, 2018, with Bozena C. Welborne, Aubrey L. Westfall, and Ozge Celik-Russell).

Asad Zaman, BS. mathematics (MIT), PhD economics (Stanford), has taught at leading universities like Columbia University in the City of New York, University of Pennsylvania, Johns Hopkins, and California Institute of Technology. Currently he is Director of Economic and Social Sciences, Al-Nafi Online Education, and member of the Monetary Committee of the State Bank (Central Bank) of Pakistan. He was vice chancellor of Pakistan Institute of Development Economics. His textbook *Statistical Foundations of Econometric Techniques* (Academic Press, NY, 1996) is widely used in advanced graduate courses. His research on Islamic economics is widely cited and has been highly influential in shaping the field. His publications in top ranked journals like *Annals of Statistics*, *Journal of Econometrics*, *Econometric Theory*, *Journal of Labor Economics*, and others have more than a thousand citations as per Google Scholar.